Score Higher
on the
SAT

Score Higher on the SAT

International Standard Book Number: 0-7897-3454-0

Library of Congress Catalog Card Number: 2005930310

Printed in the United States of America

First Printing: July 2005

08   07   06   05   4   3   2   1

Trademarks

All terms mentioned in this book that are known to be trademarks or service marks have been appropriately capitalized. Que Publishing cannot attest to the accuracy of this information. Use of a term in this book should not be regarded as affecting the validity of any trademark or service mark.

Warning and Disclaimer

Every effort has been made to make this book as complete and as accurate as possible, but no warranty or fitness is implied. The information provided is on an "as is" basis. The author(s) and the publisher shall have neither liability nor responsibility to any person or entity with respect to any loss or damages arising from the information contained in this book.

Bulk Sales

Que Publishing offers excellent discounts on this book when ordered in quantity for bulk purchases or special sales. For more information, please contact U.S. Corporate and Government Sales: 1-800-382-3419 or corpsales@pearsontechgroup.com

For sales outside the U.S., please contact international@pearsoned.com

---

Publisher
Paul Boger

Executive Editor
Jeff Riley

Interior & Cover Designer
Gary Adair

Publishing Coordinator
Cindy Teeters

Contents at a Glance

Math 53

Critical Reading 121

Practice Test 163

Welcome!

The new SAT is an important step in turning your desire to go to college into a reality. You've already done the hard part—you've decided to go. Now your job is to take advantage of the time you have between this moment and the day you sit down to take the test.

In this guide, you'll find many articles, features, and study aids to help you get ready for test day.

- *The Ins and Outs of Guessing* shows you how good guessing techniques can add 50 points or more to your score on the SAT. Learn a few simple tricks that can make the difference between random guessing and smart guessing.

- Two articles—*Your 10 Worst Fears and How to Beat Them* and *7 Super Strategies to Master Test Anxiety*—look at the things test-takers dread the most. Read these to find tips to avoid panic attacks and steer clear of the most common test-day pitfalls.

- *Slacker to Superstar—SAT Study Planners that Fit Your Lifestyle* provides a 12-month SAT planning calendar that can help you plan around high expectations, hectic schedules, and your own desire to do anything but study for the SAT.

Of course, you'll also find study guides for the Math, Critical Reading, and Writing sections—including the new Essay assignment. In *The Good, the Bad, and the Ugly—3 SAT Essays Exploded* you'll find examples of three SAT essays, along with an explanation of how they were scored. We've also included a sample test so you can see where you stack up against the scores you need for your school of choice.

All in all, preparing for the SAT is probably less fun that a lot of other things you could think of doing instead. However, it doesn't have to be a chore. Whether you start next fall in an Ivy League dorm or on a commuter train headed to city college, you'll be glad you took the time to do your best on the new SAT.

Sincerely,

Teresa Stephens

A letter from John Barnhill

Call me an optimist, but I am excited about the new SAT. It is my hope that the new writing section will help us to identify students with strengths that past assessments were not able to capture. Now in reality, I imagine that there will be a high correlation between students who did well on the old Verbal test and students that will do well on the new Writing section, but maybe, just maybe, the writing component will help us to identify potential in students that we have historically missed.

I am also eager to see the essays. This type of writing is new in admissions. We have always had essays, but they were essays that students could work on literally for months. They could edit, re-edit and solicit advice from parents, teachers, and so forth. I think it will be interesting to look at the SAT essay and compare it to the standard essay that we have historically used.

As excited as I am about the new test, it will be a couple of years before the new test is incorporated into our admissions process. We plan on doing research to see what this new measure tells us. Do students with a certain score in writing do well in their first year? Do they retain and graduate at a higher rate? Do certain essay scores do well in freshman English, so well that we could possibly award exemption credit for a certain level of performance? Is there a difference between the critical reading score and the writing score as we look at student first year performance? These and other questions will have to be answered before we can fully incorporate the new test into our process.

On a personal note, my son took the new SAT. He is a junior and he said it went really well. I love the optimism of youth. He had absolutely no issue with the essay and thought it was easy. I guess we will see how easy when his scores arrive. Also, I should tell you that I am the Chair of the National SAT Committee of the College Board, so I might be a little biased.

Sincerely,

John Barnhill
Chair of the National SAT Committee of the College Board
Director of Admissions and Records
Florida State University
Tallahassee, FL 32306

Key Facts
You Should Know About The SAT

What Colleges Want Out of the New SAT

The new SAT has been as big a change for the colleges and universities across the US as it has been for students. Admission departments nationwide have had to incorporate the new scoring procedure into their admissions requirements. As well, they've had to come up with policies to address students who took the old SAT and who want to apply for fall 2005 classes using those old scores. We've picked a few representative schools across the country and taken a look at how they're dealing with the new SAT.

Name of School	Northwestern University
Location	Evanston, IL
Website	www.northwestern.edu
Type of Institution	Private; 4-year undergraduate; Numerous graduate and post-graduate programs
Enrollment	7,789 full-time undergraduates
Rating	Highly Competitive
Policy on New SAT	Old SAT: 650-730 Verbal; 660-750 in Math. New SAT is required for 2006 freshmen admissions. The Writing section with essay is mandatory. While the new SAT is required for 2005-2006 admissions, in addition Northwestern will accept scores from the old SAT for Math and Verbal if they are higher than your new SAT Math and Critical Reading scores.
Other requirements	Northwestern recommends 3 SAT Subject Tests (SAT II) in addition to the new SAT. Northwestern also accepts the ACT with required Essay section.

Name of School	University of Texas
Location	Austin, TX
Website	www.utexas.edu
Type of Institution	State; 4-year undergraduate; Numerous graduate and post-graduate programs
Enrollment	34,000 full-time undergraduates
Rating	Moderately Competitive
Policy on New SAT	Old SAT: 540-660 Verbal; 570-690 in Math. New SAT is required for 2005-2006 admissions. UT will accept the highest individual sections scores from multiple SAT exams, but requires that those scores come from the new SAT.
Other requirements	UT also accepts the ACT with required Essay section.
Additional Information	UT Austin was the first institution in the country to announce that it would require the new SAT Writing section for all applicants. Larry R. Faulkner, speaking for the Office of the President, stated that the new SAT created incentives for students to learn to write well and for schools to emphasize writing craft.

Name of School	Dartmouth College
Location	Hanover, NH
Website	www.dartmouth.edu
Type of Institution	Private; 4-year undergraduate; Some graduate programs
Enrollment	4,000 full-time undergraduates
Rating	Highly Competitive
Policy on New SAT	660-760 Verbal; 670-770 in Math. Dartmouth will accept the highest composite of Math and Verbal scores from old SAT or Math and Critical Reading from new SAT for applicants in the 2006-2007 academic year. Starting with 2006 freshmen, the new SAT is mandatory.
Other requirements	Dartmouth also accepts the ACT with required Essay section. Dartmouth also requires 2 SAT Subject Tests (SAT II)
Additional Information	Dean of Admissions shared that the new SAT is more geared to things that make sense for curricula in high school. At Dartmouth, test scores are the 2nd most important factor in the admissions process. Transcripts are the most significant factor.

Name of School	University of California
Location	Santa Barbara, CA
Website	www.admit.ucsb.edu
Type of Institution	State; 4-year undergraduate; Numerous graduate programs
Enrollment	17,000 full-time undergraduates
Rating	Moderately Competitive
Policy on New SAT	530-630 Verbal; 560-670 in Math. New SAT is required for 2006 freshman class applicants. UCSB will accept the highest individual sections scores from multiple SAT exams, but requires that those scores come from the new SAT.
Other requirements	UCSB prefers at least 2 SAT II tests in addition to the new SAT. UCSB also accepts the ACT with required Essay section.
Additional Information	At this printing, UCSB gives equal weight to the SAT Subject Tests and the new SAT in the eligibility index.

Name of School	Florida State University
Location	Tallahassee, FL
Website	www.fsu.edu
Type of Institution	State; 4-year undergraduate; post-graduate programs
Enrollment	26,000 full-time undergraduates
Rating	Moderately Competitive
Policy on New SAT	520-620 Verbal; 530-630 in Math. For 2006-2007 admissions, the new SAT is required. FSU will accept the highest individual sections scores from multiple SAT exams, but requires that those scores come from the new SAT.
Other requirements	FSU also accepts the ACT with optional Essay section.
Additional Information	Admission standards are higher for out of state applicants than for Florida residents. See the letter on page vi from John Barnhill, Director of Admissions and Records and Chair of the National SAT Committee of the College Board.

SAT 101
Get the skinny on how to sign up and what to expect

What the new SAT looks like

You probably already know that the new SAT provides scores for three major areas: Writing, Critical Reading, and Math, each of which receives a maximum score of 800. However, on test day, you'll find that the test itself is broken into 10 sections, one of which is an essay. Each of the major scores comes from a composite of your success on three test sections. For example, your test may be organized as follows:

	Test Section	Time Limit (in minutes) (approximate)	Number of questions
1	Essay	25	1 writing prompt
2	Math (includes "grid-ins")	20	18
3	Writing	25	35
4	Reading (includes 2 long passages)	25	24
5	Math	25	18
6	Reading	25	24
7	Equating	25	30
8	Math	25	18
9	Reading	20	24
10	Writing	10	14

Typically, one section is experimental—in this case, the Equating section—and does not count toward your final score. However, you won't know which one that is on test day.

Each section of new SAT has its own special features. Let's take a 30,000-foot look at the test.

The Essay

You'll have the privilege of writing an essay in response to a writing prompt. You'll have 25 minutes to write the essay, and the writing assignment will be very specific. Two graders will each give you a score of 1-6, making a perfect score on the essay a 12. Do not write on anything other than the assigned topic. If you do, you'll get a zero.

The Writing section

In the Writing sections, you'll see four main types of questions:

1. Multiple choice questions on grammar and usage
2. Multiple choice sentence correction questions
3. Multiple choice paragraph correction questions
4. Multiple choice essay correction questions

The Critical Reading section

In the Critical Reasoning section, you'll also face four challenges:

1. Multiple choice sentence completion questions on vocabulary and logic
2. Multiple choice questions on short reading passages
3. Multiple choice questions on long reading passages
4. Multiple choice questions on paired passages, both long and short

The Math section

In the Math section, you'll see a wide variety of questions, most of which require a multiple choice response:

- Number and Operations
- Algebra I and II
- Geometry
- Statistics, Probability, and Data Analysis

You'll also see a special type of question called a grid-in. In these questions, you'll actually compute an answer and bubble it into an answer grid.

Registering for the new SAT

Just like the rest of the world, the College Board has gone digital. The easiest way to register for the SAT is to visit the College Board website at www.collegeboard.com where you can check out test dates, test centers, and other important information. You can register online and, if need be, change your registration choices.

You can still register the old-fashioned way, of course. Pick up a packet at your school counselor's office, fill out the forms, and mail it in.

If you've already registered once and you're in the College Board computer system, you can register for additional tests by phone. However, this is a fully-automated system, and it will not accept first-time registrations.

As a last resort, you can register at the test center on test day if there's room. Stand-by registration is expensive and you're not guaranteed to get a seat. However, if you must take the test on a specific day, it's worth a shot.

Upcoming test dates:

Oct. 8, 2005	SAT & Subject Tests
Nov. 5, 2005	SAT & Subject Tests
Dec. 3, 2005	SAT & Subject Tests
Jan. 28, 2006	SAT & Subject Tests
Apr. 1, 2006	SAT only
May 6, 2006	SAT & Subject Tests
Jun. 3, 2006	SAT & Subject Tests

Questionnaire

The College Board provides a student questionaire that can help you with your college search. The questionnaire lets colleges know about what you're into—your interests, activities, and plans—when your scores are reported. When you get your scores, the report will include information about the colleges you selected in comparison to other similar institutions. Completing the quetionaire also lets the College Board keep your school counselors in the loop about your scores and your plans.

SAT Subject Tests (SAT II)

As if the new SAT wasn't enough, many schools also request—or in some cases require—that you also take SAT Subject tests. The SAT Subject Tests, formerly called the SAT II, give you a chance to demonstrate your skills in 20 specific areas:

Literature
U.S. History
World History
Math Level 1
Math Level 2
Biology E/M
Chemistry
Physics
French Reading
French with Listening
German Reading
German with Listening

Spanish Reading
Spanish with Listening
Modern Hebrew Reading
Italian Reading
Latin Reading
Japanese Reading with Listening
Korean Reading with Listening
Chinese Reading with Listening

You should check the admission requirements of your selected colleges to see which subject tests they require.

Test day

You need to get to the testing center by 7:45 on test day. The test starts promptly at 8:15 and ends around 12:30. You'll get a couple of short breaks during the test, but prepare for a long morning. The test procedure is set in stone and very clearly defined. Get a good night's sleep, and eat a good breakfast. Sometime around 10:45, you'll be glad you did both.

You can't bring a whole lot with you to the SAT, but there are a few things you don't want to forget.

- Your admission ticket.
- Your photo ID.
- As many sharpened No. 2 pencils as you think you'll need, plus a couple of extras.
- An eraser. Check to make sure that the eraser really does a good job of removing the pencil marks.
- A calculator and spare batteries.
- A watch, stopwatch, or travel alarm with the audible alarm turned off.

Make it happen!

The rest is up to you. Take the time to prepare yourself for the SAT. Learn all the tricks of the test and study up on your weak spots. This book is loaded with information that can help you come out on top. Good luck and happy bubbling!

> To see an updated list of colleges' SAT Subject Test requirements visit www.collegeboard.com

The **Ins** and **Outs** of Guessing on the New SAT

At some point along the line you may have heard that random guessing won't hurt you on the SAT. So the theory goes, you get a point for each question you answer correctly and lose a quarter-point for each question you miss—which should mean that random guessing comes out as a wash. Although this idea might be theoretically and mathematically plausible, it takes away one of your most powerful weapons: smart guessing can actually add points to your SAT score.

The 10 cardinal rules for guessing on the SAT

1 Guessing is a second pass activity

Don't focus on guessing until you've made your best attempt at answering all the questions you know you can get right. You earn points for correct answers. If you have to choose between getting one question right and making three or four guesses, go for the sure thing. Return to the questions where you need to guess if you have time.

2 All questions are worth the same number of points

Wrestling with a hard SAT question instead of picking off an easy question (or three) is a waste of time. Answer the easy questions first. When you see a difficult question that you think will take a lot of time, circle it and move on. If you have time, you can come back later and take another look or make a smart guess.

3 Know where the hard questions are and what they look like

In the Math section, the higher the number, the harder the question. The same is true for the multiple choice questions in the Writing and Critical Reading sections—except for the Reading passages. This means you should be spending a lot less time on the first half of those sections than you will on the second half. Bank this time to use for guessing.

On the reading passages, the questions appear in the order the information is presented in the passage. The easy questions tend to be the ones that ask literal questions about the information in the passage. Use the question order to help you locate that information in the passage. Also, on paired passages, the easy questions tend to be the ones that ask about a single passage, not a synthesis of the pair.

4 Use POE

Process of Elimination is a powerful tool. It gives you a huge mathematical advantage over random guessing. When you can't figure out what the answer is, turn it around and ask yourself, "what *isn't* the answer?" If you can eliminate two or three answers as incorrect, your chance of getting the right answer when you guess goes up dramatically.

5 Eliminate the extremes

Eliminate answers that are extreme or out of scope. On math questions, that means answers that are obviously too small or too large—averages that are larger than any single element, distances that are too short to fit the scenario, etc. On reading questions, look for words like *always* and *never* or very strong words like *hate* or *perfect*. Usually the correct answer is somewhere between the extremes unless the question is quoting the passage literally.

6 Avoid the tiger traps

When you realize you're stuck on a hard question and you've burned over a minute, eliminate as many of the answer choices as possible and chose. If you really can't eliminate any choices, then just leave it blank. If you think you'll have time to revisit the question, circle it in your test book.

7 Plug it in

See if you can plug in an answer to get more information. Since math question answers are listed in order from smallest to biggest, use their order to help you find the bigger or smaller number you need when you're plugging in answers. If answer C is too small, then answers A and B are also too small and you can eliminate them, too.

8 The answers get trickier as the questions get harder

On very difficult questions—typically at the end of sections—the right answer is usually not the obvious one. As a rule of thumb, on the first part of a test, the answer that looks right probably is right. Toward the end of the test, beware of distracters that repeat numbers in the problem or that look simple or very familiar. Don't guess on the hardest questions unless you can eliminate two or more answers.

9 No penalty for grid-ins

Here's the exception to the random guessing rule. On the math grid-in questions, you have to bubble-in an actual number. There is no penalty for incorrect answers on the grid-ins, so bubble in your best answer before you move on. Who knows? Maybe you were right after all!

10 Random guessing is pointless—literally!

The best-case scenario for random guessing is that you get the same number of points as you'd get if you left all those questions blank. Smart guessing is your secret weapon. Use it.

From Slacker to Superstar

Exclusive SAT study planners that fit your lifestyle

Not every student approaches the SAT with the same goals. That means there isn't one study plan that fits everybody. But that doesn't mean you can't meet your goals. This section helps you create a study plan that will help you accomplish your goals.

Ivy League or bust

Francis, our Ivy League candidate, wants to go to Swarthmore. While not technically part of the Ivy League, this little Pennsylvania Liberal Arts college enjoys one of the best reputations in the U.S. It's very tough to get into—Swarthmore accepts fewer than 25% of its applicants and enrolls only 350 students in each class. Average SAT scores are 670-770 for both the Verbal and Math sections. Francis holds a 3.85 GPA and is ranked 10th in her high school class. She is active in student government and runs track.

Smart but too busy

Alex holds a 3.75 GPA despite lettering in lacrosse, editing the high school newspaper, singing in the youth chorus, and holding a 20-hour-a-week job doing web-page design for a local ad agency. Alex wants to major in Journalism at Northwestern—a highly-competitive university outside Chicago. Northwestern requires Verbal scores of 650-730 and Math scores of 660-750. Northwestern enrolls about 1,900 students each year out of more than 14,000 applicants.

The average Joe

Joey plans to go to the University of North Carolina at Chapel Hill, the largest member of the North Carolina university system. Joey lives n North Carolina, so the in-state tuition and good academic reputation of UNC are a huge incentive. UNC expects a Verbal score of 590-690 and a Math score of 600-700. UNC enrolls approximately 3,500 annually. As an in-state student Joey will have an advantage over out-of-state candidates. Joey has a 3.2 GPA and is active in several student organizations.

Slacker

Ronnie shows up for school most days. A Seattle native, Ronnie has always expected to go to the University of Washington. With a 2.8 GPA and few extracurricular activities to speak of, Ronnie needs to get a 510 Verbal and a 550 Math to meet the minimum requirements of this diverse state school. Ronnie plans to work while attending college to help pay the bills.

Ivy League or Bust

January

- Narrow your college choices to top 4 or 5 and learn about their admissions requirements. You'll probably need to schedule both the SAT and the ACT. We suggest taking the more important test for your college choices first.

- Chose the earliest possible test dates—probably March for SAT and June for the ACT. This will leave yourself enough time to prepare appropriately for the ACT or to take the June SAT, if you need to improve your scores.

- Select two or three test prep study aids for the SAT. Make sure you have 6 to 10 complete sample tests.

- Identify two to four hours weekly that you can spend studying for the SAT, including time to take one sample test every two weeks.

- Take a sample test around January 15 and record your score. This is your benchmark.

- Isolate the specific skills you need to work on. Concentrate on the areas where you need the most work.

- Take your second practice test toward the end of the month and record your score. Compare your score in each section with the requirements for the college of your choice.

February

- Concentrate on the Critical Reading section for a week. Do several long passage questions in each session. Establish a time limit for each passage, but be sure to review each of your answers to make sure understand what you missed and why.

- Create your own vocabulary study aids—flash cards that you can carry with you, audio tapes for the car. etc.

- Concentrate on Math for a week. Review the arithmetic and algebra questions to make sure you're familiar with the test questions. Focus on Geometry and Probability, which are usually the most difficult.

- Take your third practice test around the 15th of the month and record your score. Identify the sections where your scores aren't high enough for the college of your choice.

- Concentrate on Writing for a week. Write two or three practice essays. Try to write both formal and personal narrative styles to determine which is most comfortable for you. Have a mentor read you essays and assign a grade.

- Spend this week as if it were the week before the real test. Review all sections, concentrating on the areas where your practice score isn't high enough for your selected college.

- Set aside the last Saturday of the month and pretend that it's test day. Give yourself a timed practice test, following all the rules you'll have on test day—including an early start. Force yourself to take the test with minimal breaks between sections. Record your score.

March

- If your dry run has you where you need to be, take a light week and relax a little.

- The week before the test, do vocabulary drills and make sure you know all the test instructions by heart. Make sure you know exactly where to go and when you need to be there.

- Drive to the testing center a few days before the test and note how long it took you to get there.

- Nail the test.
- Take the rest of this month off. You've earned it. Your scores should be available on the web around two weeks after you take the test.

April

- Prepare for the ACT.
- If your scores are where you want them to be, consider the early admissions process for your top college choices. Identify scholarship opportunities and mage sure you report your scores to them according to their requirements.
- If your scores need to come up, determine whether you want to schedule another Spring test or to wait until Fall and find out when you need to register.

May

- Prepare for the ACT.

June

- Take the ACT.
- Enjoy your summer.

July

- Continue to enjoy your summer.

August

- Dust off you notes and repeat the February schedule.

September

- Start applying to colleges.
- Prepare for second ACT, if required.
- Take the SAT for the second time in late September or early October.

October

- Continue college applications process.
- Take second ACT, if required.

November

- Receive early admissions responses.

December

- Happy Holidays!

Smart but too busy

January

- Narrow your college choices to top 4 or 5 and learn about their admissions requirements.
- Chose the second Spring SAT test date—probably May. This will give you enough time to prepare for the SAT and still be able to take it again if your scores aren't what you need them to be.
- Select two or three test prep study aids for the SAT. Make sure you have 6 to 10 complete sample tests.
- Identify a couple of hours weekly that you can schedule for SAT study. If you're busy, putting the study on your calendar will help you actually do it.
- Schedule a three hour block for a sample test around January 15 and record your score. This is your benchmark.
- Compare your score in each section with the requirements for the college of your choice and identify the areas where you need the most work.

February

- For the first two weeks of February review the Critical Reading section. You only have a couple of hours each week, so to make the most of it, concentrate on practice questions.
- You might want to sign up for a Vocabulary Word of the Day email service.

- Pick two or three passages for each session and give yourself a time limit for each passage. After you complete the passage, go over the answers and make sure you understand what you missed and why.

- For the second two weeks of February, concentrate on the math section. Again, concentrate on the practice questions.

- Make sure you do 10 to 15 questions each practice session and review your answers carefully. If you're consistently missing the same type of question (probability, geometry, etc.) get some help in that area.

- Schedule a practice test for the end of February. Compare your scores to the January test for Critical Reading and Math. Compare your scores in these sections to the requirements for your college of choice.

March

- Take the first two weeks of March and concentrate on the Writing section multiple choice questions. Concentrate on the practice questions in your sample tests.

- The essay correction questions are the trickiest here, so make sure you include at least one or two in each practice session.

- Spend the last two weeks of March on the essay. Plan to write one essay in each of your practice sessions.

- Arrange ahead of time to have a mentor review your essays and give you feedback.

- Schedule a practice test for the end of March. Compare your scores to the January test and February tests for all sections. Compare your scores in these sections to the requirements for your college of choice.

April

- In April, concentrate on the areas where you need to improve your scores for the college of your choice.

- Include a few questions from each section in your practice sessions, but scale back in the areas where your scores are already where you need them to be.

- Review Vocabulary between study sessions. You get a lot of bang for your buck with Vocabulary review.

- Write at least one practice essay in April.

- Schedule a practice test for the end of April. Hopefully, your scores in each session should be where you need them to be on this test.

May

- If your dry run has you where you need to be, take a light week and relax a little.

- The week before the test, make sure you know all the test instructions by heart. Make sure you know exactly where to go and when you need to be there.

- Drive to the testing center a few days before the test and note how long it took you to get there.

- Nail the test.

- Take the rest of this month off. You've earned it. Your scores should be available on the web around two weeks after you take the test.

June

- Take the ACT if you need to.
- Enjoy your summer.

July

- Continue to enjoy your summer.

August

- If you need to take the SAT again, dust off your notes and repeat the February/March schedule.

September

- Start applying to colleges.
- Prepare for second ACT, if required.
- Take the SAT for the second time in late September or early October.

October

- Continue college applications process.
- Take second ACT, if required.

November

- Happy Holidays!

December

- Happy Holidays!

The Average Joe

January

- Narrow your college choices to top 4 or 5 and learn about their admissions requirements.
- Chose the final Spring SAT test date—probably June. This will give you plenty of time to prepare for the SAT. You'll still be able to take it again in the Fall if your scores aren't where you need them to be.
- Select two or three test prep study aids for the SAT. Make sure you have 6 to 10 complete sample tests.
- Take a sample test near the end of January and record your score. This is your benchmark.
- Compare your score in each section with the requirements for the college of your choice and identify the areas where you need the most work.

February

- Identify a couple of hours weekly that you can devote to SAT study.
- Sign up for Sat Question of the Day and Vocabulary Word of the Day through email.
- For the last two weeks of February review the Critical Reading section. Concentrate on practice questions.
- Pick two or three passages for each session and give yourself a time limit for each passage. After you complete the passage, go over the answers and make sure you understand what you missed and why.
- At the end of February, complete a sample Critical Reading section test. Compare your score on that section to the one you need for your school of choice.

March

- For the first two weeks of March, concentrate on the math section.
- Make sure you do 10 to 15 questions each practice session and review your answers carefully. If you're consistently missing the same type of question (probability, geometry, etc.) get some help in that area.
- At the end of the second week, do a sample Math section test and compare that score to the score you need for your school.
- Take the last two weeks of March and concentrate on the Writing section multiple choice questions. Concentrate on the practice questions in your sample tests.
- The essay correction questions are the trickiest here, so make sure you include at least one or two in each practice session.
- Schedule a complete practice test for the end of March. Compare your scores to the January test and to the requirements for your college of choice.

April

- Spend the first two weeks of April on the essay. Plan to write one essay in each of your practice sessions.
- Arrange ahead of time to have a mentor review your essays and give you feedback.
- In late April and early May, concentrate on the areas where you need to improve your scores.
- Include a few questions from each section in your practice sessions, but scale back in the areas where your scores are already where you need them to be.

May

- Review Vocabulary between study sessions. You get a lot of bang for your buck with Vocabulary review.
- Write at least one practice essay in May.
- Schedule a practice test for the middle of May. Compare your scores to the January and March tests for all sections. Compare your scores in these sections to the requirements for your college of choice.

June

- If your dry run has you where you need to be, take a light week and relax a little.
- The week before the test, make sure you know all the test instructions by heart. Make sure you know exactly where to go and when you need to be there.
- Drive to the testing center a few days before the test and note how long it took you to get there.
- Nail the test.
- Take the rest of this month off. You've earned it. Your scores should be available on the web around two weeks after you take the test.

July

- Enjoy your summer.

August

- Continue to enjoy your summer.

September

- If you need to take the SAT again, dust off your notes and concentrate on your weak spots.
- Prepare for the ACT, if required.
- Start applying to colleges.

October

- Take the SAT for the second time if necessary.
- Continue college applications process.

November

- Happy Holidays!

December

- Happy Holidays!

Slacker

January

- Recover from New Year's Eve.

February

- Recover from Valentines Day.

March

- Recover from St. Patrick's Day.

April

- Recover from Spring Break.

May

- Hang out at Starbucks alone while your geekier friends study for the June SAT.

June

- It's summer.

July

- It's still summer.
- At Mom's insistence, narrow your college choices to top 2 and learn about their admissions requirements.
- Chose the first fall SAT test date—probably late September or early October. This will give you about eight weeks to prepare for the SAT.
- Have Mom select two test prep study aids for the SAT. Make sure you have at least 4 complete sample tests.

August

- Take a sample test as close to August 1 as you can and record your score. This is your benchmark.
- Compare your score in each section with the requirements for the college of your choice and identify the areas where you need the most work.

- Starting mid-August, plan to spend 4 one-hour sessions a week on SAT study. (Chances are you only really study for one or two hours, since you're a slacker.)

- Make sure each session consists of at least one long reading section, at least 5 math questions, and at least 5 questions each from the Critical Reading and Writing multiple choice sections—about 20 questions in all.

- Write a sample essay in the last week of August. Let someone you trust give you feedback on your essay.

September

- Continue your one-hour sessions. Make sure you're getting in at least two per week.

- Around September 15 take a second sample test—with the essay. Compare your scores to the requirements for the college of your choice.

- Spend the rest of September concentrating on the area where you need the most improvement.

October

- The week before the test, make sure you know all the test instructions by heart. Make sure you know exactly where to go and when you need to be there.

- Drive to the testing center a few days before the test and note how long it took you to get there.

- Take the test. Get there on time.

- Apply to colleges.

November

- Recover from the SAT.

December

- Happy Holidays!

Writing Section

Grammar Blitz

Breeze through the Writing Section multiple choice!

It's rare that you think about the rules of grammar. Seriously, when was the last time you made sure you didn't misplace your modifiers or dangle your participles when you visited a chat room? Most of the time, though, you use good grammar out of habit. The Writing Section of the new SAT puts you through your paces grammatically, but you may be surprised at how much you already know.

In the Writing section, you'll see about 50 multiple-choice questions. Most questions consist of a sentence that contains a grammatical error. In some cases, the original sentence will be correct as-is. Your job? Find the best choice to correct the error.

The good news is that you don't need to know the technical names of the grammar rules—you just need to be able to find and fix the problems. The bad news is that the new SAT is very thorough when it comes to grammar. It tests your ability to identify the tense, form, and mood of verbs, to sort out adverbs, adjectives, prepositions, gerunds, idioms, and pronouns, and to recognize bad sentence structure and paragraph organization.

Let's look at the most common types of grammar problems you'll see in the new SAT.

Subject/Verb agreement

The verb in a sentence needs to agree in number with the subject. Simply put, a singular subject gets a singular verb. Plural subjects get plural verbs. For example:

Bill (a singular subject) calls (a singular verb) Samantha.

Bill and Samantha (a plural subject) eat (a plural verb) dinner.

Bob (a singular subject) is (a singular verb) jealous.

They (a plural subject) are (a plural verb) headed for trouble.

POWERTIP

Learn a few rules

During the exam, you'll only have to find and fix the error without naming the grammar rule it breaks. If you have time while you practice, though, try to figure out which rule you're using. On some of the trickier questions, it can help to have a list of common grammar rules in mind to figure out what, if anything, is wrong.

Geography, in addition to World History, **are offered to** the lower classmen.

Ⓐ are offered to

Ⓑ are not offered to

Ⓒ are offered for

Ⓓ is offered to

Ⓔ is offered for

You can rule out **Ⓐ**, **Ⓑ**, and **Ⓒ** because the plural verb *are* doesn't match the singular subject *Geometry*. After you've ruled out the incorrect choices, you eliminate answer **Ⓔ** because a course would be offered *to* the lower classmen, not *for* the lower classmen.

ANSWER

The correct answer is **Ⓓ**.

POWERTIP

Don't be afraid to flip it

Sometimes it's easier to check subject/verb agreement if you flip a sentence around. For example, if you rearrange the sentence:

There are lots of rumors clouding the real issue.

to read:

Lots of rumors are clouding the real issue.

It's easier to see that the plural subject "rumors" matches the plural verb "are."

Tricks to matching subjects and verbs

There are a few tricks to matching subjects and verbs. Let's take a quick look at some of the most common trouble spots.

Subjects with prepositional phrases

The prepositional phrases *in addition to*, *together with*, *along with*, and *as well as* in the subject of a sentence usually point to a singular subject.

Susan, in addition to Bill, **is** in Hawaii.

Singular pronouns

Some pronouns always identify a singular subject. The most common are *each, anyone, anybody, anything, another, neither, either, every, everyone, someone, no one, somebody*, and *everything*.

Everyone **walks** to the park on nice days.

Anything **walks** to the park on nice days.

Pronouns that won't commit

Other pronouns may identify singular or plural subjects: *none, any, some, most, more,* and *all*. You'll have to figure out what word the pronoun references to match the verb.

Singular subject: All the *cake* **is** gone. (*all = cake*)

Plural subject: All the *cookies* **are** gone. (*all = cookies*.)

Either/Or

When the subjects uses either/or or neither/nor, the verb must agree with the item that's closest to the verb.

Singular: Neither LaToya nor the *rest of the Jacksons* **visited** Neverland last year. (*the rest of the Jacksons* **visited**)

Plural: Either Bill or *his sisters* always **take** out the trash. (*his sisters* **take**)

Writing Section

9 WAYS
VERBS ARE COMMONLY USED

Verb Form	Present	Past	Future
Simple	Action is happening now	Action happened in the past	Action will happen in the future
	Example: Susan *walks* the dog around the lake	Example: Susan *walked* the dog around the lake.	Example: Susan *will walk* the dog around the lake.
Perfect	Action began in the past but that continues in the present	Action was completed in the past	Action will be completed in the future
	Example: Susan *has walked* the dog around the lake for hours.	Example: Susan *had already walked* the dog around the lake when we got home.	Example: Susan *will have walked* the dog around the lake by the time we return from shopping.
Progressive	Action is ongoing	Action was ongoing at some point in the past.	Action will be ongoing at some point in the future.
	Example: Susan *is walking* the dog around the lake.	Example: Susan *was walking* the dog around the lake.	Example: Susan *will be walking* the dog around the lake.

Verb tense

To a formal grammarian, verb tense can be a pretty complicated subject. As far as the new SAT is concerned, though, you really need to recognize nine ways that verbs are commonly used. There are three primary verb forms: **simple**, **perfect**, and **progressive**. These forms are combined with the more familiar verb tenses: **past**, **present**, and **future**. The combination of form and tense tells you when the action took place and whether or not the action is complete.

The most important thing to recognize about verb forms and tenses is whether they accurately reflect the actions described or communicated. For example, consider this sentence:

> Caroline and Gabrielle **are going** to Florida for Spring Break, and they **are having** a great time there.

The first part of the sentence suggests that they will be going to Florida at some point in the future, but the second part of the sentence suggests that they are already there soaking up the rays. This sentence would be better as

> Caroline and Gabrielle **are going** to Florida for Spring Break, and they **will have** a great time there.

POWER**TIP**

Practice speaking out

When you're practicing for the SAT, read the sentences aloud if you can. Sometimes, you'll find yourself correcting the error as you speak out of pure habit. You won't be able to read questions aloud during the actual exam— at least not without annoying your neighbors—but practicing this way can help you "hear" errors you might not "see".

Punctuating and placing participles

A participle is a verb that thinks it's an adjective. For example:

Laughing, Felicity told Josh not to call her again.

Laughing is a participle that describes Felicity.

Participles may also be part of a phrase—cleverly called a *participial phrase*—that does the same thing. For example:

Laughing in his face, Felicity told Josh not to call her again.

You'll see several questions related to participles on the new SAT. Let's look at the most common problems you'll have to fix.

1 The participle is too far from the word it modifies.

Rudolph and Cassandra left the dance early and caught a cab home *hoping to avoid the rush.*

Hoping to avoid the rush refers to Rudolph and Cassandra, but it's too far away in the sentence to make that clear. It would be better to say

Hoping to avoid the rush, Rudolph and Cassandra left the dance early and caught a cab home.

2 The participle modifies the wrong word.

Checkers caught the Frisbee thrown by his trainer, *clutching it in his teeth.*

This sentence sounds like the trainer clutched the Frisbee in his teeth. It would be better to say

Clutching it in his teeth, Checkers caught the Frisbee thrown by his trainer.

3 The participle has too many commas.

The barista, *foaming the milk,* is Geraldo's cousin.

The phrase *foaming the milk* is essential to the identification of the barista. The commas suggest that the barista is Geraldo's cousin *only while* he foams the milk. It's better as

The barista *foaming the milk* is Geraldo's cousin.

4 The participle doesn't have enough commas

Changing his pants Roscoe prepared for the day ahead.

Participles or participial phrases that begin a sentence always get a comma. This should be

Changing his pants, Roscoe prepared for the day ahead.

5 Dangling Participles

Climbing the stairs, his backpack seemed very heavy.

Dangling participles are a relatively common—and often quite humorous—writing mistake. To fix these, you may need to rephrase the sentence. In this sentence, for instance, it sounds like the backpack is the one climbing the stairs. It would be more accurate to say

His backpack seemed very heavy as he climbed the stairs.

SAMPLE QUESTION

By 1929, U.S. businesses **had been spending** $3 billion a year for advertising through newspapers, magazines, billboards, direct mail, and the new medium of radio.

- **(A) had been spending**
- **(B) has spent**
- **(C) were spent**
- **(D) were spending**
- **(E) will spent**

The first phrase of this sentence, "By 1929" sets the action in the past. The past perfect verb form "had been spending" suggests an ongoing action that was already completed in the past. The sentence, however, does not describe "spending" as a completed action.

Answer **(B)** has an agreement problem (businesses has). Answers **(C)** and **(E)** use impossible tense and form combinations—and they "sound" wrong to the ear. Answer **(D)** correctly uses the past progressive form, suggesting that the action, spending, was ongoing at some point in the past, 1929 and before.

ANSWER

The correct answer is **(D)**.

Gerunds and Infinitives

Two more unusual verb forms you'll see on the new SAT are *gerunds* and *infinitives.* In a nutshell, both gerunds and infinitives are verbs that think they are nouns. There are a couple of tricks that make them easy to spot.

Gerunds

Gerunds almost always end in *–ing.* The gerund form of *run* would be *running.* You'll see gerunds as both the subjects and objects of sentences. Like participles, gerunds may also be phrases of two or more words.

Gerund as a subject

Running is my favorite type of exercise.

Gerund as an object

My favorite type of exercise is *running.*

Gerund phrase as a subject compliment

I will be *running in a mini marathon* later this spring.

POWERTIP

Punctuating gerunds

Gerunds and gerund phrases rarely require special punctuation. You should treat the gerund or gerund phrase as if it were a single noun in the sentence and punctuate accordingly.

Pizza makes me happy.

That sentence requires no special punctuation for the noun *pizza.*

Eating pizza makes me happy.

That sentence also needs no additional punctuation, even though "*Eating pizza*" is a gerund phrase. Even "*Eating a large pepperoni pizza* makes me happy" can stand without additional punctuation.

In all cases, the gerund acts as a noun. To verify that you have a gerund, try to replace it with a pronoun.

Verifying gerund as a subject

It (*Running*) is my favorite type of exercise.

Verifying gerund as an object

My favorite type of exercise is *that* (*running*).

Verifying gerund phrase as a subject compliment

I will be *that* (*running in a mini marathon*) later this spring.

SAMPLE**QUESTION**

Climbing Mount Everest require skill, intense preparation, and a fair measure of good luck.

- **Ⓐ** Climbing Mount Everest require
- **Ⓑ** The climbing of Mount Everest require
- **Ⓒ** To climb Mount Everest require
- **Ⓓ** Climbing Mount Everest requires
- **Ⓔ** To climb the Mount Everest requires

After you recognize *Climbing Mount Everest* as a gerund phrase that acts as the singular subject of the sentence, you can eliminate answers **Ⓐ**, **Ⓑ**, and **Ⓒ** because of subject/verb agreement. It's pretty obvious that between **Ⓓ** and **Ⓔ**, **Ⓓ** is the better choice.

ANSWER

The correct answer is **Ⓓ**.

Infinitives

Infinitives are very similar to gerunds, in that you'll usually see them as verbs in disguise. Although an infinitive can function as a noun, an adjective, or an adverb, they're not that hard to recognize.

Infinitives usually consist of the simplest form of a verb combined with the word *to*. For example, the infinitive form of *sit* is *to sit*. Below are examples of the ways in which an infinitive might appear in common usage.

Infinitive as a noun

To dance is my heart's greatest desire.

Infinitive as an adjective

I have a plane *to catch*. (The infinitive *to catch* modifies the noun *plane*.)

Infinitive as an adverb

You must eat to live. (The infinitive *to live* modifies the verb *eat.)*

SAMPLE**QUESTION**

The biggest challenge facing contemporary society is the need **to balancing** the benefits of our long hours of work without sacrificing career or family.

- **Ⓐ** to balancing
- **Ⓑ** to be balanced
- **Ⓒ** balancing
- **Ⓓ** to balance
- **Ⓔ** for being good balancers of

Answers **Ⓐ** and **Ⓑ** both misuse the infinitive form, so you can eliminate them. Answer **Ⓒ** would be an inappropriate use of a gerund. Answer **Ⓔ**, while not technically correct, is far more awkward than answer **Ⓓ**.

ANSWER

The correct answer is **Ⓓ**.

Pronouns and Antecedents

A pronoun is a special type of noun that replaces another noun. Common pronouns are, he, she, it, they, them, and so forth. For the new SAT, the most important thing you need to remember about pronouns is that they must agree—or accurately represent—the nouns they replace. For example, you wouldn't use the pronoun *she* to replace the noun phrase *flock of sheep*.

Pick the pronoun

Choose the correct pronoun from the options at the end of each sentence.

1. Barbara Walters spoke with Elton John on ___ primetime special. (**she**, **her**)

2. The earth spins on ___ axis. (**its**, **their**)

3. ___ ate all his cabbage. (**He**, **Him**)

4. If anyone complains, ___ will lose a turn. (**he**, **they**)

5. Everyone needs to put away ___ own toys. (**her**, **their**)

6. ___ who need to leave should do so before the curtain rises. (**Those**, **He**)

7. ___ of you will slay the beast? (**Which**, **What**)

8. I would like some of ___ cookies. (**them**, **those**)

Answers: 1. her; 2. its; 3. He; 4. he; 5. her; 6. Those; 7. Which; 8. those

Writing Section

The antecedent

Antecedent is a fancy word for the thing to which a pronoun refers. In the sentence:

> The dog sat on his haunches.

The word *dog* is the antecedent for the pronoun *his*. On the new SAT, you may see questions that involve ambiguous pronoun references—sentences where you can't really tell which antecedent the pronoun is replacing.

SAMPLE**QUESTION**

When **Madame Curie** visited the **Queen of England**, **she** was unprepared for the way **she** would be treated.

- **A** Madame Curie Queen of England she she
- **B** she Queen of England Madame Curie she
- **C** Madame Curie her she she
- **D** Madame Curie Queen of England her she
- **E** Madame Curie Queen of England Madame Curie she

Answer **A** is a classic example of an ambiguous pronoun reference—you can't tell who is doing what to whom. Answer **C** makes the situation worse. Answer **D** suggests an incorrect pronoun, and answer **E** is just plain awkward. By rearranging the pronouns and antecedents, answer **B** makes the sentence much clearer.

ANSWER

The correct answer is **B**.

Prepositions

Prepositions are little words that show position or direction. Most of the time, you'll see prepositions as part of prepositional phrases, such as "in the house" or "under the carpet."

The new SAT tests your ability to spot two types of errors:

- Including unnecessary prepositions
- Using the wrong preposition

Unnecessary prepositions

Unnecessary prepositions can be hard to find, mostly because we're used to hearing them in ordinary speech. In the following sentences, we've eliminated the unnecessary prepositions.

> We watched the squirrel climb ~~up~~ the tree.

> Please close ~~down~~ that office—it's losing money.

> While cleaning, she found lots of dirt ~~in~~ between the stove and the refrigerator.

The following words rarely require a preposition: downstairs, downtown, inside, outside, upstairs, and uptown.

SAMPLE**QUESTION**

The bank had to **cancel out** all its accounts **after** the financial misconduct came to light.

- **A** cancel out — after
- **B** cancel out — until
- **C** cancel — until
- **D** cancel — after
- **E** cancel out — after the time when

You can eliminate answers **B** and **C** because *until* is a poor choice to replace the word *after* in the sentence. Answer **E** is an equally poor choice for the same reason. By comparing answers **A** and **D**, you can see that the preposition *out* is unnecessary and can be eliminated.

ANSWER

The correct answer is **D**.

POWER**TIP**

Expect an error

Always assume the sentence contains an error. It's tempting to jump immediately to the conclusion that the sentence is correct as given. However, sometimes the choices provide a better way to phrase an awkward sentence that isn't technically incorrect.

Incorrect prepositions

Finding the wrong preposition is a little less tricky, but there are a few that could trip you up. Following is a list of 54 common word/preposition pairs.

54 COMMON
WORD/PREPOSITION PAIRS

afraid of	careless about	give up	look up	sorry for
angry at	capable of	grasp of	love of	study for
apologize for	care for	grow up	made of	success in
approval of	concern for	happy about	make up	sure of
ask about	confusion about	hatred of	married to	talk about
ask for	desire for	hope for	need for	think about
aware of	familiar with	interested in	pay for	tired of
belief in	find out	jealous of	participation in	trust in
belong to	fond of	look for	prepare for	understanding of
bring up	fondness for	look forward to	proud of	work for
reason for	respect for	similar to	worry about	

Writing **Section**

Adjectives and adverbs

Adjectives and adverbs are both modifiers, but they modify different things. An *adjective* modifies a *noun* or a *pronoun*; an *adverb* modifies a *verb*, an *adjective*, or another *adverb*.

You probably learned to identify adverbs by looking for the "ly" suffix on the end of an adjective.

>   **Adjective:** Get that *gross* sushi out of my sight.

>   **Adverb:** Sushi is *grossly* overrated.

Not all adverbs end in "ly," as seen in the following example.

>   **Adverb:** She talks so *fast* I can't understand her.

SAMPLE QUESTION

A **strong** leader must respond **quick** to events that threaten national security.

- **A** A strong   quick
- **B** The strongest quick
- **C** A stronger   quicker
- **D** A strong   quickly
- **E** A strong   quickest

You can eliminate answers **A**, **B**, **C**, and **E** because they misuse a form of the word *quick* as an adjective.

ANSWER

The correct answer is **D**.

Comparative adjectives and adverbs

Comparative adjectives and adverbs express a difference. You'll see comparative adjectives and adverbs in two forms:

- Add the suffix "er" to the adjective, as in cold and colder.
- Precede the adjective with the word "more," as in more likely.

SAMPLE QUESTION

Which underlined portion of the following sentence contains an error?

According to **statisticians**, you are
A
most likely to be **struck** by lightning
B   **C**
than you are to win the state lottery.
D
No error
E

The phrase labeled **B** contains an error because it uses the superlative *most* to create the comparative adverb.

ANSWER

The correct answer is **B**.

Take a deep breath and remember...

You know more grammar than you think you do. You may not know what to call every part of speech, but you will probably be able to tell when a sentence contains an error. Between the rules you just learned and your years of writing and speaking English, you should be able to tackle most of the multiple choice grammar questions with confidence.

Fixing Bad Writing

The inside scoop on sentence and paragraph correction questions

It's shockingly easy to find examples of bad writing. The free-flowing grammar and loose structure of newspaper and magazine articles, email, blogs, and the like are enough to make a an editor cry.

The new SAT tests your ability to fix bad sentences and paragraphs. This part of the test is less about applying specific grammar rules and more about the structure and content of sentences and paragraphs. It may take a few practice questions to get a feel for how this section of the test works.

Sentence correction

Sentence correction questions look a lot like the ones you reviewed in the Grammar Blitz. A portion of the sentence or the entire sentence will be underlined. You have the opportunity to change the underlined portion or to leave it as-is.

Although this section reviews concepts rather than actual rules, you will apply rules you learned in the last section to make the whole sentence better.

There are two areas of sentence structure that the new SAT emphasizes:

1. Balance
2. Brevity

Let's take a quick look at each.

Balance: parallel clauses

Many sentences include pairs or short lists of words, phrases, or clauses. A good sentence uses parallel structure to balance these elements. What this means is that if a sentence lists three items, they should all be in the same form; mixing nouns and verbs, gerunds and infinitives, present and past tense, or other mismatched combinations is a writing no-no.

Let's take a look at a few unbalanced examples.

> When you go to camp, you should pack your toothbrush, your sleeping bag, and bring your iPod.

In this example, *bring your iPod* doesn't match the other items in the list. The sentence should read:

> When you go to camp, you should pack *your toothbrush*, *your sleeping bag*, and *your iPod*.

Here's another example:

> These days, it seems like I always *go to sleep late* and *wake up*.

In this sentence, *go to sleep* is modified by the adjective *late*. The phrase *wake up* remains unmodified. This sentence would be better as:

> These days, it seems like I always *go to sleep late* and *wake up tired*.

And one more example:

> Franklin was so upset he didn't know whether he should be *crying* or *to laugh*.

This sentence pairs a gerund, *crying*, with an infinitive, *to laugh*. It should read:

> Franklin was so upset he didn't know whether he should be *crying* or *laughing*.

10 THINGS
TO REMEMBER ABOUT CORRECTING SENTENCES

Here's a mental checklist to run through when you see a sentence correction question.

 Read the sentence as-is.

 Read the sentence replacing the underlined section with each of the choices.

 Check the noun/verb agreement.

 Check modifiers.

 Make sure that pronouns are clear and necessary.

 Compare the tense of the underlined portion to the rest of the sentence.

 Check for parallel structure.

 Select your answer.

 Re-read the sentence with your final choice to make sure it's worded clearly.

 Mark your final answer.

Writing Section

Brevity: less is more

You may find a sentence that doesn't seem to have any obvious grammatical errors. When this happens, check all the responses. Do any of the responses say the same thing but use fewer words to do so? If this is the case, the shorter response is the correct answer.

SAMPLE QUESTION

The result of the situation is that I am often expected to carry a heavier workload than the other employees.

Ⓐ The results is that

Ⓑ Consequently,

Ⓒ The results are that

Ⓓ The result of the situation is

Ⓔ The result of the situation is that

ANSWER

The only thing really wrong with the underlined phrase is that it's wordy. Answer Ⓑ is the best choice, as it uses one word instead of seven.

Improving paragraphs

The paragraph editing section is one of the newest components of the new SAT. In this part of the exam, you'll find an essay that needs work. Each sentence is prefaced by a number, and questions will refer to those numbers. You'll combine sentences and alter the general structure of the paragraph in one of three ways:

1. You'll improve single sentences.

2. You'll improve single sentences within the context of the entire paragraph.

3. You'll organize the paragraph's structure.

It's important to read each paragraph thoroughly before trying to answer the questions.

Remember that the point of the exercise is to consider how the sentence in question fits within the entire essay. If you don't read the actual essay, you may not see how the overall context in which a sentence appears affects the answer choices.

SAMPLE QUESTION

(1) California Governor Arnold Schwarzenegger has become the leading example of how immigrants can find success in the United States. **(2)** His drive to succeed led him from the Mr. Olympia stage to the California State House. **(3)** His ambitions may ultimately be stopped by the US Constitution, which does not permit him to serve as president.

In context, which of the following improves sentence **3** the most?

Ⓐ His desire to become president may ultimately be stopped by the US Constitution, which does not permit him to serve as president.

Ⓑ His ambitions may ultimately run afoul of the US Constitution, which does not permit Mr. Schwarzenegger to serve as president.

Ⓒ His ambitions may ultimately be stopped by the US Constitution, which does not permit those not native-born citizens to serve as president.

Ⓓ His ambitions may ultimately be stopped by the US Constitution, which does not permit those born outside the United States to serve as president.

Ⓔ His success may ultimately be thwarted by the US Constitution.

The primary problem with sentence **3** is that it doesn't explain why Mr. Schwarzenegger cannot serve as president. Only answers Ⓒ and Ⓓ attempt to correct this flaw. Of those two answers, Ⓓ is the better worded.

ANSWER

The correct answer is Ⓓ.

Getting Organized

Each sentence should be grammatically correct, and each sentence should be appropriate within the context of the paragraph's purpose. However, the way in which the sentences are organized is as important as the meaning of each sentence individually. To test your skill in paragraph organization, you may need to move, add, or delete sentences from a paragraph.

SAMPLE**QUESTION**

(1) California Governor Arnold Schwarzenegger has become the leading example of how immigrants can find success in the United States. **(2)** His drive to succeed led him from the Mr. Olympia stage to the California State House. **(3) Maria Shriver, his wife, is a celebrity in her own right. (4)** His ambitions may ultimately be stopped by the US Constitution, which does not permit those born outside the United States to serve as president.

In context, which of the following improves sentence **3** the most?

Ⓐ Maria Shriver is a celebrity in her own right.

Ⓑ Maria Shriver, his wife, comes from a political family.

Ⓒ Maria Shriver, his wife, is a celebrity in her own right and maintains an equally challenging schedule.

Ⓓ Maria Shriver, his wife, was born in the United States.

Ⓔ Delete sentence 3.

There's nothing grammatically wrong with sentence **3**. The problem is that it doesn't add to the paragraph's purpose, which is to describe the limitations of Arnold Schwarzenegger's political ambitions.

ANSWER

The correct answer is Ⓔ.

Writing Section

Take a deep breath and remember...

Sentence and paragraph correction questions are a little different from the more-familiar grammar questions. However, with a little practice, you'll get the hang of it. Just remember to pay careful attention to the meaning of the whole sentence and how it relates to the rest of the paragraph as you try to spot the errors.

Essay Cheat Sheet

The most obvious addition to the new SAT is the essay. In this section, you'll have 25 minutes to create a short essay based on a writing prompt. Depending on the assignment, the SAT may ask you to persuade your reader to agree with you, to analyze a statement or argument, to compare and contrast two ideas, or to express your opinion about a topic.

Before you tackle a sample essay, let's look at a few guidelines that can help you regardless of the essay topic.

Pick your position

When you first read the essay challenge, take a minute or two to chew on it. Jot down your ideas and choose the one that you can support with the strongest essay. Then take a stand. Nail down a clear thesis statement that you can support with two or three clear examples or arguments. You don't even have to agree with the position you take—you just need to be able to communicate and support your thesis effectively.

Build a quick outline

High-scoring SAT essays look remarkably similar to one another—an introduction that states your position or thesis, two or three paragraphs that support your position, and a brief conclusion. Your outline should be nothing more than

I. The Thesis

II. Supporting idea #1

III. Supporting idea #2

IV. Supporting idea #3 (if you need it)

V. A Conclusion that ties your ideas together

Remember that a human will be reading your essay

Unlike the rest of the new SAT, which will be graded by a computer, a real live person will be grading your essay—along with essays written by a gazillion other students. Don't be afraid to make your essay interesting and creative as long as you don't become imprecise or deviate from good structure and mechanics.

USE GOOD MECHANICS

The SAT essay readers are looking for very specific things.

AVOID

- jargon
- clichés
- redundancies
- awkward or wordy phrasing

INCLUDE

- active verbs
- interesting transitions
- varied sentence structure
- strong word choices.

Breaking the Old Rules

You may be surprised to find that the new SAT doesn't enforce many of the rules your English teacher told you were unbreakable. Here are **Four Grammar Rules** you *won't* find in the new SAT Writing section.

Rule #1:
Never end a sentence with a preposition

While most Grammar textbooks still consider this a no-no, in common speech and writing it has become acceptable to end a sentence with a preposition.

Instead of saying: "For what are you here?"

You can get away with "What are you here for?"

And "Who did you come with?" is just as good as "With whom did you come?"

Rule #2:
Never split an infinitive

The infinitive form of a verb usually begins with the word *to*, as in "to be" or "to climb." In formal English grammar, you never put a word between the "to" and the "climb." The new SAT, however, allows split infinitives.

"To boldly go where no one has gone before" works just as well as "Boldly to go where no one has gone before"

Rule #3:
Use *whom* when you need an objective case pronoun

If you get "who" and "whom" confused, don't despair. The New SAT doesn't test your ability to use who and whom correctly.

"Who were you with last Saturday?" and "Whom were you with last Saturday?" are both acceptable.

Rule #4:
Good and *Bad* are adjectives, not adverbs

You may remember (and then again, maybe not!) that "good" and "bad" are adjectives while "well" and "badly" are adverbs. However, in common speech, we use them all as adverbs. The new SAT will not test you on this distinction.

All the following are acceptable:

I feel good.

I feel well.

I feel bad.

The Essay is Your Friend

While good writing may seem as if it were a mystical art beyond your reach, anyone willing to put in the practice can do at least as well on the essay as on the rest of the new SAT. The SAT isn't looking for essays that make you weep or incite you to action. Your SAT essay needs to demonstrate to the readers that you have a specific level of skill in written communication. No magic required.

Your essay will be graded by two experts who have a very specific set of things they want to see. Here's what they're looking for.

- A well developed, insightful, and focused point of view.

- Proof that you can think critically and express your ideas in written form. You'll want to use clear and appropriate examples, anecdotes, and reasons to support your position.

- Logical organization end to end. The reader expects a smooth ride.

- A variety of writing techniques, such as varied sentence structure and length.

- Strong vocabulary and appropriate word choice. The readers won't penalize you for not including big words; they will penalize you for using words incorrectly.

- Adherence to the rules of standard written English. Your essay should be free of grammatical and spelling errors. However, a few spelling errors won't keep you from getting a 6

Regardless of your starting point, you can improve your writing. You may not be able to move from a 2 to a 6 between now and the time you sit for the exam, but you can certainly bump your score up a point or two by concentrating a few of your study sessions on writing SAT essays.

POWERTIP

Lipstick on a pig

It's still a pig even if you put lipstick on it, so the saying goes. All the creative thinking, fancy vocabulary, and complicated sentence structure won't cover up bad writing. Nail your thesis and supporting examples, use good mechanics—especially transitions—and express yourself clearly. Don't even think about getting fancy until you can do the basics without breaking a sweat.

What does the writing process look like?

If you're afraid of staring at a blank paper wondering what to write, you're in luck. The new SAT gives you a head start by giving you a subject. The assignment, sometimes called a prompt, can actually be a big help. You aren't expected to be a subject matter expert; you just need to be able to pick a thesis based on the assignment and support it with a few well-written paragraphs.

Better still, the SAT expects you to answer the question directly and answer only the question asked. Then you get to stop. While creativity is encouraged, you aren't expected to go beyond the assignment spelled out in the exam. Stick to the subject, focus on the answer, and don't be distracted by extraneous thoughts and ideas that don't necessarily support your position. Stick with what you know and fully develop each thought by using strong examples or meaningful anecdotes.

Let's take a look at a typical SAT Writing prompt.

In 1920, women across the United States won the right to vote. Back then, it was a controversial issue and many opposed it. Certainly, few seriously thought that the citizens of the United States would ever elect a woman to be the president of the United States. Now that we've entered the twenty-first century, electing a woman to be president of the United States seems inevitable.

Assignment: Do you think the United States is ready for a woman president? Write an essay that develops your point of view on this issue. Support your position with reasoning and examples taken from reading, studies, personal experience, or observation.

The assignment couldn't be much clearer. It asks you a straightforward yes or no question: Do you think the United States is ready for a woman president. It then tells you that you can support your answer with darn near anything you want—from personal observations to stuff you should have learned in school.

The only thing you have to do is pick a position on the question, nail down two or three clear reasons why you're position is reasonable, and express your ideas in clear prose. Let's take this writing assignment through the 6 steps you'd follow if you ran into it on the new SAT.

Writing Section

POWER**TIP**

Handwriting counts

Even the best essay will receive a low score if the readers can't read it. Spend some time practicing your handwriting, both cursive and printing. Ask a few people you trust to read your samples and work on correcting any problems they find.

Scoring higher on your essay

To score higher on your essay, pay close attention to content, structure, and mechanics.

Content

- **State your thesis in one sentence.** You'll lose points if the experts can't identify a clear thesis sentence in your first paragraph.

- **Supporting paragraphs should each state and develop a single argument or example.** You'll lose points if you cover more than one supporting idea in each body paragraph.

- **Supporting ideas must tie directly to your thesis.** Scrap any sentences that don't support your thesis.

- **Don't waste words.** No matter how beautifully you write, you'll lose points for including irrelevant information.

Structure

- **Most 12-point essays have only four paragraphs.** Add a fifth paragraph only if you can fully develop the additional example or thought. No matter how succinct and direct you are, you won't get a perfect score with a three-paragraph essay.

- **Don't bury your thesis and supporting arguments.** You won't lose points for putting your thesis and topic sentences at the beginning of your paragraphs. However, you will lose points if the expert readers can identify your main ideas easily.

- **Write a meaningful conclusion.** Your conclusion should restate your thesis and tie together your supporting examples. You'll lose points if your conclusion is meaningless or is missing altogether.

Mechanics

- **Be consistent.** Write your entire essay in present tense and active voice. You'll lose points if you bounce between tenses or if you use a lot of passive voice.

- **Don't use words you can't define or spell.** There are lots of good word choices out there. If you aren't confident that you know what a word means or how to spell it, choose another word.

- **Be neat.** You'll lose points if your handwriting is illegible. Take the extra few seconds required to think through each sentence before you commit it to paper.

GO FOR THE FLOW
24 TRANSITIONS THAT WILL MAKE YOUR ESSAY SILKY SMOOTH

A good essay consists of two or three arguments or examples that support your main idea. However, it's important to make sure your sentences and paragraphs flow together smoothly. Transitions are the key to good flow in an essay. Here is a list of common transitional words and phrases you can work into your essay.

although	for example	however	in no way	nevertheless	on the other hand
as a result	for instance	in addition	in other words	next	otherwise
by no means	fortunately	in contrast	likewise	now	similarly
consequently	furthermore	subsequently	then	therefore	unfortunately

Step 1: Brainstorm your way to a perfect thesis

Pick already. Is the US ready for a female commander in chief or not? Here's a clear, but boring thesis sentence that answers the question in the affirmative.

> I believe the United States is ready for a woman president.

Is this thesis clear? Yes. Can you come up with two or three good reasons to support it? Yes. Is it the best thesis sentence ever written? Not by a mile, but it will get you started toward building your essay. You know what you're going to be writing about and that's more than half the battle.

It's important to remember a couple of points. First of all, plan to take a minute or two before you start writing to brainstorm. Write down two or three possible thesis statements. At this point, it's OK if they're of the boring variety like the one above.

If you get stuck and can't decide, read your list of examples and anecdotes to see if a theme has developed. The thread that holds your ideas together may be your best thesis.

For the writing prompt you're considering at the moment, other thesis statements could be

- The United States isn't ready for a woman president.
- I am ready for a Woman president, but the United States is not.
- Given the global trend toward inclusion of women in top political roles, it is only a matter of time until the United States elects a woman as president.

Step 2: Make an outline

The key to turning a thesis statement into an essay is a good plan of attack. In this case, the best way to guarantee success is to make an outline. For the SAT essay, your outline needs to identify your thesis and the main ideas you're using to support the thesis.

The process of creating this quickie outline will often help you select the best thesis for your essay. Suppose, for example, you select the original thesis:

> I believe the United States is ready for a woman president.

Because this thesis asserts that you *believe* the United States is ready for a woman president, you could spend the rest of the essay defending your belief. Your outline might include the supporting points

- Supporting idea 1: In my home, equality of the sexes is considered to be obvious and important.
- Supporting idea 2: My teachers taught me to believe that I can do anything.
- Supporting idea 3: I cannot accept that my country is so out of touch with the modern world.

This could be an interesting essay, but it's not the strongest choice. A more definitive statement, such as the last thesis suggested, gives you gives you room to mix personal opinion with hard evidence:

> Given the global trend toward inclusion of women in top political roles, it is only a matter of time until the United States elects a woman as president.

You can support this thesis statement with points that build support in a progressive, logical argument:

- Supporting idea 1: There are no legal, biological or intellectual barriers to a woman becoming president—only social factors.

- Supporting idea 2: Women have served as leaders in India, Thailand, and even Great Britain.
- Supporting idea 3: Women have assumed increasingly more significant roles in US politics, so the US electorate has become accustomed to seeing a woman's name on a ballot.

You can write either essay and have a shot at getting a good score. The nature of the second thesis, however gives you more options. Building an outline not only organizes your thoughts for the essay, it helps you determine if your thesis is strong enough.

POWER**TIP**

You can't be more dead

Not all adjectives and adverbs can take the comparative form. For instance, terms such as *impossible*, *final*, and *unique* are absolutes.

It would be incorrect to say:

The crash was more fatal because the airbag didn't inflate.

Fatal is fatal enough by itself; more fatal is overkill.

It's enough to say:

The crash was fatal because the airbag didn't inflate.

Step 3: Choose your style

Although most good essays will have a lot in common—a strong thesis and good supporting points, and so forth—they might not all *sound* the same. A personal narrative and a formal theme can make the same points using the same supporting ideas but use radically different language.

For example, compare these two paragraphs:

Given the global trend toward inclusion of women in top political roles, it is only a matter of time until the United States elects a woman as president. Although I'm a young woman, I have lived long enough to know that the differences between men and women do not limit the potential of a woman to lead this country—my country. Further, I've long considered powerful women like Indira Gandhi and Margaret Thatcher, both of whom led their nations, to be my role models. With Hillary Clinton and Elisabeth Dole rising to national prominence in recent elections, it seems inevitable to me that a woman will soon get a shot at the top job.

Given the global trend toward inclusion of women in top political roles, it is only a matter of time until the United States elects a woman as president. The US constitution offers no barrier to a female president, and the scientific community offers no credible evidence that a woman would not be up to the task for biological reasons. Women have served successfully as national leaders in traditionally masculine countries as diverse as India and England. Even in the United States, recent elections have shown an increasing acceptance of strong women in national politics.

Both paragraphs introduce an essay using the same thesis and both follow the same outline. The choice between personal narrative and a more formal style ultimately boils down to your preference. As you practice, try writing a few of each and see which you like better. Becoming natural and comfortable with your style will help you when you sit down to one of the most *unnatural* and *uncomfortable* experiences yet devised.

By the way, you should have noticed that both these paragraphs state the thesis and then preview the outline. Your opening paragraph should let the reader know what to expect. In the SAT essay, you don't want to surprise the grader with a late plot twist or a shock ending. You want to answer the question from the writing prompt as clearly and completely as you can in 25 minutes.

POWER**TIP**

Consistency counts

Although you don't have to write in any particular tense in your essay, you will be expected to use tense correctly and consistently throughout your essay. Unless the subject calls for something else, you should probably stick with present tense in your essay.

Step 4: Write the supporting paragraphs

If you've picked a good thesis, built a solid outline with two or three strong supporting ideas, and have drafted a bulletproof introduction that communicates both the style and the substance of the essay, the rest of your job is a cakewalk. You just need to take each outline point and use it as the topic sentence of a supporting paragraph. You should have one idea per paragraph, and that idea should now appear in both your outline and your intro.

Continuing our hypothetical essay, let's tackle the first supporting paragraph. To keep things interesting, let's look at the personal narrative approach:

> No one can fail to recognize that there are real and meaningful differences between men and women. However, even the good-old-boys at my father's accounting firm agree that are no legal, biological or intellectual barriers to a woman becoming president—they just aren't ready for it. My generation is ready. We are the ones who will be writing the memos and making the tough calls when the last of the good-old-boys has gone out for his last happy hour. The world has changed around them, and like it or not, they're going to hear a woman take the oath of office on a cold January day sometime before the end of the next decade.

Let's look at what this paragraph does:

- It supports the thesis
- It follows the outline
- It continues the personal narrative style
- It sets the tone for the essay

The remaining two body paragraphs should sound about the same, but should make their respective points in support of the thesis. Now, let's wrap up our essay.

Step 5: Write the conclusion

At this point, you should put down your pencil. Take a deep breath and read everything you've just written. Your conclusion should do two very simple things, but it needs to do them both very well.

First of all, your conclusion should restate your thesis. **Do not** rewrite your thesis word for word. Summarize it. Make subtle changes to let the reader know that you've proven it beyond any shadow of a doubt. In our essay, you could try something like:

> While inevitable, change is often difficult; accepting the idea of a woman president has certainly been a big change for many Americans.

This restatement captures the sense of the thesis, but adds the sense that the majority of Americans have already adjusted to idea that a woman will be president.

The balance of the conclusion needs to tie together the supporting ideas. Let's complete this conclusion:

> While inevitable, change is often difficult; accepting the idea of a woman president has certainly been a big change for many Americans. A decade or two from now, the idea that a woman might not be welcomed as the chief executive will seem quaint and perhaps a little absurd. For now, my generation is on the front line of a new day in the great American experiment. We will carry signs, wear buttons, fight, weep, and finally cheer as the biggest glass ceiling of them all comes crashing down.

Step 6: Tidy up

Sorry to disappoint you, but your essay isn't quite finished. Your last step is to read the whole thing through, checking for proper punctuation, spelling, word choice, transitions, and everything else that you'd expect to see in a piece of finished writing. The best essay in the world won't get a perfect score if it's riddled with bad grammar, poor spelling, and missing punctuation.

You can cross out a word or even a whole sentence if necessary. You don't have to erase. The readers will disregard marked out content. Don't cross out every other word, but a few strikethroughs are acceptable. You're also allowed to insert words or even an entire sentence. Use the caret character (^) to point to phrases or words above the line

POWER**TIP**

Idioms

An idiom is a phrase that has a commonly understood meaning but which may not translate literally. The new SAT might include some questions that test your ability to recognize and use common idioms. Here are a few examples of common idioms:

come on strong

get your feet wet

all ears

got your goat

get on board

13 Keys to Writing Success

Following the steps we just covered will ensure that you write an essay with a strong thesis and a good structure. Putting the words together, however, is not a trivial exercise. Fortunately, there are about a dozen rules that will help you avoid the most common SAT essay pitfalls.

1 Know what's expected

Keep your audience in mind at all times; in this case, it's a pair of expert graders employed by the College Board. You want to produce an accurate, well-developed essay that supports your position. If the readers learn something new from your essay, so much the better. If the readers are actually inspired, great, but it's not required.

2 Address the prompt

Before you start compiling your thoughts, take the time to read and reread the writing challenge. Be absolutely sure that your response answers the question the way the readers expect it to. For instance, the challenge may ask you if you agree or disagree with a particular statement, and then you must support your position. If the challenge asks for two or more examples, don't stop with one. If asked to provide just one example, don't give them two or three. Read the instructions carefully and give them what they request—no more, no less.

3 Be specific, thorough, and personal

Be precise in your answer. If the question asks you to comment on a quote, do so deliberately and thoughtfully. It's alright to develop the subject a bit in general terms, but be sure to give them what they ask for—your response to the quote. Be specific, be thorough, and be personal. Why personal? Because sharing personal experiences and ideas is the best (and perhaps easiest) way to develop your thesis.

4 You can be informal but not imprecise

Remember, you're not writing a legal brief or a Constitutional amendment. Although your essay shouldn't be as informal as conversation, your essay can be conversation-like. You want your essay to be palatable to a wide audience. Relax, and apply grammar rules, but do so in a natural manner.

5 Find a mentor

It's very difficult to edit your own writing. It's difficult to find your own errors or improve your own work. You should find a mentor—a teacher or perhaps even a professional editor—who's willing to read and critique your writing examples.

There's simply no substitution for practice where writing is concerned. The more you practice, the more proficient you will become. Having another person read your writing forces you to confront your shortcomings.

6 Don't repeat yourself

If two sentences seem to repeat the same thought, cut one of them, no matter how fond you are of both sentences. Combine the best of both if you must, but by all means, reduce both sentences to just one. Don't repeat yourself just to make the essay longer. The judges won't appreciate the deception.

Writing Section

7 Move it along

If a sentence doesn't move your essay along, rewrite, or better yet, remove it. By itself, the sentence may be artful or even poignant, but if it doesn't support your position, delete it.

8 Use smooth transitions

Use transitions to help your reader move from thought to thought, which in this case, will probably be paragraph to paragraph. Keep in mind that there needs to be a logical choice to your use of transitions, and they aren't always necessary. Don't overuse them and make sure that they match the current thought. No reader likes a bumpy ride.

9 Don't waste words

Make every word count. Just as each sentence should move your reader to discovering your position, each word should be as specific as possible. Remove words that aren't necessary. In addition, don't use big words just because you can. Use only words you actually know well enough to use and spell correctly. The readers will probably forgive a misspelled word, but spelling does count. Avoid using a word if you're not sure of its spelling.

Also, unless you're using technical terms that are necessary within the context of the subject, avoid jargon. Technical terms can be used, if used appropriately. Never, ever, use cliché's in your writing. Phrases like "fair-weather friend" or "peas in a pod" have no place in your essay.

10 Variety helps

For the sake of variety and style, vary the sentence length and structure. Long sentences are fine, and often necessary, especially when sharing complicated ideas or circumstances. However, long sentences can be confusing and unnecessarily convoluted. A short sentence isn't the sign of a dull writer.

11 Get personal if you dare

The best essay will create a relationship between the author and the reader. One way to do so is to use personal and very specific nouns. Think of the five human senses: sight, smell, hearing, taste, and touch. However, if you're writing a formal essay, you should probably limit your use of first-person pronouns.

12 Use active voice

Active voice has an apparent subject; passive voice has an assumed subject.

Active

Who shot who?

> Joe shot Fred.

Passive

Who was shot by whom

> Fred was shot by Joe.

If the subject of your sentence isn't performing the action, the sentence is passive. Rewrite the sentence so that the subject actually performs the action.

In the best case, passive voice is boring, wordy, and weak. In the worst, case, it's misleading and imprecise.

Fred was shot is passive, and it also omits the important detail of who did the shooting.

Watch for the following verb phrases:

- Replace *to be* when possible (that includes *be, am are, is, was, were, begin,* and *been*).
- Be careful with past tense verbs such as *was* and *were*. When combined with another verb to create a verb phrase, it's probably passive voice.
- Omit *have* whenever possible. The word *have* is necessary, used correctly, but it often points to passive voice.

13 **Don't apologize**

If you say it, own it. You don't think, believe, or feel an essay. Let the thoughts and examples roll into your conclusion, and don't apologize or cushion your readers. Don't be embarrassed by what you have to share. It's unnecessary and distracting, and an apology weakens your position, and hence your essay. Avoid phrases such as

- In my opinion
- I, some, or many think
- I, some, or many believe.

POWER**TIP**

Some verbs are timeless

Some things or ideas—diamonds, good friends, The Beatles—are timeless. When you refer to these things, use *present tense*. For example:

> Even the ancient Egyptians knew that good friends are priceless.

The subject and verb agree in time and are set in past tense—*ancient Eqyptians* **knew**.

The phrase "good friends are priceless" is set in present tense and is the direct object of the sentence. It would be incorrect to say:

> Even the ancient Egyptians knew that good friends were priceless.

POWER**TIP**

Clear your throat

Before you start writing, make a quick plan for your essay. Take a second or two to think through the way a sentence will sound before your actually write it down. You might even want to write a draft of the sentence down on scratch paper before adding it to your essay. A few seconds of thought before you commit your words to paper will save you valuable minutes you'd spend trying to fix a bad sentence later in the writing process.

Take a breath and remember...

The essay is more subjective than many parts of the new SAT, but it's not voodoo. There are some very specific things you can do to make your writing better and to prepare for the SAT essay. The three or four hours it takes to write a couple of practice essays and review them with a trusted mentor will be some of the most valuable prep time you invest.

Writing Section

How You Can Grade Your Practice Essays

Two experts will read and appraise your essay. Unfortunately, neither of them will be hanging out with you at Starbucks as you study for the new SAT. To get a better idea of how your practice essays rate, it helps to know how your SAT essay will be graded.

The perfect essay is worth a total of 12 points. Each of the expert readers will each give your essay up to 6 points, and they will be looking for some very specific things. If the grades the experts assign differ by more than two points, a third expert will grade the essay.

Although the essay is new to the SAT, the SAT II has offered an essay test for many years; the grading process for the New SAT is based on that test. Although you can't duplicate the grading process exactly, but you'll get pretty close if you or someone you trust assigns 1-6 grade on each of the following points.

POWER**TIP**

Do Not Go Off Topic!

Essays written on a topic other than the one assigned will receive a score of zero. It doesn't matter how creative you are, you can't concoct the perfect essay and offer it as an alternative to the writing prompt provided.

Critical thinking

6 ☐ This essay demonstrates outstanding critical thinking and presents a compelling thesis.

5 ☐ This essay demonstrates well-developed critical thinking with a strong thesis.

4 ☐ This essay demonstrates adequate critical thinking and contains an identifiable thesis.

3 ☐ This essay demonstrates some critical thinking and contains an identifiable position but no clear thesis.

2 ☐ This essay demonstrates poor critical thinking and has an inconsistent, unclear, or missing thesis.

1 ☐ This essay demonstrates no critical thinking and no thesis.

Support for the thesis

6 ☐ This essay supports and develops its thesis with relevant and insightful support based on generally accepted facts, relevant personal experience, or insightful observations.

5 ☐ This essay supports and develops its thesis with relevant examples, arguments, and evidence.

4 ☐ This essay demonstrates support for the thesis with generally adequate but unoriginal examples, arguments, and evidence.

3 ☐ This essay provides insufficient support for the thesis and contains inappropriate, misleading, or erroneous examples, arguments, or evidence.

2 ☐ This essay provides insufficient support for the thesis due to poor or missing examples, arguments, and evidence.

1 ☐ This essay provides no identifiable thesis or support for its position.

Writing Section

Focus and progression

6 ☐ This essay demonstrates clear organization and focus, with smooth transitions and a logical progression of ideas.

5 ☐ This essay demonstrates clear organization and focus with a coherent progression of ideas.

4 ☐ This essay demonstrates clear organization and focus with a reasonable progression of ideas.

3 ☐ This essay has faults in organization and focus and uses ideas that may not logically belong.

2 ☐ The organization and focus are poor and many of the ideas are disconnected or irrelevant.

1 ☐ The problems with organization and focus are so sever that the essay is incoherent.

Use of language

6 ☐ This essay demonstrates language mastery and the vocabulary is descriptive and well-chosen.

5 ☐ This essay demonstrates language competence and the vocabulary is consistently accurate and appropriate.

4 ☐ This essay demonstrates inconsistent language usage and the vocabulary is generally accurate and appropriate.

3 ☐ This essay demonstrates basic language competence with occasional inconsistent or inappropriate vocabulary.

2 ☐ This essay demonstrates poor language skills the vocabulary is limited and frequently incorrect.

1 ☐ This essay demonstrates no serviceable facility with language and contains numerous vocabulary errors.

Writing Section

Sentence structure

6 ☐ This essay contains well-planned variation in sentence style and structure.

5 ☐ This essay contains multiple types of sentence structures.

4 ☐ This essay contains variation in sentence structure within a limited range.

3 ☐ This essay contains generally accurate sentences with little structural variety.

2 ☐ This essay contains errors in sentence structure.

1 ☐ This essay contains numerous errors in sentence structure.

Mechanics—grammar, spelling, and punctuation

6 ☐ This essay has no more than one or two mechanical errors.

5 ☐ This essay has few mechanical errors.

4 ☐ This essay has some mechanical errors.

3 ☐ This essay has multiple mechanical errors of more than one variety.

2 ☐ This essay has multiple mechanical errors that affect the reader's ability to understand some parts of it.

1 ☐ This essay has so many mechanical errors that the reader's may not be able to understand it.

The Good, the Bad, and the Ugly:
3 Essays Exploded

When it comes to writing, there's no substitute for a good example—followed by a lot of practice. Although the essay may seem more subjective than the other parts of the new SAT, the SAT graders actually have a very strict set of guidelines they use to evaluate your writing. In the following pages, we'll look at three essays designed to reflect scores of 6, 4, and 2. Each essay is based on the writing prompt below.

> In 1920, women across the United States won the right to vote. Back then, it was a controversial issue and many opposed it. Certainly, few seriously thought that the citizens of the United States would ever elect a woman to be the president of the United States. Now that we've entered the twenty-first century, electing a woman to be president of the United States seems inevitable.

Assignment

Do you think the United States is ready for a woman president? Write an essay that develops your point of view on this issue. Support your position with reasoning and examples taken from reading, studies, personal experience, or observation.

Sample essay #1

1 <u>Given the global trend toward inclusion of women in top political roles, it is only a matter of time until the United States elects a woman as president.</u> **2** <u>Although I'm a young woman,</u> I have lived long enough to know that **3** <u>the differences between men and women do not limit the potential of a woman to lead this country—</u> my country. Further, I've long considered powerful **3** <u>women like Indira Gandhi and Margaret Thatcher, both of whom led their nations, to be my role models.</u> With **3** <u>Hillary Clinton and Elizabeth Dole rising to national prominence</u> in recent elections, it seems inevitable to me that a woman will soon get a shot at the top job.

No one can fail to recognize that there are real and meaningful differences between men and women. **4** <u>However, even the good-old-boys at my father's accounting firm agree that there are no legal, biological or intellectual barriers to a woman becoming president— they just aren't ready for it.</u> My generation is ready. We are the ones who will be writing the memos and making the tough calls when the last of the good-old-boys has gone out for his last happy hour. The world has changed around them, and like it or not, they're going to hear a woman take the oath of office **5** <u>on a cold January day</u> sometime before the end of the next decade.

6 <u>Although</u> voters in the United States have not yet elected a woman to the top spot in the land, other countries offer numerous examples of powerful women in roles of national leadership. In my lifetime, Margaret Thatcher showed herself to be more than up to the challenge of leading Great Britain, one of our closest allies. Preceding her by several generations, India—one of the world's most populous nations—placed Indira Gandhi atop the political hierarchy and found her to be among their strongest leaders in their short history of independence. As I and my peers look beyond or borders, we see role models that show us what is possible in our own country.

7 <u>Even within our own country</u>, the seeds of change have been sown. In recent elections, Hillary Clinton and Elizabeth Dole have shown that blue and red voters alike recognize that women can assume roles of national leadership. **8** <u>Many men have made the leap from the Senate to the White House. Can women really be far behind?</u>

1 Strong, clear thesis responding directly to the writing prompt.

2 Introduction of personal narrative elements.

3 Supporting arguments established in opening paragraph.

4 Assertive statement and interesting use of language.

5 Strong image.

6 Transition showing contrast.

7 Transition showing support.

8 Variation in sentence structure.

Writing Section

(essay continued on next page)

(essay continued)

> **9** Restatement of thesis without repetition.

> **10** Powerful conclusion tying together theme and voice of essay.

9 <u>While inevitable, change is often difficult; accepting the idea of a woman president has certainly been a big change for many Americans.</u> A decade or two from now, the idea that a woman might not be welcomed as the chief executive will seem quaint and perhaps a little absurd. For now, my generation is on the front line of a new day in the great American experiment. **10** <u>We will carry signs, wear buttons, fight, weep, and finally cheer as the biggest glass ceiling of them all comes crashing down.</u>

Why this essay gets a 6

This essay thoughtfully and effectively presents the case that, "it is only a matter of time until the United States elects a woman as president " The writer supports this thesis by providing examples both from history and current events. As well, the author relates her own personal experience, weaving personality into the narrative. Further critical thinking comes through as the author systematically breaks down traditional arguments toward a woman's potential as a national leader, stating "there are no legal, biological or intellectual barriers to a woman becoming president." Additionally, the author asserts a clear and forceful position with statements such as, "We are the ones who will be writing the memos and making the tough calls when the last of the good-old-boys has gone out for his last happy hour." The ideas presented are coherent and well-organized, with attention to paragraph structure and mechanics. The essay demonstrates clear mastery of mechanics and a fluency with language.

Sample essay #2

1 <u>The United States is ready for a woman president</u>. **2** <u>There's no reason a woman can't be president</u>. There's **3** <u>no law against it</u>. Other countries have had women presidents. There are even **4** <u>women senators right now</u>.

5 <u>I think</u> women are just as good as men **6** <u>when it comes to leading</u>. My mom is a vice president at her **7** <u>bank and</u> she even **8** <u>makes more money than my dad</u>. The constitution of the United States says that you have to be over 35 years old and born in the United States. **9** <u>It never mentions whether or not it's OK to wear a dress.</u>

Other countries have had women leaders. There was one a long time ago in India and **10** <u>Mary Thacker</u> in England led her country. It is important for American girls to know about these women. If we would **11** <u>just be more open minded</u> we might see that a woman could be a president here too.

There are two women leaders in Washington right now. President Clinton's wife Hillary is there. So is Bob Dole's wife. If a woman can be in the senate, there's no reason **12** <u>they</u> couldn't also be president.

13 <u>In conclusion, a woman could definitely be president of the United States.</u> We just need to get rid of the old attitudes that keep us thinking that only men can be leaders. **14** <u>I hope that I can see a woman president someday soon.</u>

Why this essay gets a 4

This essay adequately presents the case that, "the United States is ready for a woman president." The writer supports this thesis with several coherent thoughts—personal experience, history, and current events—but does not develop these ideas sufficiently. The author jumps in and out of personal narrative style but does not do so effectively. The structure of the essay demonstrates some level of critical thinking, but phrases such as "I think" and "just be more open minded" are simplistic and offer little support. The author shows some fluency with language, but makes several mechanical mistakes.

1 Thesis is weak and unimaginative.

2 Offers no meaningful support for the thesis.

3 Good supporting thought but poorly stated.

4 Good supporting idea.

5 Weak paragraph opening. No transition.

6 Awkward.

7 Run-on sentence. Requires a comma.

8 Irrelevant detail. Does not support thesis.

9 Clever way to express this idea.

10 Incorrect name.

11 "Just be more open-minded" isn't strong support for thesis.

12 Agreement problem. Should be "she".

13 Weak restatement of thesis. "In conclusion" is a poor choice to open final paragraph.

14 Irrelevant sentence.

Sample essay #3

1 Thesis is weak. Includes two supporting ideas that should be in separate sentences. Run-on sentence.

2 Irrelevant information.

3 Good supporting idea, is developed inadequately in the second paragraph.

4 "It's not fair" shows little depth in critical thinking.

5 A poor choice of words, but is an attempt at a transition.

6 Poorly executed attempt to tie ideas from the essay together.

7 Whimsical touch—adds personality and relates to the personal statement in the first paragraph.

1 The US ought to have a woman president because a woman could do the job just as good as a man and it's not fair that we don't have a woman president just because she's a woman. **2** If I was old enough to be president I would do a good job and I'm a girl. There's lots of other places that have women presidents. **3** America was built on freedom and equality, and we should be able to have a woman president.

Just because you are a woman, **4** it's not fair if you can't be president. Because this is America, you should be able to do whatever you want. If a woman is the best person for the job, then she should be president. Lots of women go to college and get all the degrees that men presidents get. They should be able to be president too then.

5 I want to end up by saying that I want to be president someday. Or I want my daughter to be president. **6** If I work hard and I learn what I need to then I believe that the US would be ready for the first woman president, **7** me.

Why this essay gets a 2

This essay addresses the issue raised by the prompt, stating, "the US ought to have a woman president." The supporting arguments presented, "woman could do the job just as good as a man," "woman could do the job just as good as a man," "There's lots of other places that have women presidents," and "America was built on freedom and equality" are all reasonable ideas, but none is developed adequately. This essay relies wholly on the author's opinion and does not relate any historical facts or observations in sufficient detail. The structure and mechanics of this essay are seriously flawed, and the writer demonstrates minimal competency in use of language.

Math
Section

Going Around in Circles

You must be familiar with the basic geometry and terminology of circles to do well on the SAT math section. Let's look at a circle in all its glory.

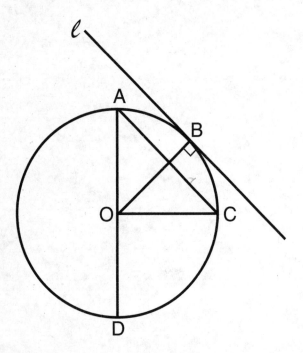

The parts of a circle.

- O is the center of the circle. The center is a point that is equidistant from every point on the circle.

- $\overline{OA}$, $\overline{OB}$, $\overline{OC}$, and $\overline{OD}$ are all **radii** of the circle. (radii is the plural of **radius**.) A radius is a line segment that extends from the center of the circle to a point on the circle. All radii of a circle have the same length.

- $\overline{AD}$ is a **diameter** of the circle. A diameter is a line segment that runs from one point on the circle to another point on the circle, passing through the center of the circle. All diameters of the circle have the same length, which is twice the radius.

- $\overline{AC}$ is a **chord** of the circle. A chord is a line segment between any two points on the circle.

- The points on the circle from A to B, or from A to C, form an **arc**. Unlike a chord, an arc is measured along the circle. You can measure an arc by the length of the portion of the circle that it contains, or by the central angle that it includes. For example, if you're told that ∠AOC is a right angle, the arc from A to C measures 90°.

- The line ℓ is **tangent** to the circle. A tangent line touches the circle at precisely one point, and is perpendicular to the radius of the circle at that point. In this case, $\ell \perp \overline{OB}$.

Circle Formulas

You should also know the two major formulas associated with the circle, both of which involve the number π, which is approximately 3.14. The circumference of a circle is the distance around the circle. If C is the circumference and d is the diameter of the circle, then

$C = \pi d$

For a circle with a diameter of 6,

$C = 6 \times \pi = 18.84$

The area of a circle also involves π. To determine the area, start with the radius r:

$A = \pi \times r^2$

For a circle with a diameter of 6, a radius of 3,

$A = \pi 3^2 = 9 \times \pi = 28.26$

POWER**TIP**

To find the length of an arc, you may be able to set up the following proportion:

The central angle of the arc/360 = the length of the arc/circumference of the circle

So, given a circle whose circumference is 40 inches and an arc whose central angle is 45°, you'd get

45/360 = Length of arc/40 or Length of arc = 5 inches

About Average

What it's called	What it is	How you get it	What it looks like
Mean (or Average)	The average of a set of values	Divide the sum of the values by the count of the values.	{2,5,6,5,8,7,4,5} The Mean is 42/8 or 5.25
Median	The middle value in a set of values arranged in ascending or descending order. **Brain jogger:** A median is also the divider in the middle of a highway.	Find the middle value in the list—the 7th value would be the midpoint in a set of 13. If you have an even number of elements, find the pair in the middle and average them—you'd average the 7th and 8th values in a set of 14.	{2,5,6,6,8,7,4,5} arranged in ascending order {2,4,5,5,6,6,7,8} The Median is the average of the two middle values. (5 + 6)/2 = 5.5
Mode	The most common value. **Brain jogger:** In French, mode means fashion. The clothes in fashion are the ones you see most frequently.	The most common value. A set with no repeated values has no mode. A set where two or more values appear with equal frequency as the most common elements would have more than one mode.	{2,5,6,5,8,7,4,5} The Mode is the most common value—5 in this set.
Range	The difference between the highest and lowest values. How far apart the bottom value is from the top value.	Locate the largest and smallest values in the set. Subtract the lower value from the higher one.	{2,5,6,5,8,7,4,5} 2 is the lowest value 8 is the highest value 8-2=6 so the Range is 6

Coordinate Geometry

The SAT will test your knowledge of coordinate geometry. Coordinate geometry uses mathematical equations to manipulate points, lines, and figures in the coordinate plane.

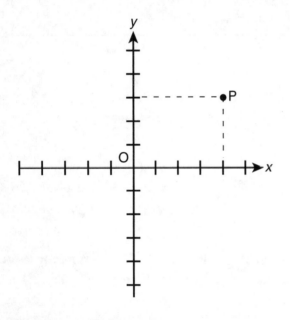

The coordinate plane.

The coordinate plane is marked off by two axes, the x axis and the y axis, which meet at a 90° angle. The tick marks on the axes indicate units of length, and the arrows indicate the direction in which the units increase. By convention, positive x is to the right, and positive y is to the top of the diagram. The point where the axes cross is the origin, labeled O in the figure. This point has an x-value of 0 and a y-value of 0. You can identify any point in the coordinate plane by giving its x-value and y-value as an ordered pair, with the x-value first. Thus, the point P in the figure is at the location (4, 3): four units to the right on the x axis and then three units up in the positive y direction.

Slope and y-Intercept

A line is represented in coordinate geometry by an equation of the form

$$y = mx + b$$

The two numbers m and b are constants, and have a special meaning:

- m is the *slope* of the line, which is defined as the change in y (*rise*) over the change in x (run). Remember, the change in y is always on top—y flies high.

- b is the *y-intercept* of the line, the point at which the line crosses the y axis.

Graphing a line

If you're given the equation of a line, you can draw it on the coordinate plane by finding any two points that fit the equation and then drawing a line that connects those points. For example, suppose you're given the equation:

$$y = \frac{1}{3}x - 2$$

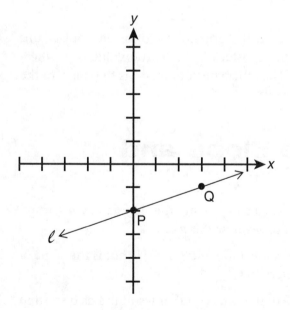

Graphing a line.

To graph the line, you need to come up with two points on the line. One easy point to find is the one where x = 0. Plug this value in to the equation to determine the corresponding y value:

$$y = \frac{1}{3}x - 2$$

$$y = \frac{1}{3}(0) - 2$$

$$y = 0 - 2$$

$$y = -2$$

So the point (0, –2) lies on the line. We've added this to the figure as point P. Another easy point to find is the one where x = 3:

$$y = \frac{1}{3}x - 2$$

$$y = \frac{1}{3}(3) - 2$$

$$y = 1 - 2$$

$$y = -1$$

Thus, the point (3, –1) is also on the line. This point is shown on the figure as point Q. Given two points, you can draw the required line *l* connecting the points.

Look back at the constants in the original equation in light of this figure. You can see that the constant b, –2, is the value of y where the line crosses the y axis. The other constant m, $\frac{1}{3}$, is the slope, or the steepness of the slant of the line.

Finding the Slope and y-intercept

If you're given two points, it's a snap to find the slope and y-intercept. Let's do a sample problem to see how this works.

A line passes through the points (3,2) and (-5, 4). What is the slope of this line? What is the y-intercept?

To find the slope, pick one of the (x,y) coordiantes to use as a starting point. Let's start with (-5,4). First, we'll find the rise, which is the change in y. Subtract the y of the starting point, 4, from the y of the second point, 2. This gives you the top of your fraction, 2. Do the same with the x coordinates, subtracting 3 from -5 to get the bottom of your fraction, -8. Your slope is 2/-8 or 1/-4.

To find the y intercept, substitute either of the (x,y) pairs into the slope-intercept form of the line; y=mx + b. Let's choose point (3,2) and use our slope 1/-4 for variable m.

2=(-1/4)3 + b

2=-3/4 +b

2 + 3/4 = b

The final equation of our line is

Y=-1/4x + 2 3/4

Let's look at an example in which you have to put the equation into slope-intercept form before you find the slope and y-intercept.

2y – 3x -4 = 0.

First put it in slope-intercept form. Move the x term and the 4 to the other side of the equation, and then divide by two. The result is

y= 3/2x + 2

Now plot the point (0,2). Finally go up 3 and over 2 to get your second point (2,5).

Math Section

Covering All the Angles

Angle name	What it is
Acute angle	An angle less than 90°
Right angle	A 90° angle
Obtuse angle	An angle between 90° and 180°
Straight angle	A 180° angle
Complimentary angles	A pair of angles whose measures add up to 90°
Supplementary angles	A pair of angles whose measures add up to 180°
Vertical angles	Angles formed when lines intersect. Vertical angles have the same measure.

Dealing with Change

You are guaranteed to see problems on the SAT in which you must calculate the percentage of increase or decrease. These problems typically show up in two forms:

1. Calculating a value based on a percentage of increase or decrease

2. Calculating a percentage of increase or decrease based on a starting and ending value.

Many students find these questions confusing, so let's take a look at how to solve these problems.

What's the percentage?

A *percent* is a ratio in which the denominator is 100. For example, 80% $= \frac{80}{100}$. Percents typically turn up on the SAT in problems involving proportion or change. For example, here's a proportion problem that uses percent:

> Thirty-five percent of the students in Advanced Placement biology are studying fish. There are 20 students in the class. How many are studying fish?

To solve using a proportion and cross-multiplication,

$$\frac{35}{100} = \frac{f}{20}$$

$$100f = 35 \times 20$$

$$f = \frac{(35 \times 20)}{100}$$

$$f = 7$$

This is a good place to remember that there's usually more than one way to solve a mathematical problem. If you recognize that 35% = .35, you can also solve this problem by a simple multiplication:

$$f = .35 \times 20 = 7$$

Percent Change—Getting a Value

Now let's look at a percent change problem where you need to find the end result of an increase or decrease.

> The pressure in a steam boiler is 250psi. If the pressure increases by 20%, what is the new pressure?

To solve this problem, first calculate the increase in pressure. The problem specifies that the increase is 20% of the original pressure, which you can calculate as follows:

20% of 250

$$\frac{20}{100} \times 250$$

$$\frac{(20 \times 250)}{100}$$

50

So the increase in pressure is 50psi. But the problem doesn't ask for the increase in pressure; it asks for the new pressure, which is the original pressure plus the increase. So the answer is 300psi.

Percent Change—Getting a Percent Change

Another type of question you'll see on the exam asks you to calculate one number as a percent of another. Suppose you're asked this question:

> A class that started with 30 students now has 27 students. What percent decrease is this?

To solve these percent change problems, you can use the following formula:

$$\text{Percent change} = \frac{(\text{amount of increase or decrease})}{\text{original amount}} \times 100\%$$

In this case, the final number is 27, and the starting number is 30. So to calculate the answer

$$\text{Percent change} = \frac{(30 - 27)}{30} \times 100\%$$

$$\text{Percent change} = \frac{3}{30} \times 100\%$$

$$\text{Percent change} = -10\%$$

So the number of students in the class has decreased by 10 percent.

Functions

The SAT will include at least one or two function questions. These aren't that hard once you figure out what's going on, but they can be tricky at first. Let's run through the basics so you can brush up a bit before you see one of these beasties on the test.

So what is a function anyway?

A mathematical **function** is a rule for associating elements from one set with elements of another set. To indicate a function, you use a special notation, as shown in this example:

$$f(x) = x^2$$

That particular function can be read as "f of x is equal to x squared." Now let's plug in a number.

$$f(3) = 3^2 = 9$$

To be a function, an equation must give only one answer for y for every x value.

Domain and Range

Two important properties of a function are its *domain* and its *range*. The domain of a function is the set of all input values for which the function is defined, or all the numbers you're allowed to plug in for x. The range of a function is the set of all values that can be produced by applying the function to values in its domain, or all the numbers the function can spit out for y.

For example, consider the function

$$g(x) = \frac{1}{x}$$

The **domain** of the function g is all the Real numbers except zero. Zero can't be in the domain, because if you plug it into the function, you get 1/0, which is undefined. Any other Real number would work, though.

The **range** is anything that the function can return based on a number you plug into it. In this case, the only value you can't get out of the function is zero. No number in the function's domain could be plugged in to get that result. Hence the range is also the entire set of Real numbers except zero.

Using functions on the SAT

If you're given a function and asked to determine the value of the function for a particular input, just plug the input in to the function and find the answer. For example, if $f(x) = 3x^2 - 7$, the notation $f(3)$ indicates the value of the function for the input 3, referred to as "f of three." You'd calculate it this way:

$f(x) = 3x^2 - 7$

$f(3) = 3(3)^2 - 7$

$f(3) = 20$

Functions can also have more than one input variable. For instance, you might have

$f(x,y) = 2x + y$

for the values (3,5)

$f(3,5) = 2 \times 3 + 5 = 11.$

Composition of Functions

Given two functions, you may be asked to work with the **composition** of the functions. The composition of two functions is a function produced by performing first one function and then using the first function's output as the input for the other. For example, consider these two functions:

$f(x) = x^2$

$g(x) = x + 2$

Then the composition $f(g(x))$ can be simplified this way:

$f(g(x)) = (x + 2)^2$

$f(g(x)) = (x + 2)(x + 2)$

$f(g(x)) = x^2 + 2x + 4$

POWERTIP

Don't go by the letter: Functions can also be indicated using $g(x)$, $h(x)$, or any other letter. Don't get confused if the SAT uses a letter other than f to indicate a function.

Math Section

How Many Ways Can You Say That?

Solving counting, permutation, and combination problems

The SAT might ask you to count some things, but it won't be as simple as tapping your pencil on a series of pictures! For counting problems, you should know the Fundamental Counting Principle: If an event can happen *m* ways and a second, independent event can happen *n* ways, the total number of ways in which the two events can happen is m times n. That's pretty abstract, so we'll put it in the form of a word problem:

> John has 7 dress shirts, 5 ties, and 6 pairs of dress slacks. How many different ways can he make up an outfit consisting of one shirt, one tie, and one pair of slacks?

To solve this problem, you can apply the fundamental counting principle. Each of the three events (choosing a shirt, choosing a tie, and choosing slacks) is independent, so the answer is $7 \times 5 \times 6 = 210$.

Permutations

In permutation problems, you're selecting from a pool of items that is not replenished, so each selection reduces the pool. To solve these problems requires some reasoning and multiplication. Here's an example:

> A bingo cage contains 75 different numbered balls. The game is played by a caller removing one ball at a time, calling out its number, and discarding the ball. How many ways can the caller call the first 5 numbers?

To solve this problem, note that the first ball comes from a pool of 75 choices, and is then thrown away, reducing the pool. The second ball therefore comes from a pool of 74 choices, and so on. The answer is

$$75 \times 74 \times 73 \times 72 \times 71 = 2,071,126,800$$

Combinations

Combination problems are like permutation problems, except that the order of results doesn't matter. An example will make this clear:

> A pond contains 15 ducks. You pick 3 ducks from the pond at random. How many different groups of 3 ducks could you form this way?

To start solving this problem, treat it as a permutation problem: For the first duck, there are 15 choices, and then 14, and then 13. So there are $15 \times 14 \times 13 = 2730$ ways to choose the 3 ducks. But not all of those ways are distinct. Suppose that the ducks are all assigned letters. If you pull out duck A, and then duck B, and then duck C, you get the same group as if you'd pulled out C, and then B, and then A. In fact, there are 6 different ways to arrange a group of 3 ducks:

A B C

A C B

B A C

B C A

C A B

C B A

So the final answer is $\dfrac{2730}{6} = \dfrac{2730}{3!} = 455$.

Math Section

POWERTIP

Factorials help

Remember, you can always find the number of repetitive arrangements by taking the factorial of the number of items you're selecting.

Knowing Math Definitions Can Unlock Tricky Math Questions

One of the most common Math section errors has nothing to do with calculations—it's misreading the questions. Guess what—you can't answer a question correctly if you don't know what it's asking. If you read a question too quickly, or if you don't understand some of the words a question uses you may wind up picking an answer to the wrong question.

Fortunately, there are several things you can do to avoid doing the right calculations but marking the wrong choice.

- Make sure you're reading with enough attention to detail.
- Look for important words like NOT, OPPOSITE, POSITIVE, and NEGATIVE that can transform the meaning of a question
- Get in the habit of circling or underlining them as you read.
- Pay special attention to words in the question that appear in **bold**, *italic*, or <u>underline</u>.
- Look for standard math symbols in the illustrations—like the little square box that tells you an angle is a right angle.

Math vocabulary?

If you thought that vocabulary on the new SAT was confined to Writing and Critical Reading, think again. As you study for the test, you'll need to make sure you're familiar with the terms you're likely to see in the Math section. Take some time to review this list so you'll be prepared to dissect whatever math question may come your way.

absolute value	The "size" of a number, measured by how far it is from zero. The absolute value of 4 and the absolute value of –4 are both 4.
Area	The area of a plane figure is the number of unit squares that it would take to exactly cover the figure.
Circumference	The circumference of the circle is the distance around the circle, which you can find using the formula $2\pi r$.
Complementary angles	Two angles are complementary angles if they add up to 90°.
Congruent	Items are congruent if they have the same size and shape, as in congruent triangles.

Consecutive numbers	Integers that are adjacent to each other on the number line.
Difference	The answer in a subtraction problem.
Digit	A number 0-9 as part of a real number. 35 is a two digit number whose second digit is 5.
Directly Proportional	Two quantities are directly proportional when they vary with each other; that is, they are related by multiplying as in A=kB for some constant k.
Distinct	Different from another item to which it is compared.
Divisible	Evenly divisible with no remainder. For example, 6 is divisible by 2 and 3 but not by 4.
Domain	All the values that you can legally plug into a function for x.
Equilateral Triangle	A triangle with all of its sides and angles equal
Even Numbers	Any integer that is divisible by 2; Zero is an even number.
Factor	The *factors* of an integer are the integers that can be multiplied together to return the original integer.
Function	A mathematical *function* is a rule for associating elements of one set with elements of another set. A function must give only one answer for y for every x value.
Greatest Common Factor (GCF)	The greatest common factor of two integers is the largest factor (prime or otherwise) that the two numbers have in common.
Integer	The positive counting numbers, their negative counterparts, and zero.
Inversely Proportional	Two quantities are inversely proportional when they are related according to an equation such as A = k/B for some constant k.
Isosceles Triangle	A triangle with two equal sides and two equal angles.
Least Common Multiple (LCM)	The least common multiple of two integers is the smallest number that has both integers as factors. 12 is the LCM of 3 and 4.
Midpoint	The point exactly halfway between the endpoints of a line segment. The midpoint formula for points (x,y) and R's would be ((x+r)/2), ((y+s)/2)
Multiples	Integers formed by multiplying a base integer by another integer. 6 and 9 are multiples of 3.
Parallelogram	A quadrilateral with two sets of parallel opposite sides.
perimeter	The distance around the entire outside of a plane figure.
Prime Numbers	A prime number is an integer that is only divisible by itself and by 1.
Product	The answer to a multiplication problem.
Quadrilateral	A polygon with four sides.
Quotient	The answer to a division problem.
Range	The set of all values a function can produce for y.
Reciprocal	A number produced by interchanging the numerator and denominator of a fraction. 4/3 is the reciprocal of 3/4.
Reflection	Creating a copy of a figure by drawing its mirror image on the other side of a specified line.
Remainder	The whole number left over after you perform a division problem. 9 divided by 4 has a remainder of 1.
Rotation	Creating a copy of a figure by rotating the figure about a fixed point.
Sum	The answer to an addition problem; to add
Supplementary angles	Two angles whose measures sum to 180°
Surface Area	The sum of the areas of every face of a 3-dimensional solid.
Symmetry	A change (rotation or reflection) that preserves the original figure.
Tangent	A line that touches a curve at precisely one point.
Translation	Creating a copy of a figure by sliding it within the plane.
Zeroes	The points at which the graph of an equation crosses the x axis.

Power and Root Operations

Powers and roots are based around the idea of multiplying a number by itself a certain number of times. A **power** is represented by an **exponent**—usually shown as a superscript to the right of a *base* number. For instance, with the expression 4^3 the *base* is 4, the *exponent* is 3, and the expression would be read as four to the third *power*.

Roots are the inverse of powers. For example, a square root represents the number that would have to be multiplied by itself two times to get the number under the root symbol. The expression $\sqrt[3]{8}$ would be read as the third *root* of eight, and is equal to 2. Roots may also be represented by fractional exponents.

Let's take a look at the power and root operations you'll need to know for the new SAT

Positive powers

To calculate the positive power of a number, you multiply the number by itself that many times. For example, four raised to the third power, expressed as 4^3, works out this way:

$$4^3 = 4 \times 4 \times 4 = 64$$

Here, 4 is the *base* and 3 is the *exponent*. The exponent tells how many times to use the base as a factor.

Negative exponents

Negative exponents have nothing to do with whether or not a number is positive or negative. A number raised to a negative exponent simplifies to 1 over that number raised to the positive exponent.

$$3^{-2} = \frac{1}{3^2} = \frac{1}{9}$$

Here's another way this might look on the SAT.

$$\frac{1}{3^{-2}} = \frac{1}{\left(\frac{1}{9}\right)} = 9$$

Roots

The root of a number is the number that you must multiply by itself the number of times represented in the root expression to get the original number.

$$\sqrt{16} = 4 \text{ meaning } 4 \times 4 = 16$$
$$\sqrt[3]{8} = 2 \text{ meaning } 2 \times 2 \times 2 = 8$$

Fractional powers

Fractional powers are the equivalent of roots. The $\frac{1}{3}$ power of a number is the same as its cube root, the $\frac{1}{4}$ power is the same as its fourth root, and so on.

$$9^{1/2} = \sqrt{9} = 3$$
$$16^{1/4} = \sqrt[4]{16} = 2$$

You need to remember a few rules when working with exponents. The table below should help you keep these rules straight.

POWERTIP

Who has the power? Watch out for negative signs when working with exponents. For example, $(-3)^2=9$, but $-(3)^2=-9$.

Math Section

Rules for working with powers and roots

The rule	An example	The answer
$X^a \times X^b = X^{a+b}$	$2^2 \times 2^3 = 2^5$	$2^5=32$
$X^a/X^b = X^{a-b}$	$2^5/2^2 = 2^3$	$2^3=8$
$(X^a)^b = X^{a \times b}$	$(2^3)^2 = 2^{3 \times 2}$	$2^6=64$
$(X \times Y)^a = X^a \times Y^a$	$(3 \times 2)^3 = 3^3 \times 2^3$	$27 \times 8 = 216$
$(X/Y)^a = X^a/Y^a$	$(4/2)^2 = 4^2/2^2$	$16/4 = 4$

Some Triangles Are Special

Right Triangles and the Pythagorean Theorem

The SAT loves right triangles and the Pythagorean theorem. You have to learn how to recognize right triangles when they appear, because you can bet your protractor you'll see at least two or three of them. Let's take a look at these special triangles along with the theorem that made Pythagoras a household name.

Right triangles

A **right triangle** is one in which one of the angles is a right angle. Some special terminology is generally used for right triangles:

- The **hypotenuse** is the side of the right triangle opposite the right angle.
- The **legs** of the right triangle are the other two sides.

A right triangle.

Note the right-angle indicator inside angle C.

Our man Pythagoras

The most important fact to know about right triangles is that every right triangle obeys the Pythagorean Theorem. The theorem may be stated in words as: The hypotenuse is equal to the sum of the squares of the other two sides. Or, using the traditional labels:

$$a^2 + b^2 = c^2$$

If you know the lengths of any two sides of a right triangle, you can use the Pythagorean Theorem to come up with the length of the third side.

Special Right Triangles

Some right triangles have additional idiosyncrasies that can help you out if you know what to look for. Let's run through the three you're most likely to see on the SAT.

3-4-5 Triangles

One right triangle you should recognize is the 3-4-5 triangle. Any triangle whose sides are in the ratio 3:4:5 (such as one whose sides are 9, 12, and 15) is a right triangle. Recognizing 3-4-5 triangles on the test can save you some valuable calculation time.

30°-60°-90° Triangles

Another special triangle is the one whose angles are 30°, 60°, and 90°. This right triangle has sides in the ratio $1:\sqrt{3}:2$.

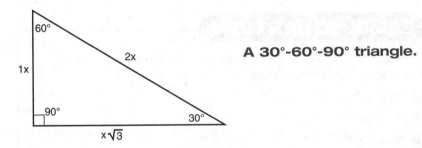

A 30°-60°-90° triangle.

45°-45°-90° Triangles

Another special right triangle is the one whose angles are 45°, 45°, and 90°. Because the two angles are equal, this means that the two legs of the triangle are also equal. The length of the hypotenuse is the square root of 2 times the length of either of the legs. The ratio of the sides is $1:1:\sqrt{2}$.

You'll also see this special triangle as the diagonal of a square

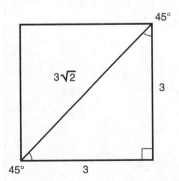

> **POWERTIP**
>
> **Which is the 30 again?**
> The 30°-60°-90° triangle can save your tons of time, but what if you forget which angle goes with which side? Just remember that the short side is opposite the small angle: 30°. The long side is opposite the big angle: 90°. On the 45°-45°-90° triangle, remember that there are two 1's but only one $\sqrt{2}$.

SAT Math Roundup

A quick assessment of your math skills

There's no substitute for practice when it comes to SAT Math. In this section, we've picked individual questions that represent the range of topics and skills you'll need to know to beat the Math section. Take a crack at each question and put a check-mark beside the ones you get right off the bat. You should be able to get a good idea of which areas you need to work on before you sit down for the real thing.

Arithmetic sequence

Ⓐ Ⓑ Ⓒ Ⓓ Ⓔ

SAMPLE QUESTION

The first three terms of a sequence are 12, 24, and 36. Which term in the sequence is equal to 12^2?

Ⓐ The 9th

Ⓑ The 12th

Ⓒ The 13th

Ⓓ The 15th

Ⓔ The 144th

ANSWER

You can see that the sequence is arithmetic, with a constant difference of 12 between the terms. The key formula here is

The nth term = the first term + the amount of change between terms × (n-1), where n is the count (as in 11th) of the term you need to find. Mathematically speaking;

$A_n = a_1 + d(n-1)$

The formula for the nth term of the sequence in our problem is 12 + 12(n-1), which is the same as 12n.

$12n = 12^2$

$12n = 144$

$n = 12$

So the 12th term is the one whose value is 12^2, and the other four answers are incorrect.

Answer Ⓑ is correct.

SAMPLE**QUESTION**

John and Arlene both leave their high school at the same time. John walks due west at 4 miles per hour, and Arlene walks due east at $2\frac{1}{2}$ miles per hour. At the end of 3 hours, how far apart are John and Arlene?

- **A** 4.5 miles
- **B** 6.5 miles
- **C** 9.5 miles
- **D** 14.5 miles
- **E** 19.5 miles

ANSWER

You can solve this by turning it into a pair of rate problems. The distance equation is D=R×T. To get distance, you multiply rate by time. John goes $3 \times 4 = 12$ miles in three hours, and Arlene goes $3 \times 2.5 = 7.5$ miles in the same time. Since they're walking directly opposite to each other, you add these two figures to get the correct answer 19.5 hours. As a shortcut, you may notice that each hour they get 6.5 miles further apart (John walks 4 miles west, while Arlene walks 2.5 miles east), so the total distance at the end of 3 hours is $3 \times 6.5 = 19.5$ miles. While we didn't use them for this problem, two other important rate formulas are:

$R_1 \times T_1 + R_2 \times T_2$ = Work Done

Workers × Rate × Time = Work Done

Answer **E** is correct.

Rate

Ⓐ Ⓑ Ⓒ Ⓓ Ⓔ

Math Section

POWER**TIP**

The power of zero: A special case of the power operator is the zeroth power. The zeroth power of any number is defined as one, so, for example,

$17^0 = 1$

$X^0 = 1$

Graphing a Parabola

SAMPLE QUESTION

Which of the following graphs corresponds to the equation $x^2 + 2x + 1$?

Ⓐ
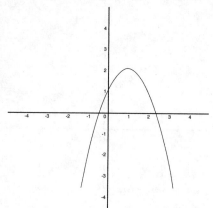

Ⓑ
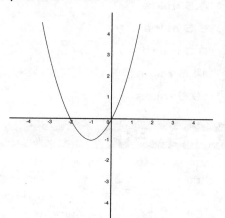

Ⓒ
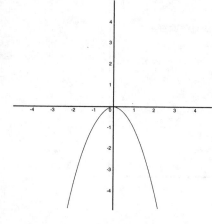

Ⓓ
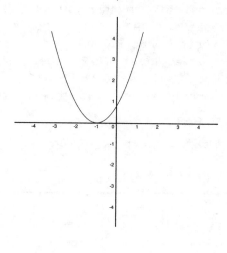

Ⓔ
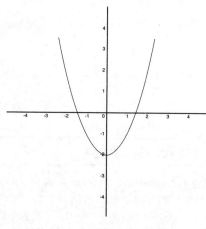

ANSWER

Because the x^2 term is positive, you know that the graph is upward. This immediately lets you eliminate answers A and C because those two parabolas are upside down for the equation. Answer B has a zero at x=0. Plugging that in to the equation gives 0 = 0^2 + 2[×2]0 + 1, or 0=1, which is not true. This eliminates answer B. Answer D has a zero at x=–1. Plugging that in gives 0 = $(–1)^2$ + 2[×2]–1 + 1, which is a true statement, so answer D is correct.

It's also good to know how to locate the line of symmetry of the x axis. If the parabola is in standard form $ax^2 + bx + c$, the x coordinate of the line of symmetry is –b/2a. You can find the vertex by plugging this x coordinate into the equation.

Answer **D** is correct.

POWER**TIP**

Watch your axes: Look carefully at graphs on the actual SAT; nothing says that the College Board will draw them to help you to correct conclusions. Sometimes you'll see a break in an axis to indicate that a series is not continuous, but this won't always be the case.

Math Section

Types of Numbers

Mathematicians have assigned names to specific groups and types of numbers. Below is a table showing the names and definitions of the number types you may encounter on the new SAT.

Type of Number	Definition	Examples
Real	The set of Rational and Irrational numbers.	0, 1, -15, .5, .333, π, $\sqrt{2}$, $\sqrt{3}$
Rational	Real numbers that can be expressed as the ratio of two integers.	0, 1, .5, -15, .5, .3333
Irrational	Real numbers that cannot be expressed as the exact ratio of two integers, such as repeating digits or imperfect roots.	π, $\sqrt{2}$, $\sqrt{3}$
Integer	Zero, the positive counting numbers, and the negatives of the counting numbers	...,-2, -1, 0, 1, 2, ...
Whole	Zero and the positive counting numbers	0, 1, 2, ...

Variation

Ⓐ Ⓑ Ⓒ Ⓓ Ⓔ

SAMPLE**QUESTION**

If x is directly proportional to $\frac{y}{5}$, and x has the value 12 when y has the value 10, what is the value of x when y has the value of $\frac{27}{4}$?

Ⓐ $\frac{10}{81}$

Ⓑ $\frac{81}{10}$

Ⓒ $\frac{4}{27}$

Ⓓ 15

Ⓔ $9\frac{1}{10}$

ANSWER

The question tells you that there is a direct relation between x and $\frac{y}{5}$:

$$x = k\left(\frac{y}{5}\right)$$

$$x = \frac{ky}{5}$$

Now plug in the known values of x and y from the second clause to determine k:

$$12 = \frac{10k}{5}$$
$$6 = k$$

The equation for the proportion is:

$$x = \frac{6y}{5}$$

Now plug in $\frac{27}{4}$ for y and solve to get x:

$$x = \frac{\left(6 \times \frac{27}{4}\right)}{5}$$

$$5x = \frac{(6 \times 27)}{4}$$

$$5x = \frac{162}{4} = \frac{81}{2}$$
$$x = \frac{81}{10}$$

Remember:

- Varies directly: x=ky
- Varies Indirectly: x=k/y

Answer Ⓑ is correct.

The SAT Math section will offer several questions in which the order of mathematical operations is critical to getting the correct answer. Students have been using the mnemonic phrase *Please Excuse My Dear Aunt Sally* for decades—if not centuries—to remember that you compute mathematical operations as follows:

Parenthesis

Exponents

Multiplication

Division

Addition

Subtraction

When you're faced with a complex mathematical expression to simplify, you must perform the operations in a particular order to get the right answer:

1. Perform any operations inside of parentheses or brackets. If there are multiple sets of parentheses or brackets, start from the innermost set and work your way out.

2. Perform power and root operations in order from left to right.

3. Perform multiplication and division operations in order from left to right.

4. Perform addition and subtraction operations in order from left to right.

Here's an example showing how to calculate the value of an expression one step at a time using these rules:

$22 + (5 \times 3) \times 2^2 + \sqrt{9} - 4 \div 2$

$22 + 15 \times 2^2 + \sqrt{9} - 4 \div 2$

$22 + 15 \times 4 + 3 - 4 \div 2$

$22 + 60 + 3 - 2$

83

If an expression is in the form of a fraction, you can simplify the numerator and denominator separately. Then as a final step, either perform the division or leave the answer in the form of a fraction.

Please Excuse My Dear Aunt Sally

Combination

Ⓐ Ⓑ Ⓒ Ⓓ Ⓔ

SAMPLE**QUESTION**

A teacher is assigning teams of 2 students each for tennis doubles. There are 24 students in the tennis class. How many different choices are there for the first team chosen?

Ⓐ **23**

Ⓑ **24**

Ⓒ **276**

Ⓓ **552**

Ⓔ **1,104**

ANSWER

This is a classic combination problem. There are 24 choices for the first student, and then 23 choices for the second student on the team (because the first student can't be assigned to the same team twice). But a team consisting of Bill and Joe is the same as a team consisting of Joe and Bill, so you need to divide the number of potential teams by 2!, which is 2 × 1. The final number is given by (24 × 23)/2! = 276.

Remember, to solve a combination problem, start by finding the number of permutations using the information given. Then, because order doesn't matter, divide that result by the factorial of the number of things you are selecting.

Answer Ⓒ is correct.

POWER**TIP**

Batteries not included: Remember, you *can* use a calculator on the math sections of the SAT—but you're not *required* to do so. Don't use a calculator just because you can: Doing so may rob you of precious time that could be better used working on another question.

SAMPLE**QUESTION**

The cost of belonging to the homeowners' association goes up by 5% each year. This year the cost was $132.30. What was the cost two years ago?

(A) $118.00

(B) $119.40

(C) $120.00

(D) $122.30

(E) $126.00

ANSWER

Call the cost two years ago C. Each year the cost goes up by 5%, which means that it is multiplied by 1.05. So,

$c \times 1.05 \times 1.05 = 132.30$

$c = \dfrac{132.3}{1.05 \times 1.05}$

C = 120

Answer **C** is correct.

Percent Increase

Ⓐ Ⓑ Ⓒ Ⓓ Ⓔ

SAMPLE**QUESTION**

Let the symbol r[[s]]t represent $x^r + sx + t$. What are the zeroes of 2[[6]]8?

(A) 0 and 1

(B) –2 and –4

(C) –1 and –2

(D) 6 and 8

(E) –6 and –8

ANSWER

Tackle this one in two steps. First, convert the special symbol to standard notation. If you substitute, you'll find that 2[[6]]8 is $x^2 + 6x + 8$. Now you could graph the function or use the quadratic formula to find its zeroes, but the simplest way to proceed is to factor the polynomial. To do this, note that you need a pair of integers whose sum is 6 and whose product is 8. Two and 4 fit the bill, so $x^2 + 6x + 8 = (x + 2)(x + 4)$.

Now remember that the zeroes of the function are values that eliminate one or the other of those terms: –2 and –4. To check, substitute back in to the formula: $(-2)^2 + 6(-2) + 8 = 4 - 12 + 8 = 0$ and $(-4)^2 + 6(-4) + 8 = 16 - 24 + 8 = 0$.

Answer **B** is correct.

Special Symbol

Ⓐ Ⓑ Ⓒ Ⓓ Ⓔ

Math Section

Math Section

Number Word Problem Grid-in

SAMPLE**QUESTION**

SAMPLE**QUESTION**

The sum of three consecutive integers is 15. What is the ratio of the largest of these integers to the smallest of these integers?

ANSWER

To solve this problem, you first need to find the three integers. Because they're consecutive, you can do this with an equation based on the smallest integer:

$x + (x + 1) + (x + 2) = 15$
$3x + 3 = 15$
$3x = 12$
$x = 4$

This tells you the smallest of the integers is 4, so the largest must be 6. The ratio of the largest to the smallest is 6 to 4. You can solve this as $\frac{6}{4}$, $\frac{3}{2}$, or 1.5.

Remember, you can't grid in $1\frac{1}{2}$.

Grid in 1.5 or 6/4.

You may also encounter problems with even consecutive integers or odd consecutive integers. On these, you'd use (n) + (n+2) + (n+4). If n starts even it'll stay even. Like your brother Fred, if n starts odd, it'll stay odd.

Number word problem

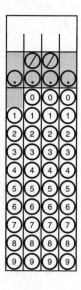

SAMPLE**QUESTION**

The marching band decided to raise money by selling candy bars. They invested $50 in advertising, and sold the candy bars for a profit of $2 per box. If they sold 311 boxes of candy bars, what was their total profit after advertising costs were deducted? (Disregard the dollar sign and any cents when gridding your answer. For example, if the answer is $230.00, grid 230.)

ANSWER

This problem asks you to convert words into an equation. Start with the profit per box times the number of boxes:

$P = 311 \times 2$

You then need to reduce this number by the advertising costs:

$P = (311 \times 2) - 50$
$P = 622 - 50$
$P = 572$

Grid 572.

SAMPLE **QUESTION**

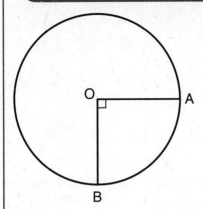

In the figure above, O is the center of the circle and the total perimeter of the sector OAB is $4 + \pi$. What is the circumference of the circle?

A 2π

B 4π

C $8 + 2\pi$

D $16 + 4\pi$

E $16 + 8\pi$

Circumference of a Circle

Ⓐ Ⓑ Ⓒ Ⓓ Ⓔ

Math Section

ANSWER

To see this, note that OA and OB are both radii of the circle, so the diameter of the circle is 2OA. You know that the total circumference of the circle is π times the diameter. Because the slice has a right angle at its center, the length of the curved part is one fourth of the total circumference. Putting all this together, you get an equation you can solve for OA:

$$OA + OB + \frac{2\pi OA}{4} = 4 + \pi$$

$$2\,OA + \frac{2\pi OA}{4} = 4 + \pi$$

$$8\,OA + 2\pi OA = 16 + 4\pi$$

$$OA = \frac{16 + 4\pi}{8 + 2\pi}$$

$$OA = 2$$

If the radius OA = 2, the diameter of the circle is 4 and the circumference is 4π.

Don't confuse Circumference and Area. Area = πr^2

Answer **B** is correct.

Parallel Lines

Ⓐ Ⓑ Ⓒ Ⓓ Ⓔ

Math Section

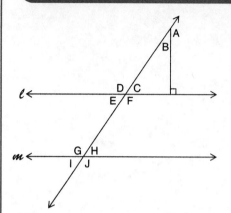

Note: Figure not drawn to scale.

In the figure above, lines *l* and *m* are parallel. If angle A is 105°, what is angle I?

Ⓐ 10°

Ⓑ 15°

Ⓒ 45°

Ⓓ 75°

Ⓔ 105°

ANSWER

If ∠A = 105°, ∠B = 75 because they add up to a straight line. Now consider the triangle with B and C as two of its angles. The figure gives you the third angle as a right angle, 90°. Because the sum of the angles in the triangle is 180°, this means that ∠C = 15° (180-90-75). All the acute angles formed by a line cutting a pair of parallel lines are the same, so ∠I = 15° as well.

Answer Ⓑ is correct.

POWER**TIP**

Don't trust your eyes: On the exam, you cannot assume that two lines are parallel unless you're explicitly told so, or unless you can prove it from some other fact.

SAMPLE**QUESTION**

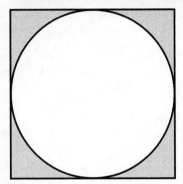

The figure above shows a circle embedded in a square, with the sides of the square tangent to the circle. Each side of the square is 2 units long. What is the ratio of the unshaded area to the area of the square?

A 1:2

B 1:π

C 1−π:1

D 1−$\frac{\pi}{4}$:1

E 2:1

ANSWER

Start by calculating the area of the two figures. The area of the square is 4, the product of the sides. The radius of the circle is 1, so the area of the circle is πr^2, or π. So the area of the unshaded region is 4 − π, and the ratio is 4 − π:4, or (1−$\frac{\pi}{4}$):1.

Answer **D** is correct.

Area of Shapes

Ⓐ Ⓑ Ⓒ Ⓓ Ⓔ

Math Section

Distance Formula or Pythagoreum Theorum

Ⓐ Ⓑ Ⓒ Ⓓ Ⓔ

SAMPLE**QUESTION**

The coordinates of three points in the xy plane are

A = (2, 2)
B = (2, 6)
C = (5, 2)

What is the distance BC?

Ⓐ 3

Ⓑ 4

Ⓒ 5

Ⓓ 6

Ⓔ 7

ANSWER

You can work this out from the general formula for distance in the plane, but there's a faster way. If you plot the three points on a graph, you'll see that they form a right triangle with AB = 4 and AC = 3. You should recognize these as two sides of the 3-4-5 right triangle, so BC = 5.

Answer Ⓒ is correct.

Spatial Perception

Ⓐ Ⓑ Ⓒ Ⓓ Ⓔ

SAMPLE**QUESTION**

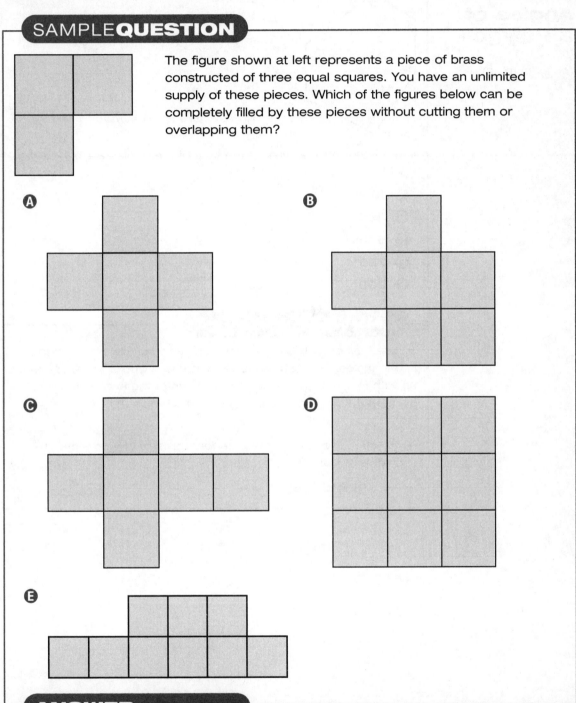

The figure shown at left represents a piece of brass constructed of three equal squares. You have an unlimited supply of these pieces. Which of the figures below can be completely filled by these pieces without cutting them or overlapping them?

ANSWER

Answer Ⓑ is correct. This is one of those problems in which you just have to "see" the answer, though it's easy to tell that answer A is incorrect: You can't cover five squares with a multiple of three squares.

Sum of Interior Angles of a Polygon

Ⓐ Ⓑ Ⓒ Ⓓ Ⓔ

SAMPLE**QUESTION**

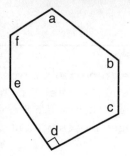

Note: Figure not drawn to scale.

In the figure above, what is the sum of the angles a + b + c + d + e + f?

Ⓐ **180°**

Ⓑ **360°**

Ⓒ **540°**

Ⓓ **720°**

Ⓔ **900°**

ANSWER

To see this, draw lines between vertices to divide the hexagon into triangles. You'll find that no matter how you do this, you end up with four triangles. Because the sum of the angles in a triangle is 180°, the sum of the angles in the hexagon is 4 × 180° = 720°.

Remember, the sum of the *exterior* angles of any polygon, the answer is always 360°.

Answer Ⓓ is correct.

SAMPLE**QUESTION**

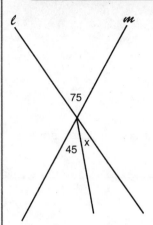

In the figure above, *l* and *m* are lines. What is x?

A 25°

B 30°

C 45°

D 50°

E 75°

ANSWER

The vertical angles between two lines are equal, so 45° + x = 75°. This gives x = 30°.

Answer **B** is correct.

Vertical Angles

Ⓐ Ⓑ Ⓒ Ⓓ Ⓔ

Math Section

POWER**TIP**

It's plane to see: Unless you're told otherwise, you can assume that all drawings on the SAT geometry section lie in the plane. That is, they're completely "flat" with no third dimension.

**Pythagorean
Theorem**

Ⓐ Ⓑ Ⓒ Ⓓ Ⓔ

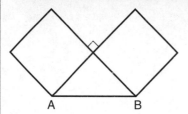

A   B

The figure shows two squares joined at one corner. Each square has the area 72. What is the distance AB?

Ⓐ 6

Ⓑ $6\sqrt{2}$

Ⓒ 12

Ⓓ $12\sqrt{2}$

Ⓔ 36

ANSWER

If the squares have an area of 72, they each have a side of $\sqrt{72}$ = $6\sqrt{2}$. AB is then the hypotenuse of a right triangle with two sides of $6\sqrt{2}$. This allows you to calculate the length using the Pythagorean Theorem:

$$AB = \sqrt{\left(6\sqrt{2}\right)^2 + \left(6\sqrt{2}\right)^2}$$

$$AB = \sqrt{72 + 72}$$

$$AB = \sqrt{144}$$

$$AB = 12$$

Answer Ⓒ is correct.

Math Section

SAMPLE**QUESTION**

In rectangle ABCD, BC = 12 and BD = 13. What is the perimeter of the rectangle?

ANSWER

If you draw the rectangle, you'll realize that BD is a diagonal distance, not one of the sides. You know that the side BC = 12 and need to find the length of the other side. You can calculate this length AB as $\sqrt{13^2 - 12^2}$. Doing the math, you'll find that AB = 5. (You may also remember that 5-12-13 is a right triangle, and save yourself from doing the math at all.) So the perimeter is 2(5 + 12) = 34.

Fill-in grid 34.

Pythagorean Theorem Grid-in

SAMPLE**QUESTION**

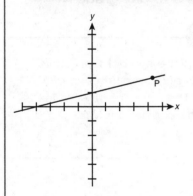

Note: Figure not drawn to scale.

Point P lies on the line, which has a slope of $\frac{1}{4}$ and which crosses the y axis at y = 1. If the y coordinate of P is 2, what is its x coordinate?

ANSWER

From the slope and y-intercept, you can immediately write the equation of the line: $y = \frac{1}{4}x + 1$. Substitute y = 2 and solve for x:

$$y = \frac{1}{4}x + 1$$

$$2 = \frac{1}{4}x + 1$$

$$8 = x + 4$$

$$x = 4$$

Fill-in grid 4.

Slope Intercept

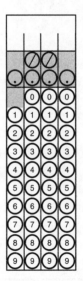

Math Section

**Reading
a Graph**

Ⓐ Ⓑ Ⓒ Ⓓ Ⓔ

SAMPLE **QUESTION**

Flights Per Year

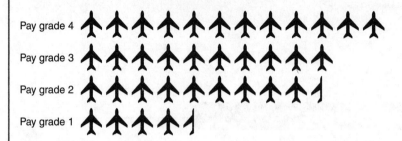

 = 3 flights

According to the pictograph above, which of these changes in pay grade would result in 10 1/2 extra flights per year?

Ⓐ **A promotion from pay grade 1 to pay grade 2**

Ⓑ **A promotion from pay grade 1 to pay grade 3**

Ⓒ **A promotion from pay grade 2 to pay grade 3**

Ⓓ **A promotion from pay grade 2 to pay grade 4**

Ⓔ **A promotion from pay grade 3 to pay grade 4**

ANSWER

Note from the answer key that each plane symbol represents three flights per year. Thus, you want to find a difference of 3 1/2 symbols to account for 10 1/2 flights. The rows for pay grades 2 and 4 differ by this amount, so D is the correct answer.

Answer Ⓓ is correct.

Math Section

POWER**TIP**

A picture is worth 1000 words (or maybe 2000): If you see a pictograph on the SAT, be sure that you understand what each symbol represents. Without reading the key, you might be misled into assuming that 5 symbols mean 5 instead of 15 or 100.

SAMPLE**QUESTION**

A class with 17 students is averaging 85% on exams. Three students drop out, and the remaining students are averaging 88% on exams. What was the average exam score of the three students who dropped out?

Ⓐ 69

Ⓑ 70

Ⓒ 71

Ⓓ 80

Ⓔ 82

ANSWER

The total score before the three students dropped out was 85 × 17 = 1445. The total score after the three students dropped out was 88 × 14 = 1232. That leaves a difference of 213 points to be accounted for by the three students, and their average score is 213/3, or 71.

Answer **Ⓒ** is correct.

**Average
(Mean)**

Ⓐ Ⓑ Ⓒ Ⓓ Ⓔ

Median

Ⓐ Ⓑ Ⓒ Ⓓ Ⓔ

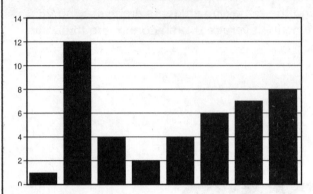

SAMPLEQUESTION

Net Weight, Ounces

What is the median of the observations shown on the graph above?

Ⓐ 3

Ⓑ 4

Ⓒ 5

Ⓓ 5.5

Ⓔ 6

ANSWER

The median is the middle of a set of numbers. Because there are an even number of observations on the graph, the median is the mean of the two central observations. But remember: You have to sort the numbers in order from lowest to highest to find the median! If you do that, you'll find that the set is 2,3,5,6,8,8. The two numbers in the middle are 5 and 6, and their average is 5.5.

Answer Ⓓ is correct.

SAMPLE**QUESTION**

In freshman calculus, the three quizzes each count the same toward the final grade, and the final exam counts as much as two quizzes. Mary scored 75, 81, and 93 on the three quizzes. Her final average score in the course was 85. What was her score on the final exam?

A 85

B 88

C 89

D 90

E 91

ANSWER

You can treat this as a weighted average problem, with x representing the score on the final:

$$\frac{75 + 81 + 93 + 2x}{5} = 85$$

$249 + 2x = 5 \times 85$
$249 + 2x = 425$
$2x = 176$
$x = 88$

Answer **B** is correct.

Weighted Average

Ⓐ Ⓑ Ⓒ Ⓓ Ⓔ

Math Section

Probability

Ⓐ Ⓑ Ⓒ Ⓓ Ⓔ

SAMPLE**QUESTION**

A drawer contains 4 red socks, 2 blue socks, and 6 green socks. You reach into the drawer and, without looking, take out 2 socks. What is the probability that you have drawn a matching pair?

Ⓐ 1/6

Ⓑ 1/5

Ⓒ 1/4

Ⓓ 1/3

Ⓔ 1/2

ANSWER

Let's think about the red socks first: There are 4 ways to draw a red sock, and then 3 ways to draw another red sock, making 12 ways to get a red pair. For the blue socks, there are 2 ways to do it (first sock 1 and then sock 2, or vice versa). For the green socks, there are 6 ways to draw the first sock and then 5 ways to draw the second sock, for a total of 30 ways to get the desired outcome. So there are a total of 12 + 2 + 30 = 44 ways to get the desired outcome of a matching pair. Overall, there are 12 socks. The total number of possible outcomes is 12 × 11 = 132 (12 ways to draw any sock, followed by 11 ways to draw another sock). So the probability of a pair is 44/132, or 1/3.

Answer Ⓓ is correct.

Math Section

SAMPLE**QUESTION**

You roll three standard six-sided dice. What is the probability that at least one of the dice will display a 2?

Ⓐ 1/216

Ⓑ 3/216

Ⓒ 91/216

Ⓓ 125/216

Ⓔ 215/216

ANSWER

You could list out all the possibilities, but it's easier to take advantage of the fact that you're dealing with three independent events here. For each die, the probability of *not* displaying a 2 is 5/6. So the probability of there being no die displaying 2 is

$$\frac{5}{6} \times \frac{5}{6} \times \frac{5}{6} = \frac{125}{216}$$

So, there are 125 chances out of 216 of not seeing a 2. The probability of seeing at least one 2 is given by the remaining 91 chances of 216.

Answer **Ⓒ** is correct.

SAMPLE**QUESTION**

A box contains red and blue balls. The probability of drawing a red ball is 24%. There are 190 blue balls in the box. How many red balls are in the box?

ANSWER

Because the probabilities must add up to 1, the probability of drawing a blue ball is 76%. Call the total number of balls in the box *x*. So this gives you 190/x = .76. (The probability of drawing a blue ball is the number of blue balls divided by the total number of balls.) Then you know that .76x = 190. Solving for x, you get 250 total balls in the box. If 190 of the balls are blue, that leaves 60 red balls.

Fill-in grid 60.

Probability

Ⓐ Ⓑ Ⓒ Ⓓ Ⓔ

Probability

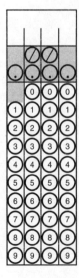

Math Section

Geometric Probability

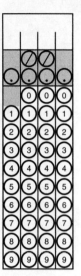

SAMPLE**QUESTION**

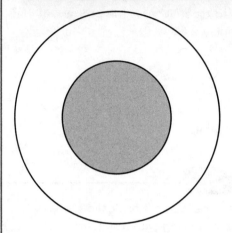

The figure above shows two circles, with the smaller circle completely inside the larger one. The larger circle has a radius of 4. A point is chosen at random in the larger circle. There is a 25% chance that the point will also lie in the smaller circle. What is the diameter of the smaller circle?

ANSWER

To work this geometric probability problem, you must determine the areas of the two circles from the formula $A=\pi r^2$. The area of the larger circle is thus 16π. Now, if there is a 25% chance of a point from the larger circle being in the smaller circle, the smaller circle must have 25% of this area, of 4π. This means that the smaller circle must have a radius of 2. But note that the question asks for the diameter of the smaller circle, not its radius. Multiply the radius by 2 to get 4, the correct answer.

Fill-in grid 4.

SAMPLE**QUESTION**

Which of the answer choices is equivalent to the expression:
–|8| + |1–7|

- **Ⓐ** -14
- **Ⓑ** -2
- **Ⓒ** 0
- **Ⓓ** |8|
- **Ⓔ** 14

Absolute Value

Ⓐ Ⓑ Ⓒ Ⓓ Ⓔ

ANSWER

This problem tests your ability to add and subtract negative numbers and to use absolute values. The absolute value of 8 is 8. The minus sign outside the absolute value symbols means that the first term evaluates to -8. The second term takes the absolute value of 1-7, an expression equivalent to -6. The absolute value of -6 is 6. The resulting expression is -8 + 6, which is equal to -2.

Answer **Ⓑ** is the correct answer.

Math Section

Powers and Roots

Ⓐ Ⓑ Ⓒ Ⓓ Ⓔ

SAMPLE**QUESTION**

Which of the answer choices is equivalent to the expression:

$$\frac{(4^{\frac{1}{2}})(4^{-2})}{(4^2)(4^{\frac{1}{2}})^2}$$

Ⓐ 2/1024

Ⓑ 1/16

Ⓒ 4

Ⓓ 16

Ⓔ 512

ANSWER

This question tests your knowledge of powers and roots. The easiest way to solve this is to simplify each term.

$(4^{\frac{1}{2}})$ is the square root of 4, or 2.

(4^{-2}) is the reciprocal of 4^2, or 1/16.

(4^2) is equal to 16.

$(4^{\frac{1}{2}})^2$ is equal to $4^{\frac{1}{2} \times 2}$ which is equal to 4

The result can be expressed as

$$\frac{2}{(16)(16)(4)} \text{ or } 2/1024.$$

Answer Ⓐ is correct.

SAMPLE**QUESTION**

Which of the answer choices is equivalent to the expression:
$-3^2 + (6+3)^2((4+9)^3(15-2)^{-3}))$

Ⓐ 72

Ⓑ 90

Ⓒ 1062

Ⓓ 2024

Ⓔ $-9 + (6+3)^6$

ANSWER

This order of operations question also tests your knowledge of a few rules of power and root operations. Evaluate the first term by squaring 3 to get 9 and *then* applying the minus sign to get -9. Evaluate the second term by adding 6+3 to get 9 and then squaring that result to get 81. Evaluate the third term by summing the expressions within the parentheses to get $(13)^3 \times (13)^{-3}$. Then, add the exponents to get 13^0, which is equal to 1. The resulting expression is $-9 + (81 \times 1)$ or 72.

Answer Ⓐ is correct.

Order of Operations

Ⓐ Ⓑ Ⓒ Ⓓ Ⓔ

SAMPLE**QUESTION**

How many prime numbers fall between 60 and 100?

Ⓐ 1

Ⓑ 7

Ⓒ 11

Ⓓ 15

Ⓔ Cannot be determined from the information given

ANSWER

First, you eliminate all even numbers. Next, you eliminate all multiples of 3—63, 69, etc. Then, eliminate all multiples of 5—65, 70, etc. You should be left with the numbers 61, 67, 71, 73, 79, 83, 87, 89, 91, 93, and 97.

Answer Ⓒ is correct.

Divisibility

Ⓐ Ⓑ Ⓒ Ⓓ Ⓔ

Math Section

Volume of a prism

Ⓐ Ⓑ Ⓒ Ⓓ Ⓔ

What is the volume of the right prism shown below:

AB=14   CE=8
DE=10   BD=20

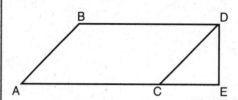

Ⓐ **40**

Ⓑ **40 √2**

Ⓒ **200**

Ⓓ **400**

Ⓔ **1600**

ANSWER

First, calculate the area of the end of the prism using the formula for the area of a triangle 1/2b×h. The base (b) is segment CE and the height (h) is segment DE. 1/2 × 8 × 10 = 40. Next, multiply that result by the length of the prism represented by segment BD. The result is 40 × 20, or 800.

Answer Ⓓ is correct.

POWER**TIP**

Everyone does it that way:
By convention, uppercase letters such as **P** and **Q** refer to points, and lower-case script letters such as **l** and **m** refer to lines.

SAMPLE**QUESTION**

How many axes of reflective symmetry are present in the figure above?

ANSWER

Each line from a point of the star through the center of the star is an axis of reflective symmetry because the figure won't change if it is reflected across that line.

Fill-in grid 5.

Symmetry

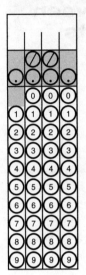

SAMPLE**QUESTION**

Which answer choice shows the equation of a line perpendicular to the line represented by

y=3x+2
and passing through point (3,2)

- **A** y=6x+3
- **B** y=3x+5
- **C** x=1/3y+b
- **D** y=-1/3x +3
- **E** y=1/3x +5

ANSWER

The slope of a perpendicular line is the negative reciprocal of the initial line's slope. The slope of our initial line is 3, so the slope of the perpendicular line must be -1/3. You can immediately elimi-nate any answers with other slopes. Next, you plug the point (3,2) into the new line equation: 2=-1/3(3) + b, or b=3. The equa-tion of the perpendicular line is y=-1/3x+3.

Quick trick: If you came up with the correct slope for the new line, when you multiply the slopes together you'll get -1.

Answer **D** is correct.

Perpendicular Slope

Ⓐ Ⓑ Ⓒ Ⓓ Ⓔ

Math Section

Distance Between Points

Ⓐ Ⓑ Ⓒ Ⓓ Ⓔ

SAMPLE**QUESTION**

What is the distance between (5,6) and (-3,-2)

Ⓐ 2

Ⓑ 8

Ⓒ $8\sqrt{2}$

Ⓓ 16

Ⓔ 64

ANSWER

There are several ways to calculate the distance between points. The distance formula works, but will probably slow you down. It's usually easier to just use the Pythagorean Theorum, as the distance can always be expressed as the hypotenuse of a right triangle drawn on the coordinate grid. Here, the distance between the x coordinates is 8, calculated as 5-(-3), and the distance between the y coordinates is also 8, calculated as 6-(-2). With both legs of a right triangle being equal, you can use the 45°-45°-90° triangle trick to determine that the hypotenuse—the distance between our points—is $8\sqrt{2}$.

Answer Ⓒ is correct.

POWER**TIP**

Recognizing shortcuts like the special triangle can be the difference between taking three minutes on this problem or taking only a few seconds. Or, more to the point, possibly the difference between a 570 and a 640 on the math section.

Mastering the Grid-in

The new SAT includes a new type of math question format—the *student-produced response*, more commonly called the *grid-in*. Unlike multiple choices questions where you select from several possible choices, with grid-ins you actually bubble in a numeric answer. The types of questions you'll encounter are similar to the multiple-choice questions, but you need to be careful when you enter the answer.

The rules

Follow these simple rules to ensure you handle grid-in questions effectively.

Start at the left

Although technically you can start anywhere in the box you like so long as you have room for your answer, but it's best to start in the leftmost column just for the sake of consistency.

Don't round your numbers

Bubble in as many decimal places as you can calculate.

No mixed numbers

Fractions cannot be entered as mixed numbers. To grid in 1 _ you'd have to convert the number to the form 7/4.

No negative numbers

None of the grid-in answers will require a minus sign. This is a tip-off that none of your answers will be negative numbers.

Use your calculator

The calculator helps with grid-ins, especially when you wind up with lots of decimal places.

No penalty for guessing

Unlike other SAT questions where you lose points for incorrect choices, the grid-in questions have no penalty for wrong answers. If you get any answer at all, you're better off gridding it than leaving it blank.

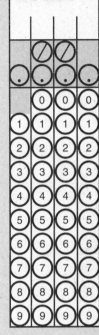

This Doesn't Look Like Math!

Dealing with word problems

If the new SAT just gave you mathematical formulas to work with, the math section would be pretty easy. But you're more likely to be asked to apply your mathematical and reasoning skills to problems laid out in words rather than equations. You need to know how to convert word problems to equations so that you can solve them.

Converting word problems to equations

One of the keys to solving word problems is to convert them to equations as you're reading them. There are a few key words and phrases that you'll see frequently on the new SAT. Recognizing these will give you a boost in solving word problems. The table below lists some of the key phrases and words to watch out for.

KEY WORDS AND PHRASES FOR WORD PROBLEMS

Words	Convert to	Example
is, has, was	=	John is 57 years old **J = 57**
more than, greater than, farther than, older than, sum of	+	The blue bowl contains ten more balls than the red bowl. **B = R + 10**
Difference, less than, younger, fewer	–	Betty is two years younger than John **B = J – 2**
of	× or %	50% of the students take calculus. **C = .5S**
for, per	÷, ratio	Bill paid \$5 for every \$3 that Mary paid. $\frac{B}{5} = \frac{M}{3}$

You'll also run into the terms *directly proportional* and *inversely proportional*. Two quantities are directly proportional when they vary with each other[md]that is, they are related by multiplying by some constant. For example, if you're told that the number of bolts is directly proportional to the number of assemblies, and that 30 assemblies require 270 bolts, you can write the equation

$$30A = 270k$$

This simplifies to $A = 9k$: For each assembly, there are 9 bolts.

Two quantities are inversely proportional when they are related according to an equation such as

$$A = \frac{k}{B}$$

for some constant k. For example, you may be told that a company's profits are inversely proportional to the current price of wheat. This tells you that

$$P = \frac{k}{W}$$

You'd need more information to determine the constant k, but you already know that as the price of wheat goes up, profits go down, and vice versa.

Math Section

What to do if you're clueless

No matter how you slice it, you're probably going to hit at least one question that leaves you scratching your head. There's no easy fix for the completely clueless, but there are a few tips you can try to help jog your mathematical memory banks.

Identify the problem type

You'd be surprised how often a light goes off when you recognize, "Hey! This is just a rate problem!" The Math Roundup article on page 72 can help you here.

Brainstorm connections

Mentally list everything you know about the problem—for example, suppose you see an isosceles right triangle. You automatically know the measures of all three angles and that the length of the hypotenuse is the length of either side multiplied by $\sqrt{2}$.

(continues)

What to do if you're clueless
(continued)

You also know that the measures of the smaller angles are each 45°. Sometimes it looks like you don't have enough information, but if you list all the facts, you'll see connections that weren't obvious at first.

Create a similar but easier problem

Try substituting different numbers or objects. You may be able to eliminate information you don't need to solve the problem. Say you're facing a problem like $9^{50} \times 9^{27}$—numbers so big you can't calculate them in your head. If you don't immediately remember the exponent rule, you might change the problem to one you can calculate, such as $3^2 \times 3^3$. If you calculate this one the long way, you will be able to see the pattern[md]add the exponents when you multiply.

Use concrete numbers for abstract problems

When a question asks you to create a general equation for a problem such as:

The phone company charges you $40 per month. There's an additional fee of .10 per minute. How much does the phone cost per year. Set up an equation that represents your monthly fee if M is the minutes used.

To crack this problem, plug in some real numbers. Assume you used the phone 85 minutes. You'll see that you multiply $85 \times .10$ and add the monthly fee. The general equation is then obvious:

$$M \times .10 + 40$$

Look for shortcuts

We've tossed in dozens of tips throughout this book that can help you save time. Sometimes an "impossible" problem becomes very easy when you see that you're dealing with something like a 3-4-5 right triangle. Another example, is if you're asked to find the solutions of two equations, instead of solving the system of equations, you might recognize that you can plug the answer choices in and choose the numbers that make both equations true.

Plug in values from the answers

In a lot of questions, it's easier to just plug the values from the answer choices into the equation given to find the right one. Only one answer is correct, so the rest of them will fail when you plug them in.

When all else fails, make an intelligent guess

See the article, "The Ins and Outs of Guessing" for a bunch of great guessing techniques.

Understanding Basic Probability

Probability problems are new on the SAT. You won't be quizzed on any advanced probability topics, but you do need to understand the difference between independent and dependent events. You'll also need to be able to calculate probabilities.

Distinguishing between Independent and Dependent events

One of the key concepts that you need to understand is the distinction between **independent** and **dependent** *events*. Two events are independent if the outcome of one event has no effect on the outcome of the other. But if the outcome of one event can affect the outcome of the other, the two events are dependent events.

Independent events

For example, consider these two events:

- Your car's engine stops working.
- You win $1,000 in the lottery.

These are most likely independent events: The state of your car's engine has no effect on whether you win the lottery, and vice versa.

Dependent events

Now consider these two events:

- Your car's engine stops working.
- You drive to the mall for dinner.

These two events are likely dependent events. If your car's engine stops working, that has a direct influence on whether you can drive to the mall for dinner. As you'll see in the next section of the chapter, calculating probabilities follows different rules for dependent events than it does for independent events.

Calculating Probabilities

The **probability** of an event is a number between zero and one (inclusive), indicating how likely an event is to occur. A probability of zero indicates that an event is impossible. A probability of one indicates that an event is certain.

What about events that are neither impossible nor certain? The basic rule for calculating probabilities is to divide the number of ways that the event can occur by the number of possible outcomes. That may sound a bit confusing, but it's easy enough in practice. For instance, what is the probability that a coin will turn up heads if you flip it once? There's one way that this can happen (the coin turns up heads) and two possible outcomes (heads or tails). Thus the probability is 1/2, or .5.

The total of all the probabilities in an entire set of outcomes will always add up to one. For example, a coin can either come up heads or tails, nothing else. If you know the chance of the coin coming up heads is .5, the chance of the coin coming up tails must also be .5.

What is the probability that a coin will come up once on heads and once on tails if it is tossed twice? To answer this question, start by enumerating the possible outcomes. Using H for heads and T for tails, flipping the coin twice can give you four possible outcomes: HH, HT, TH, and TT. Of these, two have one head and one tail, so the probability is 2/4, which is again .5.

What is the probability of rolling a total of 4 with two dice?

Second Die	First Die					
	1	2	3	4	5	6
1	2	3	4	5	6	7
2	3	4	5	6	7	8
3	4	5	6	7	8	9
4	5	6	7	8	9	10
5	6	7	8	9	10	11
6	7	8	9	10	11	12

Probability with a pair of dice.

The chart shows the possible outcomes from rolling two dice. Across the top are the values for the first die; down the left side are the values for the second die. The cells inside the chart show the totals. The three shaded cells are the three ways to roll a total of 4, and there are 36 cells in all. So the probability of rolling a 4 is 1/12, which is about 0.083.

Put it together

To find the probability of two or more independent events occurring together, multiply the probabilities of the events. Here's an example:

> You plant five tomato seeds. The seeds are in separate containers and have no effect on one another. Each of the seeds has a 40% chance of germinating. What is the chance that none of the seeds will germinate?

The first thing to note about this question is that it introduces an alternative way to talk about probability. In terms of problem solving, the chance of an event is the same as the probability of the event. Also, it doesn't matter whether you represent the chance as a decimal number, a percentage, or a fraction—.4, 40%, and 4/10 all mean the same thing.

Math Section

Now, note the second sentence of the question. This sentence tells you that the probability of each seed sprouting is an independent event. Also, you're told that the chance of a seed germinating is .4, which means that the chance of a seed *not* germinating is .6.

Think about the event that you're interested in: none of the seeds germinating. This is composed of five independent events:

1. Seed A not germinating
2. Seed B not germinating
3. Seed C not germinating
4. Seed D not germinating
5. Seed E not germinating

Because these are independent events, you can multiply the individual probabilities together to get the answer: .6×.6×.6×.6×.6 = 0.07776, or nearly 8%.

Working with Geometric Probability

You may also run across SAT questions dealing with geometric probability. These are just regular probability questions based on geometric figures. Here's one to try:

> The figure below shows a cube of side 1 with a right cylinder embedded in it. The cylinder has a radius of .5 and the circular face of the cylinder exactly touches the cube at the center of each side as shown. A point is chosen at random from the interior of the cube. What is the probability that this point will lie within the cylinder?

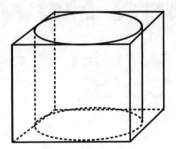

A geometric probability problem.

The key to solving this problem is to understand that it's asking for the ratio of the volumes of the two solids. The chance of a point being in the cylinder (the desired outcome) is proportional to the volume of the cylinder; the total number of outcomes is proportional to the volume of the cube. So you can figure the probability this way:

$$\frac{\pi\,(.5)^2 \times 1}{1 \times 1 \times 1}$$
$$= .25\pi$$

Thus the answer is $\pi/4$, or about 79%.

Your 10 Worst Fears
—And How to Beat Them!

The SAT Worst Case Scenario Survival Guide

Let's face it. We all have a few fears nagging at us in the pits of our stomachs. You know, those absurd little worries that keep us up late at night. When it comes to the SAT, some of your worst fears might be justified. Let's take a look at a few worst-case scenarios and how to deal with them.

1 I've missed a question and all my bubbles are off by one

The trick, of course, is not to find yourself in this situation. Train yourself to check the number of the question with the number of the bubble on every question. The easiest place to get into trouble is when you skip a question in the test booklet but not on the answer sheet. When you skip a question, you should mark it in the test booklet by circling that question number. This will be a cue to also leave a line blank on the answer sheet.

If, Heaven forbid, you discover that you're off by a line, do the following. Quickly look in your test booklet for questions you've skipped. These should be circled. There should be a blank line on the answer sheet for the skipped question. If you find your mistake, quickly transpose your answers to the correct line. It may be easier to work from the last answer you bubbled incorrectly, moving that bubble down a line and then erasing the line above it thoroughly. You can then repeat that procedure until you reach the blank you should have skipped.

2 I don't know how to use my fancy new calculator

If your calculator is too fancy, you might have a couple of problems. First of all, there are specific rules about what kind of calculator you can use on the SAT. (You'll find some of these guidelines in the SAT Helpdesk article.) The SAT Math section requires you to compute squares and square roots and to do calculations using negative numbers. If you understand how to use a calculator that can handle exponents, scientific notation, and fractions, you're ahead of the game. For the record, you can use scientific and graphic calculators. If you know how to use one, it can be an advantage to have a sophisticated device, but the night before the test is a bad time to start learning the features of a new calculator.

3 I used up too much time on a really hard question

Practice budgeting your time early. Keep a watch with you as you do practice questions. You will have about a minute a question in most sections and 25 minutes to do your essay. Especially practice reading the long passage questions, as these can really rob time. If you get stuck on a question, circle it and move on. The next question is worth the same number of points, as will be the ones at the end of the section that you'll never see if you burn all your time. Use process of elimination to weed out the obviously wrong answers, take your best guess, and keep moving. If you're really short of time, look for the easy questions and use the guessing strategies from The Ins and Outs of Guessing.

4 I sent my scores to the wrong colleges

You made a $9 mistake. After you take the test, you can go to the College Board website (www.collegeboard.com) and report your scores to additional schools at a cost of $9 for each report.

5 I got a really bad score

Take the test again. If you really studied for the test and were still disappointed, you might try a SAT prep course, where an instructor will help you identify the best strategies for you. As well, you should look to see if your school choices will accept the ACT and give that test a shot. If these options aren't available to you, you should discuss your score with your college's admissions office. The SAT isn't the only criteria they use, and you might be able to make your case to them. It can be really devastating to see those cold, hard numbers, but it's not the end of the world.

6 It's the night before the test, I haven't studied at all, and this magazine is the only study aid I have

Bottom line: you aren't going to pick up a whole lot of new math facts, vocabulary words, or essay writing skills in 24 hours. However, there's still a lot you can do to help yourself out.

- Know the directions for every section
- Work a few sample questions from each section so you'll know the question formats

- Read the article on guessing
- Learn how the Grid-in questions work in the Math section
- Go to bed early. An all-nighter isn't going to help you.

7 My girlfriend dumped me yesterday

You can't always predict the little twists and turns life is going to throw at you. If you know you're going to be off your game in a major way, reschedule the test. The College Board will not allow you to cancel a scheduled test and receive a refund. However, you can move a test to a future test date by calling (609) 771-7600. As of this printing, the cost to change a test date is $19. If you just don't want to see your ex on test day, you can use the same number to chance your testing center—also $19.

8 I missed the signup deadline, but I have to take the test

The College Board makes provisions for standby registration. Standby registration is on a space-available basis, so at a busy test center or on a busy test date, you might be out of luck. However, if you require a standby registration, go to the test center (early) with a completed registration form sealed in an envelope along with a check made out to The College Board for the full registration fee plus the $35 standby registration fee.

9 I have a panic attack in the middle of the math section

If you're prone to panic attacks, you need to be prepared to deal with one during the test. Use whatever relaxation techniques you've relied on in the past to bring yourself back

Math Section

down to earth. It helps to be prepared, to know what to expect, and to have a plan in case you get flustered. Read the article Seven Super Strategies to Master Test Anxiety for more information.

10 I experience a personal emergency during a test section

You'll get a break at the end of each hour of testing. The break will be short, but it should be sufficient for you to attend to any pressing personal needs. If you have an emergency during a test section, you should alert the test proctor. You may be allowed to leave, but you will not be allowed to return and complete that section.

Bonus anxiety: I showed up naked

Even if you're not actually naked, it can be a big problem if you forget your ID, your pencils, or your calculator. Double-check the things that you're bringing to the testing center. You might want to put them all into a backpack or purse the night before:

- Your admission ticket
- Your photo ID
- As many sharpened No. 2 pencils as you think you'll need, plus a couple of extras
- An eraser[md]and check to make sure that the eraser really does a good job of removing pencil marks!
- A calculator
- Spare batteries for the calculator
- A watch, stopwatch, or travel alarm with the audible alarm turned off.

7 Super Strategies

to Master Test Anxiety

1 Be prepared—know the test and don't let yourself be surprised by anything.

New situations are always an opportunity for stress. It's natural to feel some anxiety when you sit down for the SAT. However, if you do your homework, nothing on the SAT should come as a shock. The instructions for each section are available for you to learn and they will not change on test day. The practice tests in this book and others show you exactly what the test will look like. If you give yourself a few timed tests, you should even be ready for the fatigue that inevitably sets in as you do the later sections of the SAT. Know what the test is about and you'll be much more confident on test day.

2 Visualize yourself being successful—don't let yourself or others give you negative messages

Start out your practice sessions with an affirmation: You're taking this test to give yourself the best shot at a good college and a good future. Keep a positive outlook and plan to get the score you need for the school of your choice.

3 Allow plenty of time before your college application deadlines.

You may need to take the SAT twice. Many (if not most) students shooting for a competitive school take the SAT at least two times. Sign up for an early Spring test date and plan to take the test again early in the fall if you need to.

4 Give yourself lots of time the morning of the SAT

Many a student has spent a little too much time in bed on SAT day and wound up sliding into a parking space, sprinting to the registration desk, and breathlessly sitting down to write an essay. Don't let this be you. Know exactly how long it takes to get to the test center. Give yourself time for a good breakfast, and arrive at the test center at least 15 minutes before the scheduled start time.

5 Pick a relaxation strategy that works for you if you panic on the test

A panic attack in the middle of the SAT can wreck an otherwise great test. Learn a few relaxation techniques and practice them beforehand. Some things you might try are deep breathing exercises, clenching your fists and then relaxing and wiggling your fingers, or visualizing an image with positive connections—such as a favorite vacation spot.

6 Promise yourself a treat afterwards

Knowing that something pleasant awaits you after you finish the SAT can really help you get through those long study sessions as well as the test itself. If you can avoid it, don't plan to go to work right after the test. Give yourself a "me day." Go out with friends or plan to catch a matinee. You've earned it. You're special.

7 Have reasonable expectations for yourself

Even the smartest kids and the best test takers rarely get perfect scores. Start by knowing what scores you really need. You can get a 550 in the math section, for example, by answering only a little more than half the questions correctly and using good guessing techniques on the remaining questions. Your practice tests should be a good indicator of what you can expect on the actual test.

Getting Personal: Faces of the New SAT

We checked in with a couple of brave students who took the new SAT on March 11, 2005. Here's what they had to say about themselves and the test.

Carly

Tell us a little bit about yourself

I am Carly, and I am seventeen. I enjoy the pressure school puts on you to not only succeed, but to explore the world of knowledge. I have always thrived on pressure and tried to meet the expectations of people—especially in school.

Do you participate in any clubs?

I am a section editor for the school paper. I am junior class vice-president, I participate in DECA and have recently been elected District 4/5 State President, I am a Greyhound Kick-off Mentor—a mentor program for incoming freshman, I am a member of National Honor Society, and I participate in Model UN.

What activities do you enjoy?

I run cross country and am team captain. I enjoy running in my free time and playing pretty much any sport. I spend a lot of time with my friends, too.

What majors are you considering?

I am looking to pursue a major in public relations.

What is your grade point average?

My grade point average is 3.92.

How did the writing section go?

I think the writing section went pretty well thanks to all the writing I do in school. The prompt was a little different than I expected, but it allowed me to draw on a lot prior knowledge. My strategy was that of any essay I write in class or on a test. The time limit, 25 minutes, is very similar to what I am used to. I first read through the question and developed a thesis from which I could write a five paragraph essay. My one bit of advice I would pass on is to begin writing right away. Don't spend too much time planning out what you have to say, instead just say it.

What did you think was most difficult about the test?

The writing prompt probably created the most anxiety for me and was most difficult. The only way I can share to overcome this is write as much as possible. In my block class at school, AP American Literature and AP U.S. history, we write essays or take an essay test at least once a week. Once you get use to writing under a time constraint it takes away a lot of the difficulty of the new SAT.

What did you do to prepare for the new SAT?

I actually did not do anything special to prepare for the new SAT. For one of the previous times I took the old SAT I looked over a friend who got their test sent back to them and looked up any words I didn't know. A few of the words actually ended up being on the test I took.

What's your advice for other students?

First of all, don't get too nervous. It's just like any other test you take and school and the best part is if you don't do well you can always take it again. With that in mind, you have still take it seriously if you want to do well. Look over some practice materials the weeks before and sometimes having the stuff fresh in my brain helped. My other bit of advice is read as much as you can. I can't believe how many of the words I didn't know on the test I've since encountered in my reading.

Greg

Tell us a little bit about yourself

My name is Greg, and I'm a junior. I'm 17 years old and have one brother who is 15. My ethnic background is Filipino American, and I am half-Christian and half-Jewish due to mixed religion marriage. I am a very outgoing, nice guy who can get along with almost anyone. I like to make people laugh, and I enjoy helping people out in whatever way I can. In school, I enjoy working on group projects and learning new things that I didn't know before. It's always helpful to learn things that'll be useful to you later on in life.

Do you participate in any clubs?

I run in varsity track and field for Carmel High School and I play guitar in the High School Jazz Band. I have been in the Rising Stars Drama Club, Student Venture, the Club Club, and National Honors Society.

What activities do you enjoy?

I enjoy acting and I play electric guitar for Community Church Worship Band. I also enjoy art and participate in several art classes at school.

What majors are you considering?

A major that I have my sights set on in college is Media Arts and Animation where I would do a lot of artistic things that deal with computers.

What is your grade point average?

My GPA is about 3.75—mostly As and some Bs.

How did the writing section go?

The writing section was a bit tough and awkward at first, to tell you the truth. The prompt was not really what I expected. The reason for this was that the question was quite broad. For mine, the question was basically "Do you think majority rules is a good way to make big decisions?" For me, this gave me a multitude of things to talk about.

What did you think was most difficult about the test?

The problem was, we only had 25 minutes and just two pages to write. I felt rushed because it seemed as if I didn't have enough time to plan and say everything I needed to say. Basically all you could do was just cite a bunch of examples of where it works and try to organize that into an essay.

What did you do to prepare for the new SAT?

I took an SAT preparation course. I didn't have a specific strategy that my SAT prep teacher gave me, but I had written several essays during U.S. History class and English, as well as other classes. I felt that this sufficiently prepared me for any essay writing. The thing was that the essays I took in class gave me enough time and I already had ideas on what to say and had a more narrowed field of information to talk about. I felt like my strategy was a little less effective as the broad question caught me off guard a bit.

What's your advice for other students?

The only advice I could give to other students is to not think too much about the essay question, but just write quickly and persuasively. Organize your ideas for a few moments and use a lot of examples. Don't go into detail too much about one topic, but don't jump around from topic to topic quickly either. Stay relaxed and try your best.

Critical Reading Section

Are You Gonna Finish That?

Completing your sentences in the Critical Reading section

The new SAT has abolished the infamous analogies that were the bane of your parents' pre-college days. However, that doesn't mean vocabulary isn't important. On the contrary, in the new SAT's 19 sentence completion questions you need to be able to recognize the correct word or words to finish an incomplete sentence.

The sentence completion section of the new SAT is mostly about vocabulary, but it also tests your ability to understand complex sentences. You'll see sentences that are missing one or two words, and you'll choose the appropriate word or words from a list.

Understanding the types of questions

There are two types of sentence completion questions:

1. vocabulary-in-context
2. logic

Vocabulary-in-context

In these questions, you'll have to figure out which word or words bests fits the sentence based on the meaning of the missing words.

SAMPLE**QUESTION**

The congressman's ____ responses in regards to the missing funds might cost him votes in the ____ election.

Ⓐ exemplary...sector's

Ⓑ considerate...forthcoming

Ⓒ impetuous...special

Ⓓ evasive...subsequent

Ⓔ incriminating...preceding

ANSWER

The correct answer is Ⓓ. The congressman's *evasive* answers cost him votes in the *subsequent* election.

Logic

In these questions, the missing words are usually more familiar, but you'll need to determine which word is best based on the content of the sentence.

Now, let's take a look at a few strategies that will help you crack the sentence completion questions.

SAMPLE**QUESTION**

The jury's hasty decision was cause for a(n) ____.

Ⓐ reprimand

Ⓑ appeal

Ⓒ mistrial

Ⓓ retrial

Ⓔ dismissal

ANSWER

The correct answer is Ⓒ. This question tests your ability to logically connect the consequences of a judge acting too quickly to a negative outcome—a mistrial

Choose your answers wisely

Even when you aren't completely sure of the right answer, selecting the best response isn't just guesswork. You may be surprised how many times you will recognize the correct answer when you plug it into the sentence. When you encounter one of these questions, try the following steps.

1. Read the entire sentence and actually say "blank" for the missing words. It helps you to get a feel for how the sentence sounds.

2. If you see any unfamiliar words in the sentence, try to discern their meanings before you start plugging in answers.

3. Before reading the answers, try to fill in the blank using your own words.

4. After choosing a word of your own, review the answers for a word that's similar to yours. If you don't find an exact match, choose the word that's the closest to your word.

5. If you don't find a good match, repeat the sentence and fill in the blank with each response. Be sure to review each response—don't stop with the first one that seems right.

Putting the five steps to work

Let's work through a sample question following these steps:

Alexis' exquisite artwork was ____ by those who admired it.

Ⓐ feared

Ⓑ lauded

Ⓒ criticized

Ⓓ purchased

Ⓔ misunderstood

How should you break down this question? The following items will help you:

1. Say the sentence as follows: "Alexis' artwork was blank by those who admired it."

2. More than likely, you know all the words in this sentence. However, if you were unsure of the meaning of the word *exquisite* in this context, you might take a moment to think through exactly what it means here.

3. Before reading the possible responses, think of any words that might fill the blank appropriately. For example, you might think of *complemented* or *remembered*.

4. Search the list and see if you can find any word that's close to one of your own. *Lauded* is a synonym for *complimented*, so that would seem a good choice.

5. Quickly scan the sentence using the other words. In this case, answer B is clearly the best choice.

Be careful, though. Although this is a logic question, you still need to know the meaning of the word "lauded" to get the right answer. In this example, *purchased* could work, but *lauded* is better. Remember that you are looking for the best response, not just any response that fits.

Use the process of elimination

If you've ever watched Who Wants to Be a Millionaire, you know that one of the most valuable lifelines is the one where the contestant drops a couple of answers and narrows the choices. Regis won't be able to help you on the new SAT, but you may be able to reduce your answer options by the process of elimination.

Let's look at a question where elimination may make the difference between choosing among 5 words and having a 50/50 shot—even if you don't have a clue what the right answer really is.

> ## POWER**TIP**
>
> ### Write it down, Man!
>
> **Transfer each word to an index card.** The process of writing the words and their definitions will go a long way toward committing them to memory.

Putting the art of elimination to work

Try your hand at the following question.

The principal preferred to use the _____ "retained" instead of saying "failed" when a student was forced to repeat a grade.

A parenthetical

B hypothesis

C eulogy

D euphemism

E antonym

From the context of this sentence, you can pretty easily figure out that you need to supply an answer that means "synonym" or "nicer word." Although you may not know which answer fits the bill, you probably *do* know that answers A, B, and E aren't even close. Choosing between *eulogy* and *euphemism* gives you a much better chance at success than a random shot between A and E.

> ## POWER**TIP**
>
> ### Can you hear me now? Good!
>
> **Make an audio tape or CD of your word list.** Play the tape anytime you have a few minutes.

> ## POWER**TIP**
>
> ### The weirder the better
>
> **Wacky images stick in your head.** Create visual clues to help you remember difficult words. For example, to help you remember the word "abduct," you might visualize a man kidnapping a duck.

Pay close attention to keywords

Sometimes little words can make a big difference. Words like *not*, *but*, *also*, *however*, and *yet* can completely change a sentence's meaning. They can also help you understand the sentence. For instance, the words *although*, *even though*, and *nevertheless* indicate a conflict or contrast between the main thoughts in a sentence. For example:

> Although Alexis sold all of her work, she was a *pariah* in the art community.

> Alexis was *panned* by the art critics, but she sold all of her work.

> Alexis remains an *obscure* figure in art circles, yet she continues to sell every piece almost as soon as the paint dries.

All these sentences have a similar purpose—to express Alexis' success even though she is not a big name in the art community. In each case, the keyword is a tip that the underlined word—which, of course, would be missing in a SAT question—is in conflict or contrast with the phrase that follows the keyword. Thus, even if you don't know a *pariah* from a poltergeist you can probably determine that the word means "outcast."

Watch for these keywords

Other keywords to watch for include:

As a result

Consequently

Resulting in

Subsequently

Subsequent to

Therefore

Rather than

Instead of

Due to

> ## POWER**TIP**
>
> ### Beyond multiple choice
>
> **Improving your vocabulary** won't just help you out in the Critical Reading section of the New SAT. A solid vocabulary, used correctly, will improve your essay score, as well. Pick a few good, all-purpose SAT vocabulary words and keep them handy for your essay.

Use logic

Sometimes you can crack a difficult sentence by picking it apart logically. It helps to remember that there are five logical relationships in most sentences:

1. Contrast
2. Support
3. Cause and effect
4. Definition
5. Restatement

Specific words and phrases can clue you in to the type of relationship in use. Once you've defined the relationship, a little reasoning can help you figure out the meaning of any unfamiliar words.

Contrasting keywords

although, but, conversely, despite,
even though, however, in contrast,
in spite of, instead of, nevertheless,
nonetheless, on the contrary, on
the other hand, rather, yet,

and so on

Supporting keywords

additionally, also, besides,
furthermore, in addition, likewise,
moreover, similarly,

and so on

Cause and effect keywords

as a result, because, consequently,
due to, if...then, in order to, since,
so, subsequently, therefore,

and so on

Definition keywords

am, are, as, especially, for example,
for instance, including, to be, is,
means, refers to, that is,

and so on

Restatement keywords

that is, or, in other words, in a
nutshell,

and so on

POWER**TIP**

Say what?

**Lots of words have more than
one meaning, and some of
those meanings can be rather
obscure.** This part of the exam will
stick with the standard definitions. You
won't be expected to know little known
uses for the word.

SAMPLE**QUESTION**

The _____ accident knocked the old
man off his guard.

Ⓐ unexpected

Ⓑ prestigious

Ⓒ elite

Ⓓ monumental

Ⓔ auspicious

In this question, you know that you're
looking for an adjective. While all the
choices are adjectives, answers B, C,
and E wouldn't ordinarily describe the
word "accident." Between *unexpected*
and *monumental*, *unexpected* is a better
match for the supporting phrase *knocked
off his guard*.

ANSWER

The correct answer is **Ⓐ**.

SAMPLE**QUESTION**

Despite the child's angelic
appearance, she was quite _____.

Ⓐ beautiful

Ⓑ ugly

Ⓒ wicked

Ⓓ careless

Ⓔ playful

Here, the keyword *despite* telegraphs
the contrast between the child's angelic
appearance and some less-than-angelic
aspect of her character. Answer C is the
best response. No other choice captures
the contrast between appearance and
behavior.

ANSWER

The correct answer is .

SAMPLE**QUESTION**

_____ **is the expensive process of** separating the salt from sea water.

Ⓐ Desalinization

Ⓑ Evaporation

Ⓒ Mining

Ⓓ Ionization

Ⓔ Fusion

The word "is" clues you in right away that you're looking at a definition relationship. Answers B, C, D, and E are all incorrect because they do not match the definition. You can use elimination to zap answers C, D, and E because you know that they are not connected to the removal of salt from seawater. Between A and B, you might correctly choose _desalinization_ just because it sounds more expensive than _evaporation_.

ANSWER

The correct answer is Ⓐ.

POWER**TIP**

Questions get harder toward the end

If you're really guessing—as in you have no clue whatsoever—pay attention to what part of the test you're in. The questions get harder as you get farther into each section. Toward the end of a section, don't try to guess unless you can eliminate at least one answer.

SAMPLE**QUESTION**

The company's _____ was a result of poor planning and a lack of resources.

Ⓐ success

Ⓑ origin

Ⓒ demise

Ⓓ termination

Ⓔ confinement

The keywords _result of_ let you know this is a cause and effect question. Answer **C** is the correct answer. Something bad happened (_demise_) to the business _as a result_ of these things (_poor planning and a lack of resources_).

ANSWER

The correct answer is Ⓒ.

POWER**TIP**

Watch your colon

Semicolons and colons always indicate a supporting relationship, but they aren't interchangeable. Semicolons are used when the second clause develops the first. Colons are used when the second clause explains the first.

Take a deep breath and remember...

Vocabulary may not be your thing, but that doesn't mean you have to lose points on the Sentence Completion section of the new SAT. Practice recognizing common sentence patterns, keywords, and context clues, and you'll be sure to jack up your score by at least a few points. If you become a master of elimination, you'll even have a better shot at questions that have you totally stumped.

Know your word parts

You can't possibly memorize every word that might appear on the exam. The next best thing is to be familiar with the pieces that make up common SAT words. By learning the following set of prefixes, suffixes, and root words, you stand a better chance of guessing correctly when you're uncertain of a word's meaning.

Common word elements

Word Element	Meaning	Example
a	without or not	amoral
ad	toward; near	adjacent
ambi	both; around	ambidextrous
an	without or not	anaerobic
ante	before	antebellum
arch	ruler	monarch
archy	one who rules	monarchy
bi	two	biped
cata	down	catastrophe
co	together	commingle
con	together	conspire
contr	against or opposite	contrary
corp	body	corpse
counter	against or opposite	counterproductive
cracy	government	democracy
crat	supporter	democrat
de	down, away, or apart	descend
dec	ten	decathlon
di	two; away from	divert
dic	speak or say	dictate
e	out	evict
em	out	embark
en	into or in; to put in	employ
ence	full of	preference
ex	out	expel
fac	make	manufacture
her	to stick	adhere
hyper	over or beyond	hypersonic
hypo	under or below	hypodermic
ian	person who	librarian
ify	make	typify
il	not; in or into	illogical
im	not	impervious
in	not	insubstantial
ir	not	irrelevant
intra	within	intramural
inter	between	interstate

Word Element	Meaning	Example
ist	person who	artist
ium	relating to	tedium
ive	relating to	passive
lat	side	lateral
min	small	minimum
mit	to send	transmit
mono	one	monophonic
mor	manners or behavior	morals
mort	death	mortician
non	not	nonplussed
nov	new; nine	novitiate
ology	the study of	biology
omni	all	omnivore
pan	all; also	pantheistic
pathy	feelings	empathy
ped	foot	biped
ped	child	pediatric
penta	five	pentathlon
philo	love of	philosophy
pod	foot	podiatrist
port	carry	transport
pre	before; preceding	preempt
quad	four	quadraped
re	back or again	repeat
sion	act of or state of	transition
sive	relating to; of	progressive
soph	wise, wisdom	sophistry
spec	see	speculate
temp	time	tempo
term	end	terminate
tion	act of or state of	transition
trans	across or change	transfer
tri	three	tricuspid
un	not	unfriendly
uni	one	universe
vi	life	vital
viv	life	vivacious

Dissecting the Reading Passages

There's not much point to reading something if you don't understand what it means. The new SAT challenges you to master three types of reading passages—short passages, long passages, and paired passages.

Types of questions you'll see

In this section of the exam, you'll encounter three types of questions:

- **Extended Reasoning Questions.** These questions will expect you to evaluate information and draw a conclusion. These questions do not have a literal or direct answer within the actual passage content; you will have to infer the answers from the reading. In other words, you will have to reason through the question.

- **Vocabulary-in-Context Questions.** These questions will test your understanding of word usage within the context of the passage. It's important to keep context in mind when answering these questions. Words often have more than one meaning, and reading just the sentence in which the word is used won't always be enough.

- **Literal Comprehension Questions.** These questions ask about the facts presented in the passage. You are not expected to apply your interpretation or opinions in these questions. As Jack Friday of Dragnet would say, "Just the facts, ma'am."

Now, let's take a look at each type of question in depth. There's no better way to prepare than to know what to expect. The new SAT has some very specific skills it's trying to test, and some of the questions are trickier than others.

Extended reasoning questions

Extended reasoning questions are just what the title suggests. There's no literal fact in the passage to turn to—you must reason through what you've read to figure out the most likely response. You can identify most extended reasoning questions just by their wording, but watch for the following words and phrases:

- According to the author/passage
- Apparently

- Implies
- Inferred
- Probably
- Seems
- Suggests

One key to answering extended reasoning questions correctly is recognizing what's a fact and what isn't. Both a narrative and an argumentative passage may imply or suggest an idea, and you must know the difference between a universally accepted fact and the author's opinion.

Sometimes the difference is subtle and hard to spot. Watch for is the use of personal pronouns such as *I*, *me*, *my*, and *mine*. These are clues that the author is speaking from personal experience or expressing a personal opinion. Consider the following example:

> Martha screamed at the first firefighters to arrive on the scene, "Where have you been? I called nearly 20 minutes ago! My house is completely gone! Save my 10 cats!"

> Which of the following is the most factual?

Ⓐ Seventeen minutes lapsed between the first call to 911 and the fire truck's arrival.

Ⓑ Something surely went wrong if it took nearly 20 minutes for the first fire truck to arrive.

Ⓒ Nearly 20 minutes lapsed between the first call to 911 and the fire truck's arrival.

Ⓓ Kids call Martha "that crazy cat lady."

Ⓔ Nearly 20 minutes lapsed between Martha's first call and the fire truck's arrival.

This question is clearly asking for you to use your reasoning ability to determine which responses state only the facts in the passage and which require you to make an inference. Answer Ⓔ is correct, as it is the only statement that repeats only facts we know from

the passage. Let's look at why the other answers are poor choices.

Answer Ⓐ states that 17 minutes lapsed. From the passage, you know only that it was nearly 20 minutes.

Answer Ⓑ is incorrect because there's no way to discern from the timing of events that something went wrong. Seventeen minutes might actually be normal for that area.

Answer Ⓒ requires you to infer that Martha dialed 911. The passage doesn't say whom she called.

Answer Ⓓ is also incorrect. The children may indeed call Martha "the crazy cat lady," but the passage doesn't say so.

Vocabulary-in-context questions

Your vocabulary skills get a real workout in the SAT exam. Unlike the more straightforward sentence completeion questions, in the short passage section you must be able to discern the author's intent by keeping context in mind.

The word in question will most likely have many meanings, and you can expect the answers to utilize all those meanings. It's up to you to find the appropriate answer within the context of the passage.

POWERTIP

By the way, there's no way around it. You are going to have to read the passage to answer the questions. Don't try to just skim the passage for answers in an effort to save time. You'll need the context of the passage to answer most of the questions.

Often you don't have to know the exact definition—that's what reading comprehension is all about. You can get the word's meaning because of the context in which the word is used. Consider the following example that requires you to find the definition to the word *sage*.

> The old woman's *sage* advice saved the day.

The word *sage*, as used in the above sentence, most nearly means:

Ⓐ A plant that grows in the desert

Ⓑ Wise

Ⓒ Bad

Ⓓ Uneducated

Ⓔ Worldly

Answer Ⓑ is the best answer. You know from the phrase "saved the day" that the wise advice worked.

Literal comprehension questions

Literal comprehension questions are fact-based questions. It's as simple as that. These questions will ask you to find the answer within the passage. These types of questions sometimes use qualifying terms such as *except*, *only*, *not*, *other than*, and so on.

Answers will seldom appear in the same word-for-word form, though. In addition, you may have to review the passage to get the most specific and correct answer. Don't depend on your memory or prior knowledge on the subject. Take the time to reread the appropriate section of the passage if necessary. Let's look at an example:

> Except for the wolf hawk, which hunts in packs, hawks are solitary hunters.

Which statement about hawks is the most accurate?

Ⓐ Hawks are solitary hunters.

Ⓑ Wolf hawks are solitary hunters.

Ⓒ Wolf hawks hunt in packs.

Ⓓ All hawks hunt in packs.

Ⓔ Wolf hawks are the only hawks that hunt in packs.

Answer Ⓔ is correct. Let's look at how this question tries to trip you up.

Answer Ⓐ implies that *all* hawks are solitary hunters. This can't be true, as the passage itself offers the counterexample of the wolf hawk. Remember that it only take *one counterexample* to disprove an absolute such as *all* or *never*.

Answers Ⓑ and Ⓓ are factually incorrect and can be eliminated immediately.

Answer Ⓒ is *verrrrry* tempting. It's absolutely true and is supported by the passage. However, it's not the *best* answer.

Answer Ⓔ both captures the information in answer C and highlights the relevance of it by pointing out the unique nature of the wolf hawk's hunting style.

Watch for words like *except*, *only*, *all*, and *never* in the question and in the passage. The answers here also demonstrate clearly that you should read all the responses before making a choice.

┌─────────────────────────┐
│ **POWERTIP**   │
└─────────────────────────┘

Order please

The long passage questions are always given in the order that you'll encounter the answers in the passage.

POWER**TIP**

Take a deep breath

Many students dread this reading section. However, this section might be the easiest section of the exam if you approach it enthusiastically. Read each passage with the attitude that you're simply learning something new. Don't sweat the questions that are coming. If you can relax, you'll recall more about the passage. Remember, the answers to the questions are in the passages. It's the only "open book" section of the SAT.

Answering questions effectively

Unlike math and grammar, reading isn't an exact science. However, there are definitely some ways to improve your chances of success on the short passages questions. Let's take a look at a few strategies you can use to improve your performance on this section.

Rephrase tough questions

If you don't understand the question, or if more than one answer seems to be correct, rephrase the question as an open-ended question. Then try to answer that question as fully as possible.

For instance, let's take a look at a typical SAT question that requires a multiple choice response.

> The author's attitude toward the role of men in feminism is best characterized by which of these responses

(A) Even the best of men is likely to become a burden before too long.

(B) Men have no constructive role to play in the feminist movement.

(C) How could any reasonable man object to the idea that a woman could be his equal?

(D) Men stand to benefit the most from feminism.

(E) Lorena Bobbit had the right idea!

Now, let's look at the same question rephrased as an open-ended question:

> How does the author feel about feminism?

As you summarize the author's view, the passage's purpose will become clearer and one of the answers will usually stand out

Avoid absolutes

If you can't choose between two similar answers, go with the less absolute of the two. Statements with words such as *never*, *always*, *only*, and *so on* are less likely to be true because it only takes one counter-example to disqualify that choice.

For example, the statement:

> **It never rains in New Mexico.**

would be disproved by one spring shower. The statement:

> **It rarely rains in New Mexico.**

is much more likely to be true.

POWER**TIP**

She blinded me with science

The topics you'll see in the SAT reading passages range from science to literature. It's tempting to be frightened by the subject matter. However, these questions aren't testing what you know, but rather what you discern while reading. Everything you need to answer each question will be in the passage.

Watch for extremes

In a typical passage, extreme statements are less likely to be true. For instance, on a passage describing the decline in natural scenery along public highways, the answer:

> Billboard advertising along the roadway is a horrific public nuisance and should be abolished

is less likely to be the correct choice than would be:

> Advertisers should consider the impact their signs will have on the natural beauty of the roadway

These answers may mean roughly the same thing, but it's your job to decide which is the most appropriate. More often than not, the less extreme response would be the right answer.

Bear in mind, the passage may be directing the reader toward an extreme position. If the language in the passage represents an extreme position, then an answer that reflects that opinion would be appropriate.

Stick with what the passage says

In SAT passages, you should be able to find all the information you need to answer the questions *in the passage itself.* You should not try to bring in information you learned from other sources. If a passage asserts a position with which you disagree or facts you believe are inaccurate, answer the questions based on what the passage actually says.

POWER**TIP**

Read the text

There's simply no substitute for reading the passages, questions, and answers carefully. You can expect some answers in this particular section to add additional pieces of information with the correct information in an effort to trick you. Do *not* be fooled. Choose the answer that includes only information from the essay.

Don't try to read the author's mind

Sometimes, two answers will sound similar, but one calls on you to interpret the author's feelings while the other merely asks you to interpret the facts presented in the passage. For example, consider these two statements:

> The author loves her border collie.

> Border collies are highly intelligent and easily trained.

Each sentence may be true, but unless the passage explicitly states the author's feelings toward her dog, the second is easier to support from the facts. This author, by the way, loves her border collie.

Watch for cues in the questions

When a question refers to a specific sentence, reread that sentence before trying to answer the question. When a question says something like, "In line 7 of the first passage, the author asserts…" you should stick to the meaning of line 7 rather than interpreting that statement based on other parts of the passage. When you're supposed to draw conclusions, the questions will direct you to do so.

> **POWERTIP**
>
> **Answer the easy questions first**
>
> Easy questions are **worth** the same as hard questions.

Take a deep breath and remember…

Practice makes perfect! There's no question about it. The more you practice your critical reading skills, the better you'll become at answering the questions in this section. Don't skimp on this part of your study for the new SAT because you're a fast reader or a great writer. Just like the other sections of the test, success here is a matter of knowing what to expect and being ready for it.

The **3 types** of reading passages

Identifying *narrative*, *argument*, and *analysis* on the test

One of the most important things you can do in cracking both short and long reading passages is to figure out what the passage is trying to do. If you can determine what type of passage you're reading, you'll be better able to answer the questions.

Although the passages will cover a wide range of topics, each will have a specific purpose. The most common types of passages are the *narrative*, the *argument*, and the *analysis*. Let's take a look at each of these. With any luck, you'll be able to identify each type when you see it on the test.

Narrative

A *narrative* is a story. Narrative passages are probably the easiest ones to identify. These passages will describe a main character's ordeal or conflict. Biographies and memoirs are narratives. The most obvious distinguishing characteristics of a narrative are:

- Discussions of an individual's motivations or actions

- Presentation of subjective information

- A clear timeline

- Personal touches, such as personal pronouns or less-formal language.

- Often describes a conflict or challenge faced by the author

Narrative questions will contain a mixture of fact-based questions and more subjective idea-oriented questions. While all the information you need to answer the questions will be in the passage, you may need to decode an author's personal reflections or observations to retrieve the information.

Argument

An *argument* attempts to persuade the reader to a specific point of view. Although these types of passages often include facts, they may be subjective in content and not purely factual. It's not that tough to recognize an argument if you remember a few key points about this style of passage:

- The author is trying to convince you to agree with a specific idea or position. If you feel like you're being sold something, you're probably reading an argument.

- The author has no reason to be even-handed. Unlike the *analysis* format, which you'll see in a minute, an argument doesn't always present the opposing viewpoint. Many arguments leave you saying, "Yeah, but what about..."

- An argument usually ends with a clear statement endorsing a specific conclusion. It may sound something like: "Therefore, it's clear that records set by baseball players convicted of using steroids should be removed from the record books."

Analysis

An *analysis* informs the reader by providing facts in an objective format. Just the opposite of the *argument*, an analysis presents facts and offers no attempt to persuade. These passages often result in the easiest questions, because they present facts without bias and don't try to draw conclusions for you.

Remember, in Critical Reading questions, you're trying to work out the passage's *purpose*, *main idea*, and *structure*. Identifying which of the previous forms the passage follows can help you figure out what you're reading.

Reading
short
passages

Short passages is the term the new SAT uses for writing examples that are no more than a paragraph or two in length—roughly 100 to 300 words. You see examples of short passages in everything from news articles to email.

Apart from special circumstances (such as poetry or music), most short passages are designed to communicate information. As far as the SAT is concerned, you should know three things after reading a short passage:

1. The passage's *purpose*
2. The passage's *main idea*
3. The passage's *structure*

The subjects covered are similar to those you'll encounter in college texts. Passages vary both in style and content. The questions in this section test your ability to:

- Identify and compare facts
- Draw conclusions based on facts, opinion, or anecdote
- Use context to define unfamiliar or subjective terms

POWER**TIP**

If you can improve your speed and accuracy with short passages, you'll have more time to spend on the trickier long passages.

POWER**TIP**

Special circumstances

It's possible for students with some specific learning or physical disabilities to get extra time for this portion of the test. If you believe you might qualify, see your guidance counselor for more information.

What short passages look like

Most passages in the short passage section are only 1-2 paragraphs long. Let's take a look at typical short passage question.

> By the time of the Civil War, more than two centuries after the first colonist arrived in New England, half the nation's land was still nearly empty. The frontier—a ragged line of settlements from the East—ran through part of Minnesota, along the border of Iowa, Missouri, and Arkansas and then swung westward into Texas. Reaching in from the West Coast there was also a thin line of settlements in California, Oregon, and Washington. Between these two frontiers there were only a few islands of settlers, such as the Mormons in Utah, the miners in Colorado, and the Mexican Americans in New Mexico. Even in the "settled" areas on the edge of the open land, it was often a long way between neighbors.
>
> By 1860, there were two frontiers. List their border states.
>
> **A** New England and New Mexico
>
> **B** Minnesota, Iowa, Missouri, and Arkansas; California, Oregon, and Washington
>
> **C** Minnesota, Iowa, Missouri, and Texas; California, Oregon, and Washington
>
> **D** Utah, Colorado, and New Mexico
>
> **E** Minnesota, Iowa, Missouri, Arkansas and Texas; California, Oregon, and Washington
>
> This passage would make a good introduction into the discussion of what topic?
>
> **A** settling the great plains between the two 1860 frontiers
>
> **B** westward expansion
>
> **C** the hardships faced by pioneers
>
> **D** how Mormons, miners, and Mexicans settled the great plains
>
> **E** discovering the western half of the United States

As it typical in the short passage section, the first asks a purely factual question. The passage states very clearly that the eastern settlements are bordered by Minnesota, Iowa, Missouri, Arkansas and Texas and the western settlements by California, Oregon, and Washington. Answer **E** is correct.

The second question tests your ability to correctly identify the main point of the passage. In this case, the passage paints a picture of widely spread out settlements on and between the frontiers. Answer **A** captures the sense of what the reader would naturally expect to follow this passage

On the other hand...

The new SAT also offers a second type of short passage question. Instead of one passage, you'll see two smaller passages, each of which presents its own set or facts or point of view. Your job is to read both passages and determine the best responses to questions that ask you to compare, contrast, and synthesize the information presented.

Passage 1

(Line 1) People can continue to use the known supply of fossil fuels at current rates for many years. New technology makes finding and extracting oil, coal, and natural gas easier. For example, in 1978, scientists thought there was about 648 billion barrels of oil remaining worldwide. However, with new discoveries and improved technology, optimists now think there may be as much as 3 trillion barrels remaining. **(Line 5)**Even if the use of oil increased, scientists would still have several hundred years to develop alternative fuels and new refining processes. In addition, technologies are reducing the amount of sulfur dioxide and nitrogen oxides released when fossil fuels are burned.

Passage 2

(Line 1) Advances in technology will serve only to speed up the rate at which oil is extracted from oil reserves. The amount of oil available for consumers will rise, and people will feel no need to conserve. At some point, production will decrease as supplies dwindle. The emissions produced when fossil fuels burn put society as a whole at risk. **(Line 5)**Despite more efficient methods of combustion, more than 6 billion tons of carbon dioxide was released into the atmosphere in 1997. Developing alternative sources of energy now will reduce pollution in the future. These alternatives also free fossil fuels for use in the production of plastics, paints, medicines, and other essential materials.

1. **Both passages are primarily concerned with the subject of**

   Ⓐ how to reduce the use of fossil fuels.

   Ⓑ the need to reduce the use of fossil fuels.

   Ⓒ modern techniques for drilling and refining fossil fuels.

   Ⓓ the availability of fossil fuels.

   Ⓔ developing alternate fuel sources.

   (See answer next page)

2. **After reading both passages, what is the main issue that needs to be resolved regarding the use of fossil fuels?**

   Ⓐ Finding safer ways to burn fossil fuels.

   Ⓑ Determining whether the conservation of fossil fuels is necessary.

   Ⓒ Agreeing upon a way to reduce our dependency on fossil fuels.

   Ⓓ Determining how much of the remaining fuel deposits should be used.

   Ⓔ Without alternative energy sources, we will use up all the fossil fuel.

   (See answer next page)

3. **Both passages discuss the following subjects, within the context of the position the passage supports.**

   Ⓐ Advances in technology and pollution

   Ⓑ The amount of remaining oil, advances in technology and pollution

   Ⓒ The amount of remaining oil, advances in technology and pollution, and alternate energy sources

   Ⓓ Advances in drilling and refining technologies, and fossil fuel as a pollutant

   Ⓔ Advances in technology, other uses for oil besides energy, and cleaner ways to burn fossil fuels

   (See answer next page)

continues

continued

1. Answer **C** is correct; the passages both discuss oil conservation and consumption, but they take opposing positions. Answers A, B, and D, and E are all incorrect. These subjects are part of the discussion, but they are not the main point.

2. Answer **B** is correct. The first passage concludes that there's plenty of oil and conservation isn't necessary. The second passage supports the idea of reducing the amount of fossil fuel we use. Answers A, C, D, and E are all incorrect. Although these points are all made in at least one passage, they aren't the main disagreement between the two passages.

3. Answer **D** is correct. The answer is essentially the same as Answer A, but it's more specific. Answer A is incorrect because it's incomplete. Answers B and C are incorrect because passage 2 doesn't discuss the amount of fossil fuel remaining. In fact, passage 2 makes the point that conservation is necessary regardless of the amount left. Answer E is incorrect because passage 1 doesn't discuss alternate uses for fossil fuels.

Take a deep breath and remember...

The short passage questions are arguably the easiest part of the new SAT. Each passage has only a couple of questions and the answers are in the passage itself. Spend at least some of your practice time on short passages.

Say what?
Knowing these basic literary terms helps you crack critical reading questions

Most of the vocabulary you're required to know in the Critical Reading section will be tested in the multiple-choice sentence completion questions. However, there are a few special vocabulary terms you'll see in Critical Reading questions. Even if you understand the passage, you won't get far if you don't know what the question is asking. This portion of the SAT exam may use the following words in the questions.

Anecdote

An *anecdote* is a personal story that usually illustrates a point. For example:

> As a youngster, I didn't understand how witches made it into the Pledge of Allegiance—"...and to the republic for witches stands...".

How anecdotes might look in an SAT question

The author's *anecdote* about witches is intended to

- **A** entertain the reader
- **B** inform the reader
- **C** etc.

Counterexample

A *counterexample* contradicts a point that has already been made. For example:

Statement: All prime numbers are odd.

Counterexample: Two is both an even number and a prime number.

How a counterexample might look in an SAT question

Passage 1 states that the amount of Mercury in the groundwater has minimal impact on the health of American children. As a *counterexample*, passage 2 states:

- **A** The primary adverse health effects from Mercury result from eating contaminated fish, not from drinking water.
- **B** etc.

Hyperbole

A hyperbole exaggerates a point. For example:

> That woman can talk a mile a minute.

How a hyperbole might look in an SAT question

In asserting that llamas make the best pets, which of the author's statements is the greatest hyperbole:

- **A** Were it not for the lack of speech and opposable thumbs, llamas might well have become the dominant species on Earth.

continues

continued

    B Llamas are intelligent, empathetic, and loyal.

    C etc.

Irony

Irony produces results you didn't expect, but that are understood once all the facts are known. For example:

> "Who would have guessed that our sweet and outgoing little niece would be the murderer? She was always so happy and well-adjusted," stated our mother. "That seems true, but now that we know her mother's life was regularly threatened it isn't a stretch to see why she acted like that," father interjected.

How irony might look in a SAT question

The *irony* in the passage above might best be summarized by which of the following statements:

    A The individual who appeared least likely to do harm to another person, was, in fact, the most brutal

    B etc.

Metaphor

A *metaphor* describes something by comparing it to something else. For example:

> This past week has had more ups and downs than a yo-yo.

How a metaphor might look in a SAT question

Which of the following metaphors might best replace the one used by the author in line 5 of the passage above:

    A This week has been a real roller coaster ride.

    B The many unexpected events of the past week made it especially challenging.

    C etc.

Simile

A *simile* compares two things using words such as *like* or *as*. For example:

> My life has been like a yo-yo lately—up and down, up and down.

How a simile might look in a SAT question

In line 7, the author refers to the bluegrass song, "Life is Like a Mountain Railroad." Which of the following statements best captures the meaning of that simile.

    A In one's life, one may expect to encounter dangerous and challenging situations and unexpected changes in direction.

    B One should always enjoy the view out the window when traveling.

    C etc.

Going Long
Managing long passages in the Critical Reading section

The long passages on the new SAT are a lot like the short passages except—you guessed it—they're longer. These passages run 400 to 850 words—about the length of a typical newspaper article. You'll still need to answer the same types of questions about each passage, but the passages themselves may be more complex, and can include both purely informational and literary passages.

With the longer passages, your skill at identifying the overall structure of the passage and finding relevant information for each question takes top priority. You simply won't have enough time to reread the entire passage for each question. We won't review all the basics of critical reading here; instead, we'll concentrate on the areas that make long passages tricky.

Determining the Structure of a Longer Passage

Unlike shorter passages, where the structure is generally pretty consistent, the longer passages you'll see on the new SAT offer quite a bit of variety. You should keep in mind three things when reading a longer passage:

1. What is the overall theme, structure, and style of the passage?
2. What is the purpose of each paragraph within the passage?
3. What are the important transitions between paragraphs?

Answering these three questions will help you understand the structure of the passage, which in turn will help you answer the questions. The goal is to transform reading from a passive practice to an active one.

For more tips on active reading, read the "6 Ways to Maximize Your Reading Time" article on page 154.

POWER**TIP**

When you make notes, highlight sentences, and otherwise work with the text, you'll find that it's easier to recall the information in the passage.

Now, let's look at a typical longer passage.

The following passage is an excerpt from a modern earth sciences textbook.

During most of the late Paleozoic, organisms diversified dramatically. Some 400 million years ago, plants that had adapted to survive at the water's edge began to move inland, becoming land plants. These earliest land plants were leafless vertical spikes about the size of your index finger. However, by the end of the Devonian, 40 million years later, the fossil record indicates the existence of forests with trees tens of meters high.

In the oceans, armor-plated fishes that had evolved during the Ordovician continued to adapt. Their armor plates thinned to lightweight scales that increased the organisms' speed and mobility. Other fishes evolved during the Devonian, including primitive sharks that had a skeleton made of cartilage and bony fishes—the groups to which virtually all modern fishes belong. Because of this, the Devonian period is often called the "age of fishes."

By late Devonian time, several fish became adapted to land environments. The fishes had primitive lungs that supplemented their breathing through gills. Lobe-finned fish likely occupied tidal flats and small ponds. Through time, the lobe-finned fish began to use their lungs more than their gills. By the end of the Devonian period, they had developed lungs and eventually evolved into true air-breathing amphibians with fishlike heads and tails.

Modern amphibians, like frogs, toads, and salamanders, are small and occupy limited biological niches. However, conditions during the remainder of the Paleozoic were ideal for these newcomers to the land. Plants and insects, which were their main diet, already were very abundant and large. The amphibians rapidly diversified because they had minimal competition from other land dwellers. Some groups took on roles and forms that were more similar to modern reptiles, such as crocodiles, than to modern amphibians.

By the Pennsylvanian period, large tropical swamps extended across North America, Europe, and Siberia. Trees approached 30 meters, with trunks over a meter across. The coal deposits that we use today for fuel originated in these swamps. These lush swamps allowed the amphibians to evolve quickly into a variety of species.

The Paleozoic ended with the Permian period, a time when Earth's major landmasses joined to form the supercontinent Pangaea. This redistribution of land and water and changes in the elevation of landmasses brought pronounced changes in world climate. Broad areas of the northern continents became elevated above sea level, and the climate became drier. These climate changes are believed to have triggered extinctions of many species on land and sea.

By the close of the Permian, 75 percent of the amphibian families had disappeared, and plants had declined in number and variety. Although many amphibian groups became extinct, their descendants, the reptiles, would become the most successful and advanced animals on Earth. Much of the marine life did not adapt and survive. At least 80 percent, and perhaps as much as 95 percent, of marine life disappeared. Many marine invertebrates that had been dominant during the Paleozoic, including all the remaining trilobites as well as some types of coral and brachiopods, could not adapt to the widespread environmental changes.

Now, let's break this passage down a little bit based on the main things you should be looking for in a longer passage.

What is the overall theme of the passage?

No tricks here. This passage tells you what it's up to right off the bat:

> During most of the late Paleozoic, organisms diversified dramatically.

This thesis tells you that the passage deals with the diversification of life during the Paleozoic period. Underline the thesis.

Here's what you should know at this point:

1. This passage is a straight-forward science passage not a literary passage.

2. This passage is going to present facts not argue a position.

3. This passage is probably going to use some scientific terminology

Here's what you should not know at this point:

1. What *Paleozoic* means—although you can probably guess it was a long time ago.

2. Anything at all about the development and proliferation of life during the Paleozoic period.

3. Anything about the author's motivation or background.

Here's what you should expect:

1. A 450-800 word discussion of life in the Paleozoic period where each paragraph has a specific topic related to the thesis.

2. Lots of facts to organize and sift through.

3. About 8 questions.

If you're really on the ball, you might even guess that the information is gong to be organized into chronological chunks examining the diversification of life in the Paleozoic period over time. The keyword *during* and verb *diversified* suggest that the main idea here is related to change over time—*diversified during*. You might want to circle these important words in the thesis sentence.

Knowing these things about the structure and purpose of this passage will give you a better clue on how to read this passage. You're looking for facts—probably in chronological order—that relate to changes in life on ancient Earth.

POWER**TIP**

2x2

You'll encounter at least one pair of related passages on the exam. Questions will ask you to compare the passages in some way. Be careful to read each question carefully. Questions may ask for choices that both passages share or may ask about one passage in particular.

POWER**TIP**

Beat the clock

If you're running out of time and you have only a few minutes left for a long passage, take a look at the first few questions before you start reading. The questions that ask you about specific facts in the passage are easier. Answer these first. It's better for your score to answer a few questions correctly than to guess blindly on all of the questions.

Breaking it down

Next, you should try to identify the purpose of each paragraph. With this selection, you should underline these sentences and fragments:

> Plants that had adapted to survive at the water's edge began to move inland, becoming land plants.

> The Devonian period is often called the "age of fishes."

> By late Devonian time, several fish became adapted to land environments.

> The amphibians rapidly diversified because they had minimal competition from other land dwellers.

> Lush swamps allowed the amphibians to evolve quickly into a variety of species.

> This redistribution of land and water and changes in the elevation of landmasses brought pronounced changes in world climate.

> By the close of the Permian, 75 percent of the amphibian families had disappeared,

You should also write the word "extinctions" next to the final paragraph because it talks about how many different types of organisms died out. The net effect of this underlining and note taking is to provide a sort of roadmap of the passage.

Watch the transitions

While you're identifying the main idea of each paragraph, be aware of the transitions between paragraphs. In this case, the transitions are fairly obvious: The narrator is moving forward through time, describing what happened in each successive period.

The keyword *by* appears at the start of three paragraphs, suggesting movement through time. As well, the construction

> Had evolved ... continued

in the second paragraph and the contract between *modern amphibians* and their Paleozoic precursors reinforce the idea that this passage deals with the development of life.

At this point, you should be familiar with the flow of the passage and have a good sense of how the author has supported the thesis. As well, you should have underlines or marked several key words, phrases, or sentences to make them easier to find when you go through the questions. As well, you've examined the transitions between the paragraphs to get a feel for the time line and the way the topics depend on each other.

POWER**TIP**

Underlining key sentences helps the structure of the passage stand out.

Use the questions for information

You should consider reading the question stems before reading the longer passages. Although this strategy may not work for everyone, some research shows it to be very effective. The biggest down-side is that it can take a little longer; you have to practice reading the questions quickly or else you'll run out of time.

On the positive side, if you know what you're looking for before you read the passage, you may retain those pieces a little bit better. To show you how this is done, let's see what we can learn from a set of questions without the passage to which they belong.

1. The phrase "household duties" in line [A] describes

   Ⓐ work brought home from the office.

   Ⓑ household chores such as cooking and ironing.

   Ⓒ anything requiring effort at home.

   Ⓓ taxes paid by a freeman for the privilege of living in a house.

   Ⓔ teaching and cooking.

2. According to the author, the Greeks regarded dinner as a time for

   Ⓐ eating simply and good conversation.

   Ⓑ killing time that would otherwise pass too slowly.

   Ⓒ feasting and heavy drinking.

   Ⓓ enjoying meals cooked with their own hands.

   Ⓔ making appointments for later discussions.

3. The word "vulgar" in line [B] is used to mean

   Ⓐ Crudely indecent

   Ⓑ Deficient in taste, delicacy, or refinement

   Ⓒ Associated with the common people

   Ⓓ Off-color

   Ⓔ Used in everyday language

4. The main theme of the passage is that

   Ⓐ the few freemen in ancient Greece rested on the backs of many slaves.

   Ⓑ only men could be truly free in Greek society.

   Ⓒ eating is a dreary thing that is best avoided.

   Ⓓ the Greek ideal of freedom required living a moderate and simple life.

   Ⓔ in a free civilization, the family unit is the core of society.

You should not attempt to answer any of these questions now regardless of how much you might know about Greek society. The idea here is to help you focus your reading. You're looking for clues that will help you get the right pieces from the passage. Let's see what these questions told us about the passage.

Question 1 tells you exactly which words in which line you need to understand. At this point, you could underline the words "household duties" on line [A] as a reminder that you need to understand their meaning in context. Put the number 1 in the margin of the passage to note that this is where you'll find the information for question 1.

Question 2 doesn't include a line number, but it does include the word "dinner." That should tip you off to keep an eye out for portions of the passage that deal with dinner.

Question 3 again points you at a particular line and word. Underline "vulgar" on line [B] and put the number 3 in the margin. Now you know the answer to question 2 should be somewhere between the two numbers you've marked in the margin.

Question 4 asks about the overall theme of the passage. As soon as you realize this is an "overall" question, move on. This question is going to require you to understand the whole passage, not to focus in on one particular section.

Remember, you don't have time to dawdle here. If there are a dozen questions, and it takes you twenty seconds to skim each one, underline words, and write numbers in the margin, you've just spent four minutes on the questions without reading the passage at all. Four minutes might not sound like much time, but in a 25-minute Critical Reading section of the real thing it could be very important.

Skim the questions but skip the answers. You don't have to read the questions in detail. You need only to identify the themes and line numbers to watch out for.

> **POWERTIP**
>
> **The best advice we can give is that you** need to practice both ways (reading the questions first or reading the passage first) and decide which way works best for you.

Budget your reading time

The long passages on the new SAT can get you into time trouble. It's easy to get sucked into a long passage and burn a lot of time looking for answers to a specific question. This can be a big problem. If you spend too much time on one passage, you won't have time to even try the other questions in the section.

As a rule of thumb, you have about one minute per question in the SAT Critical Reading section—including reading time. You can allow a bit of extra time for the long passages because the short passage questions will go much more quickly.

> **POWERTIP**
>
> **As a rough rule of thumb,** you should give yourself no more than 15 minutes for a long passage. Practice your time management skills as well as your accuracy.

Learn common question types

As you work through SAT practice exams, you'll realize that the SAT uses some types of questions over and over again. By recognizing the patterns in these questions, you'll be better prepared to read the passages with an eye for important information. Here are some of the question types that you should be prepared for:

- **Some questions will ask you what a particular word or phrase refers to.** Most often the question wants the meaning of term in the context of the passage. If you have trouble with one of these questions, try substituting each of the possible answers in the sentence containing the phrase to see whether the sense of the sentence remains the same.

- **Some questions will ask why a particular sentence or image occurs in the passage.** To answer these questions, you'll need to understand the argument that the author is making. Identify the theme of each paragraph and of the passage as a whole to answer these questions.

- **Some questions will ask you what a particular word or phrase emphasizes or highlights.** Watch out for these questions! Remember, your job is to pick the best answer, not the first true answer that you run across. Make sure that you read all of the answers to these questions so that you can pick the best one.

- **For analytical passages, questions will often ask you to identify a fact:** Why did something happen, or what was the result of an action? On these questions, pay close attention to what's in the passage, rather than to any knowledge of the field you might already have. You need to answer questions based only on what's in the passage that you read.

Working with paired passages

According to the College Board—and they should know—there will be at least one pair of long passages and at least one pair of paragraph-sized passages on the exam. In these pairs, one passage will support, oppose, or complement the point of view of the other passage. Here's an example:

> *The following passages represent two views on the state of mind of the French people in the years leading up to the French revolution. Passage 1 is from a French historian, originally published in 1880. Passage 2 is from a history written in 1892 by an American historian.*

Passage 1

To comprehend their actions we ought now to look into the condition of their minds, to know the current **[A]**train of their ideas, their mode of thinking. But is it really essential to draw this portrait, and are not the details of their mental condition we have just presented sufficient? We shall obtain a knowledge of them later, and through their actions, when, in Touraine, they knock a mayor and his assistant, chosen by themselves, senseless with kicks from their wooden shoes, because, in obeying the national Assembly, these two unfortunate men prepared a table of taxes; or when at Troyes, they drag through the streets and tear to pieces the venerable magistrate who was nourishing them at that very moment, and who had just dictated his testament in their favor. Take the still rude brain of a contemporary peasant and deprive it of the ideas which, for eighty years past, have entered it by so many channels, **[B]**through the primary school of each village, through the return home of the conscript after seven years' service, through the prodigious multiplication of books, newspapers, roads, railroads, foreign travel and every other species of communication. [ ]Try to imagine the peasant of the eighteenth century, penned and shut up from father to son in his hamlet, without parish highways, deprived of news, with no instruction but the Sunday sermon, continuously worrying about his daily bread and the taxes, "with his wretched, dried-up aspect," not daring to repair his house, always persecuted, distrustful, his mind contracted and stinted, so to say, by misery. His condition is almost that of his ox or his ass, while his ideas are those of his condition. He has been a long time stolid; "he lacks even instinct," mechanically and fixedly regarding the ground on which he drags along his hereditary plow. In 1751, d'Argenson wrote in his journal: "nothing in the news from the court affects them; the reign is indifferent to them....the distance between the capital and the province daily widens. ...Here they are ignorant of the striking occurrences that most impressed us at Paris....The inhabitants of the country side are merely poverty-stricken slaves, draft cattle under a yoke, moving on as they are goaded, caring for nothing and embarrassed by nothing, provided they can eat and sleep at regular hours." They make no complaints, "they do not even dream of complaining;" their wretchedness seems to them natural like winter or hail. Their minds, like their agriculture, still belong to the middle ages.

Passage 2

There are two ways in which the French Revolution may be considered. We may look at the great events which astonished and horrified Europe and America: the storming of the Bastille, the march on Versailles, the massacres of September, the Terror, and the restoration of order by Napoleon. The study of these events must always be both interesting and profitable, and we cannot wonder that historians, scenting the approaching battle, have sometimes hurried over the **[D]**comparatively peaceful country that separated them from it. They have accepted easy and ready-made solutions for the cause of the trouble. Old France has been lurid in their eyes, in the light of her burning country-houses. The Frenchmen of the eighteenth century, they think, must have been wretches, or they could not so have suffered. The social fabric, they are sure, was rotten indeed, or it would never have gone to pieces so suddenly.

There is, however, another way of looking at that great revolution of which we habitually set the beginning in 1789. That date is, indeed, momentous; more so than any other in modern history. It marks the outbreak in legislation and politics of ideas which had already been working for a century, and which have changed the face of the civilized world. These ideas are not all true nor all noble. They have in them a large admixture of speculative error and of spiritual baseness. They require today to be modified and readjusted. But they represent sides of truth which in 1789, and still more in 1689, were too much overlooked and neglected. They suited the stage of civilization which the world had reached, and men needed to emphasize them. Their very exaggeration was perhaps necessary to enable them to fight, and in a measure to supplant, the older doctrines which were in possession of the human mind. Induction, as the sole method of reasoning, sensation as the sole origin of ideas, may not be the final and only truth; but they were very much needed in the world in the seventeenth and eighteenth centuries, and they found philosophers to elaborate them, and enthusiasts to preach them. They made their way chiefly on French soil in the decades preceding 1789.

1. **In line [A] of passage 1, the word "train" most closely means**

   Ⓐ a long line of moving people or animals.

   Ⓑ a set of linked mechanical parts.

   Ⓒ a part of a formal gown that trails behind the wearer.

   Ⓓ a string of gunpowder used as a fuse to explode a charge.

   Ⓔ an orderly succession of related items.

2. **The author of passage 1 lists means of communication (lines [B]–[C]) in order to**

   Ⓐ emphasize the rate of progress in the modern world.

   Ⓑ help the reader understand why peasants in pre-revolutionary France might not have advanced ideas.

   Ⓒ show how revolutionary ideas propagated from Paris to the French provinces.

   Ⓓ hint that things were really not so bad for French peasants.

   Ⓔ demonstrate that the French revolution was a good thing for the peasantry.

3. **In passage 2, the phrase "comparatively peaceful country" (line [D]) means**

   Ⓐ the years leading up to the French revolution.

   Ⓑ the Netherlands, where no revolution occurred.

   Ⓒ the French agricultural provinces.

   Ⓓ areas of France that Napoleon's armies did not ravage.

   Ⓔ an area behind the battlefront where no troops are active.

4. **In speaking of "another way of looking at the great revolution," the author of passage 2**

   Ⓐ sees the French revolution as part of a long process rather than as a singular event.

   Ⓑ suggests that ideas of reason rather than popular discontent drove the French revolution.

   Ⓒ introduces a conspiracy theory to explain the French revolution.

   Ⓓ claims to have the final and only truth about the origins of the French revolution.

   Ⓔ proves that he is more interested in the causes of the French revolution than its effects.

5. **The author of passage 2 would most likely view passage 1's view of the failings of the pre-revolutionary peasantry as what sort of an explanation of the revolution?**

   Ⓐ Important

   Ⓑ Sufficient

   Ⓒ Glib

   Ⓓ ncorrect

   Ⓔ Insightful

continues

continued

As you can see, the paired passages give rise to three types of questions:

1. **Questions about the first passage**

2. **Questions about the second passage**

3. **Questions about both passages together**

Thus, to answer all of the questions, you need to understand not just the two passages independently, but also the way in which they relate to one another. Here's how you can reason your way through the five sample questions that you just saw:

Question 1 asks you to find the appropriate definition of "train" in the sentence, "To comprehend their actions we ought now to look into the condition of their minds, to know the current train of their ideas, their mode of thinking." You can answer this question by substituting each proposed definition in turn back into the original sentence. This makes it clear that answer E, "an orderly succession of related items," is the best fit. Note that both answers A and D contain imagery that might make you think of the mass of people preparing for a revolution, but they're not supported by the context.

Question 2 checks your ability to reason through a complex passage. You might find it helpful to reduce the author's argument to simple terms: Contemporary peasants have all these means of communication, but eighteenth century peasants didn't. This points to answer B. If you've studied the French revolution, you might be tempted by any of the other answers—but remember, what you've studied is irrelevant. Only what the author says in the passage counts.

Question 3 is designed to trap you into a wrong answer if you're reading quickly. Although answers B, C, D, and E all refer to land, which is the usual definition of "country," they're all wrong. That's because the author of the passage is using "comparatively peaceful country" in a figurative sense to mean the time before the revolution.

Question 4 checks that you understand the main point that the author of the second passage is trying to make. Again, depending on what you know, you might read too much into the answers. If you summarize the two paragraphs, though, you'll see that the first one is about a traditional understanding of the causes of the revolution, whereas the second paragraph suggests another theory. Answer B is the only one that mentions two theories, and it's the correct answer.

Question 5 asks you to compare the two passages. It should be evident from your reading that the two authors disagree: The first sees the mass of discontented peasants as the cause of the revolution, whereas the second points to new ideas. This lets you dismiss answers A, B, and E because the second author is unlikely to use positive words about the first one. Of the remaining terms, "glib" (answer C) is a better choice than "incorrect" (answer D). The second author makes it clear that he thinks other authors make the easy choice in blaming wretched social conditions for the definition without thinking—a perfect definition of "glib."

When you have to choose between answers that both seem correct but are subtly different, it can be helpful to ask, "How does the author want me to feel about this subject?" This question can help you clarify the author's tone, which may make the most correct answer stand out.

Developing a strategy for paired passages

Remember, paired passage questions may be about either passage individually or the two passages taken together. By far, the easier questions are the ones that address the passages individually. If you're pressed for time, answer these questions first—before the questions that ask you to compare and contrast the passages.

Consider the three ways that the paired passages might be related in a bit more detail:

1. The second passage may support the first passage.

2. The second passage may oppose the first passage.

3. The second passage may complement the first passage.

If you can identify which of these situations applies to a particular pair of passages, you'll have a good idea of what to look for:

- **If the second passage supports the first passage**, expect questions about what evidence each passage brings to bear on the question at hand. But beware of attempts to trick you by assuming that both passages say exactly the same thing. For example, say the first passage condemns large cars for wasting gasoline. The second passage condemns large cars for causing accidents. Even though both passages condemn large cars, the authors may not agree on why. In some cases, they may even disagree in the reasons. For example, the first writer

may believe that large cars are safer, but still condemn them for wasting gasoline.

- **If the second passage opposes the first passage**, be prepared for questions about how the author of one passage would view a word, phrase, or idea from the other passage. You might also be asked to determine how or why the two passages present opposing viewpoints: Does the second depend on more recent research, different underlying assumptions? Is there different experience on the part of the authors?

- **If the second passage complements the first passage**, you should expect them to be about the same general subject but to each contain their own information and point of view. You might also be asked to pick out statements on which the two authors agree. In some cases, you'll find that passage 1 says X and Y, while passage 2 says Y and Z. You may need to identify the unique information in each passage as well as the overlap. In some cases, you may be asked to identify reasons why the information differs in the two passages.

POWERTIP

Are you implying that I should infer...

Don't mix up imply and infer. The author implies something. The reader infers the author's intent.

Take a deep breath and remember...

The long passages questions on the new SAT can be tricky for several reasons. The passages are often on unfamiliar topics, and the questions themselves are designed to put you through your intellectual paces. You can also find yourself in a race against the clock unless you budget your time wisely. Practicing long passages to get faster and more accurate in your answers will pay off, though. You'll not only improve your score on this section, but you'll help yourself along at least a little by reviewing additional vocabulary and by learning the structures that will help you write your own essays.

6 ways to maximize your reading time

Sure you know how to read, but you don't usually expect to be quizzed after you finish a few pages of John Grisham. If you miss a detail here or there in a Yahoo! News article about Napoleon Dynamite, you'll probably get by, but the new SAT is less forgiving. It helps to have a strategy for active reading. Here are a few tips that will maximize the time you spend with each reading passage.

Read the questions first

Most people benefit from reading—or at least skimming—the questions before reading the passage. You don't need to read the answers at this point, just the question. This will help you hone in on the facts within the passage.

> **POWERTIP**
>
> **Reading the questions before reading** the passage does require some time, so don't spend too much time on this step.

Take notes

While reading through the passage, make brief notes in the margins. Don't get carried away, and keep these notes specific to the three questions you'll be expected to answer:

1. What is the *purpose*?
2. What is the *main idea*?
3. What is the *structure*?

Also consider writing a few clues or keywords about each paragraph in the margin. That'll help you find the right facts later when you're answering questions.

Underline key sentences

In addition to your margin notes, feel free to underline important ideas or words in the test booklet. You should be looking for the topic sentence of each paragraph. Once you've found it, underline it. This method highlights main ideas and makes it easier to go back and find specific topics in the passage.

Visualize it

One way to anchor thoughts in your mind is to visualize what you read. Relax and allow your mind to commit what you read to pictures. You'll find the information much easier to access when answering questions.

Slow it down

Reading too quickly may actually slow you down. If you find yourself referring back to the passage too often when trying to answer questions, you may actually have to reread large sections. If you're prone to reading too fast, practice summarizing each paragraph before you move on to the next one. Doing so will force you to slow down.

Focus on content

Be careful to keep your own opinions separate from the author's. It's fine to form an opinion, but you must be careful not to confuse your thoughts with the passage's point. The questions will concern the passage's literal content, not any opinions you might form while reading.

SAT Help Desk:

Answers to 14 Commonly Asked Questions

What should I eat for breakfast?

Your SAT-morning breakfast deserves some thought as well. Eat a mix of protein (eggs, bacon, sausage) and carbohydrates (cereal, toast, grits) so that you'll have both quick-energy and slow-energy foods working in your system. Remember, this breakfast has to get you through until lunchtime with no snacks. If you usually have coffee with breakfast, go for it. But if you don't, the day of your SAT is not the day to try coffee for the first time. Three hours and 45 minutes of concentration doesn't fit well with caffeine-induced jitters. And just like your sleep schedule, don't try to change your eating habits all at once. If you usually skip breakfast, start changing your habits a week or two before the SAT, not the day of the test.

You wouldn't be the first student to smuggle an energy bar or a bag of M&Ms into the testing center, although the SAT rules say you can't do this. If you get caught eating by a particularly tough proctor, you could have your test cancelled.

Can I use a calculator on the Math section?

Yes, you can use a calculator on the math sections. Speaking of the calculator, there are more than a few rules about what type of calculator you can bring with you. Not everything the size of a calculator is legal. You are not allowed to use a PDA, laptop computer, anything with an alphabetic keyboard, anything with pen input, anything with a printer, anything that makes "unusual noise," or anything that requires an electrical outlet. The intent is to let you check basic match calculations while forbidding anything that you might use to smuggle answers into the SAT, or that might distract other test takers.

Make sure that you put fresh batteries into the calculator (or charge it, if they're rechargeable) and that you understand how to use it. An expensive scientific calculator won't do you much good if you can't figure out how to figure a square root with it.

What else should I bring with me?

Here's a list of things you should bring with you:

- Your admission ticket.
- Your photo ID.

- As many sharpened No. 2 pencils as you think you'll need, plus a couple of extras.
- An eraser. Check to make sure that the eraser really does a good job of removing the pencil marks.
- A calculator and spare batteries.
- A watch, stopwatch, or travel alarm with the audible alarm turned off.

How much scratch paper should I bring?

You don't get scratch paper for the SAT, but you can write as much as you like on your test booklet. Don't be afraid to make notes or underline in the reading sections or work out problems in the mathematics section. But keep your answer sheet clean, except for filling in the answer ovals: Extraneous marks might be misread as wrong answers.

How do I know how many questions will be in each section?

Each section of the SAT tells you right at the top how many questions it contains and how long you get to work on it. Make a note of the time when you start, and keep track of how much time is remaining.

Which questions are most important? Which ones can I afford to skip?

Every question on the SAT is worth the same number of points, so you should do the easy questions first. On most sections of the SAT the questions are arranged from easiest to hardest, so the easy questions come first. The exceptions are the passage-based reading and improving paragraph questions. These are arranged in the order the information is presented in the passage. On these sections, you'll probably want to quickly skim the questions to pick out the ones that seem easiest—usually the ones asking about literal facts from the passage—and answer those questions first.

How many times should I take the SAT?

Whether it helps your scores or not, taking the SAT twice is a risk-free strategy. Many college admissions offices take into account your highest score on each section. With these schools, if you get 650 reading, 720 writing, and 550 math the first time, and 630 reading, 710 writing, and 700 math the second time, you'll be seen as a 650-720-700 student as far as your overall SAT scores are concerned. All you have to lose is a little more time studying and another long morning taking the exam. What you have to gain is getting in the college you *really* want. Not a bad tradeoff.

What if I get confused by the directions?

There are only eight different sets of directions for the SAT—and they're in the practice test in this book. There's one set for sentence completions, one for passage comparisons, and so on. Read them, learn them, and understand them. That way, you won't waste any of those precious minutes on test day reading the instructions. If you have questions about the instructions, answer them *before* you get to the exam.

What is a perfect score?

A perfect score on the new SAT is a 2400. There are 800 points possible for the Math, Critical Reading, and Writing sections. You'll also get a separate score for the essay, from 2 to 12.

Do I have to take the SAT?

Not all colleges require the SAT. In fact, not all colleges will even accept the SAT as an admissions test. You should check with your college's admissions department to determine if you need to take the SAT or the ACT. If you're applying to several colleges, you may need to take both.

When should I take the SAT?

It's a good idea to allow yourself time to take at least two cracks at the SAT. Many students take the SAT in the spring of their junior year and again, if need be, in the fall of their senior year. Make sure you know what your college's application deadlines are and allow sufficient time to get your best score into them on time.

How do I get my scores? How long does it take?

Scores are available on the Internet or by phone approximately 15 days after you take the test. You can retrieve your scores on the web for free. It costs $9 to retrieve your scores by phone. Scores will be mailed out approximately three weeks after the test date.

How do colleges get my scores?

Most colleges require that they receive your scores directly from the College Board. Be sure to report your scores to the colleges who will need to receive them. On or before test day, you can request four free reports that go to the colleges of your choice. Additional reports are $9 each.

What if I have a learning disability or a physical handicap?

The College Board has many programs designed to help students with disabilities. However, not all services are available at all test locations on all test dates. You can visit the College Board website at http://www.collegeboard.com/ssd/student/ to get the eligibility requirements and other details.

Online Resources

www.collegeboard.com

The College Board has its own website at http://www.college-board.com, and every SAT taker should visit it at least once. You can register for the SAT online, get the "SAT Practice Question of the Day", and even download another complete practice test. This is also where you'll download your scores or report your scores to additional colleges.

www.examcram.com

On the Exam Cram website you'll find links to other SAT prep respources on the web. You'll also be able to sign up for a Vocabulary Word of the Day sent automatically through email.

www.number2.com

Number2.com offers free online SAT preparation materials. Its "question of the day" and "word of the day" are an easy way to sneak in a little extra practice.

www.freevocabulary.com

If you're worried about the size of your vocabulary, check out the "5000 Free SAT Words" page. Don't try to memorize it all at once, though!

Other valuable sites

Numerous other sites offer free online quizzes, email services, or access to free or fee-based SAT Prep options. If you're surfing, you might also check out:

> www.testprepreview.com
>
> www.freesat1prep.com
>
> www.act-sat-prep.com
>
> www.powerscore.com
>
> www.eduprep.com
>
> www.nytimes.com/learning/students/satofday/
>
> www.kaptest.com

24 Hours to the SAT— Dos and Don'ts Before You Take Your Exam

Friday

8:00 am

You'll probably be in school. You should try to complete any major projects a day or two in advance so you're not stressed-out the day before the test.

4:00 pm

If you can, try to avoid after-school activities or work. You'll need time to get your things together for the test, and you'll also need a good night's sleep. It would be a good idea to avoid a lot of caffeine this afternoon, since you'll be going to bed early.

6:00 pm

Do something that will relax you. Have dinner with family or friends, go for a run, or watch a funny movie.

8:00 pm

Do a pre-test inventory:

❑ Find your ID

❑ Find your admission ticket

❑ Find your calculator and make sure it has new batteries

❑ Find at least two #2 pencils with good erasers

❑ Find your glasses (if necessary)

❑ Find your watch—make sure it's working!

❑ Pack these things in a backpack and put them somewhere you won't forget them.

❑ Review the directions to the test center or confirm your transportation.

9:00 pm

❑ Get your breakfast items together. You need to eat breakfast, and you won't have time to stare into the refrigerator for 15 minutes in the morning!

❑ Put out your clothes. It's a good idea to dress in layers, as you don't know how hot or cold the test center will be.

Don't go out with your friends for a pre-SAT bash!

9:30 pm

- ❏ Set your alarm clock for 6:30.
- ❏ Set your other alarm clock for 6:30.
- ❏ Tell Mom to make sure you get up at 6:30.
- ❏ Go to bed.

Saturday

6:30 am

Get up and eat breakfast.

7:00 am

Gather your backpack with the test items and hit the road.

7:30 am

Arrive at the test center. Stretch a little and go check in for the test.

8:00 am

Showtime!

Practice Test with Answer Keys

How to take the practice exam

The following practice exam consists of 170 questions and an essay section, and you should complete it within 3 hours and 45 minutes. The practice exam is divided into timed sections. You should carefully time yourself on each section so that you do not go over the allotted time.

We strongly suggest that when you take this self test, you treat it just as you would treat the actual exam at the test center. Use the following tips to get the maximum benefit from this test:

- Before you start, create a quiet, secluded environment where you are not disturbed for the duration of the exam.

- Allow yourself only the things that you can bring to the real SAT: pencils, a timepiece, and a calculator.

- Don't use any reference material during the exam.

- Pay close attention to the time limits! One of the most important skills you can gain from the practice tests is to learn how to pace yourself.

Test yourself!
Drill and practice your way to a higher score

Essay

SECTION 1

Time—25 minutes

Turn to page 2 of your answer sheet to write your ESSAY.

The essay gives you an opportunity to show how effectively you can develop and express ideas. You should, therefore, take care to develop your point of view, present your ideas logically and clearly, and use language precisely.

Your essay must be written on the lines provided on your answer sheet—you will receive no other paper on which to write. You will have enough space if you write on every line, avoid wide margins, and keep your handwriting to a reasonable size. Remember that people who are not familiar with your handwriting will read what you write. Try to write or print so that what you are writing is legible to those readers.

You have twenty-five minutes to write an essay on the topic assigned below. DO NOT WRITE ON ANOTHER TOPIC. AN OFF-TOPIC ESSAY WILL RECEIVE A SCORE OF ZERO.

Think carefully about the issue presented in the following excerpt and the assignment below.

Throughout its history, the United States has attempted to balance its drive to grow and expand through harvesting the natural resources within its borders with the desire to preserve the natural beauty of is forests, waters, and open wilderness. In recent year, this tension has heightened due to an increased dependence on foreign energy sources and raw materials.

Assignment: Should the preservation of undeveloped lands within the United States take precedence over the harvesting of natural resources? Support your position using information from current events, readings, and your own observations.

DO NOT WRITE YOUR ESSAY IN YOUR TEST BOOK. You will receive credit only for what you write on your answer sheet.

BEGIN WRITING YOUR ESSAY ON PAGE 2 OF THE ANSWER SHEET.

If you finish before time is called, you may check
your work on this section only. Do not turn to any
other section in the test.

Section 1

SECTION 2

Time—25 minutes

24 Questions

Turn to Section 2 of your answer sheet to answer the questions in this section.

Directions: For each question in this section, select the best answer from among the choices given and fill in the corresponding circle on the answer sheet.

Each sentence below has one or two blanks, each blank indicating that something has been omitted. Beneath the sentence are five words or sets of words labeled A through E. Choose the word or set of words that, when inserted in the sentence, <u>best</u> fits the meaning of the sentence as a whole.

EXAMPLE:

The Internet is _____ now, being available in 78% of all American households.

Ⓐ unimportant

Ⓑ transitory

Ⓒ migrating

Ⓓ negligible

Ⓔ ubiquitous

Answer: **Ⓔ**

---

1. The _____ countryside offered little opportunity for an aspiring engineer.

   Ⓐ pristine

   Ⓑ barren

   Ⓒ rolling

   Ⓓ agrarian

   Ⓔ pastoral

2. Despite their _____ size, the girls were quite healthy and _____.

   Ⓐ enormous . . petite

   Ⓑ petite . . fragile

   Ⓒ unusual . . charming

   Ⓓ small . . frail

   Ⓔ diminutive . . robust

3. Alfred Nobel was _____ in many languages and wrote his own business letters because he did not trust anyone to _____ for him.

   A accomplished . . speak

   B fluent . . translate

   C knowledgeable . . compose

   D lacking . . write

   E illiterate . . perform

4. Jet and rocket technologies developed during World War II were later _____ to create new crafts that _____ the edge of space.

   A combined . . probed

   B abandoned . . reached

   C utilized . . explored

   D refurbished . . investigated

   E pooled . . studied

5. Many _____ of the first American colleges had themselves never _____ college but had faith in education.

   A educators . . completed

   B professors . . appreciated

   C founders . . attended

   D students . . finished

   E employees . . considered

The passages that follow are followed by questions based on their content; questions following a pair of related passages might also be based on the relationship between the paired passages. Answer the questions on the basis of what is <u>stated</u> or <u>implied</u> in the passages and in any introductory material that may be provided.

Questions 6–9 are based on the following passages.

Passage 1:

The biggest mistake with the current legal status of computer software is the attempt to apply outdated legal systems, developed for an age of printed books, to computer programs. Software

Line can vastly benefit the public only if it is freely available to all:
5 free to use, free to copy, free to improve. Software is unique in that it is not a limited good. If I give you a copy of a program, that doesn't keep my copy of the program from running. By freely sharing software and its source code, and encouraging everyone who can do so to modify and improve the software, developers can
10 help to improve the human condition. In the long run, attempts to restrict access to software through inappropriate concepts such as copyrights, patents, and property rights are doomed to failure.

Passage 2:

Modern history has shown again and again the immense benefits to be gained by giving inventors the exclusive use of their inventions. This "intellectual property" is typically granted for a period

Line of years through mechanisms such as patents and trademarks,
5 and it encourages invention by providing a reward for inventors. Although software may not seem to resemble plows and lightbulbs, the same drives sustain inventors in the programming field as in more traditional engineering fields. If a software developer is unable to make a reasonable living by selling his or her creations,
10 he or she will have to find another line of work. In the long run, attempts to remove copyright and patent protection from software are foolish and dangerous. If they succeed, there will be less software innovation and the promise of computers will be stillborn.

6. Both of these passages are designed to
   Ⓐ explain the history of intellectual property protection.
   Ⓑ demonstrate the importance of computer software in the modern world.
   Ⓒ teach the reader how to program a computer.
   Ⓓ persuade the reader of the author's point of view.
   Ⓔ convince the reader to support changes in the law.

7. The author of passage 2 would most likely consider the second sentence of passage 1
   Ⓐ shortsighted and unrealistic.
   Ⓑ illegally dangerous.
   Ⓒ reasonable but incomplete.
   Ⓓ novel and possibly true.
   Ⓔ true with qualifications.

8. Compared to passage 2, passage 1 is

    Ⓐ anchored more firmly in real experience.

    Ⓑ a better piece of advocacy for software patents.

    Ⓒ more concerned with the rights of society than the rights of individuals.

    Ⓓ about a wider range of computer software.

    Ⓔ less likely to have been written by a software author.

9. If software were no longer subject to patent or copyright protection, which of these words would more aptly describe the author of passage 2 than the author of passage 1?

    Ⓐ relieved

    Ⓑ ecstatic

    Ⓒ confused

    Ⓓ tired

    Ⓔ crestfallen

Questions 10–14 are based on the following passage.

The earliest Indian civilization is cloaked in mystery. It emerged in the Indus River valley, in present-day Pakistan, about 2500 B.C. This civilization flourished for about 1,000 years, then vanished
Line without a trace. Only in this century have its once prosperous
5 cities emerged beneath the archaeologists' picks and shovels.

Archaeologists have not fully uncovered many Indus Valley sites. We have no names of kings or queens, no tax records, no literature, no accounts of famous victories. Still, we do know that the Indus Valley civilization covered the largest area of any
10 civilization until the rise of Persia more than 1,000 years later. We know, too, that its cities rivaled those of Sumer.

The two main cities, Harappa and Mohenjo-Daro, may have been twin capitals. Both were large, some three miles in circumference. Each was dominated by a massive hilltop structure,
15 probably a fortress or temple. Both cities had huge warehouses to store grain brought in from outlying villages.

The most striking feature of Harappa and Mohenjo-Daro is that they were so carefully planned. Each city was laid out in a grid pattern, with rectangular blocks larger than modern city blocks.
20 All houses were built of uniform oven-fired clay bricks. Houses had surprisingly modern plumbing systems, with baths, drains, and water chutes that led into sewers beneath the streets. Merchants used a uniform system of weights and measures.

From such evidence, archaeologists have concluded that the
25 Indus Valley cities had a well-organized government. Powerful leaders, perhaps priest-kings, made sure that the tens of thousands of city-dwellers had a steady supply of grain from the villages. The rigid pattern of building and the uniform brick sizes suggest government planners. These experts must also have
30 developed skills in mathematics and surveying to lay out the cities so precisely.

As in other early civilizations, most Indus Valley people were farmers. They grew a wide variety of crops, including wheat, barley, melons, and dates. They were also the first people to cul-
35 tivate cotton and weave its fibers into cloth.

Some people were merchants and traders. Their ships carried cargoes of cotton cloth, grain, copper, pearls, and ivory combs to distant lands. By hugging the Arabian Sea coast and sailing up the Persian Gulf, Indian vessels reached the cities of Sumer.
40 Contact with Sumer may have stimulated Indus Valley people to develop their own system of writing.

From clues such as statues, archaeologists have speculated about the religious beliefs of the Indus Valley people. Like other ancient people, they were polytheistic. A mother goddess, the
45 source of creation, seems to have been widely honored. Indus people also apparently worshipped sacred animals, including the bull. Some scholars think these early practices influenced later Indian beliefs, especially the veneration of, or special regard for, cattle.

50 By 1750 B.C, the quality of life in Indus Valley cities was declining. The once orderly cities no longer kept up the old standards. Crude pottery replaced the finer works of earlier days.

We do not know for sure what happened, but scholars have offered several explanations. Damage to the local environment
55 may have contributed to the decline. Possibly too many trees were cut down to fuel the ovens of brick makers. Tons of river mud found in the streets of Mohenjo-Daro suggest that a volcanic eruption blocked the Indus, which flooded the city. Other evidence points to a devastating earthquake.

60 Scholars think the deathblow fell about 1500 B.C., when nomadic people arrived in ever larger numbers from the north. The newcomers were the Aryans, whose ancestors had slowly migrated with their herds of cattle, sheep, and goats from what is now southern Russia. With their horse-drawn chariots and
65 superior weapons, the Aryans overran the Indus region. The cities were soon abandoned and eventually forgotten.

10. In the context of the passage, the phrase "vanished without a trace" (lines 3–4) means that

    Ⓐ no physical traces have ever been found of the Indus River civilization.

    Ⓑ we don't know why the Indus River civilization collapsed.

    Ⓒ there is no written record of the Indus River civilization.

    Ⓓ the Indus River civilization no longer exists.

    Ⓔ the Indus River civilization was destroyed by the Arya.

11. The sentence "Merchants used a uniform system of weights and measures" (line 23) is used to indicate that

    Ⓐ fraud has always been a problem wherever commerce was present.

    Ⓑ weights and measures are important to maintaining a military class.

    Ⓒ the Indus River cities included craftsmen who were responsible for shaping weights.

    D the Indus River civilization was advanced and organized.

    E a merchant class can only exist after accurate measure ment is perfected.

12. Words such as "perhaps" (line 26) and "suggest" (line 29) in the passage indicate that

    A the authors of the passage have not had time to read the most recent research on the subject.

    B readers should draw their own conclusions.

    C there are alternative explanations for the evidence that has been discovered.

    D the authors haven't made up their mind which set of experts to believe.

    E Archaeology is an inherently speculative science.

13. In line 44, the word "polytheistic" most nearly means

    A aggressively religious

    B feminist

    C worshipping many gods

    D retiring

    E venerators of cattle

14. The author of this passage would most likely agrees that

    A early civilizations were unable to stand up to nomadic pressures at all.

    B more research is needed to fully appreciate the scope of the Indus River civilization.

    C modern civilizations offer more freedom than ancient ones.

    D our civilization will be destroyed by environmental damage.

    E the domestication of the horse was more important than the invention of writing.

Questions 15–24 are based on the following passage:

The following passage is from a collection of short stories by the nineteenth century American writer Stephen Crane.

Four men once came to a wet place in the roadless forest to fish. They pitched their tent fair upon the brow of a pine-clothed ridge of riven rocks whence a boulder could be made to crash *Line* through the brush and whirl past the trees to the lake below. On 5 fragrant hemlock boughs they slept the sleep of unsuccessful fishermen, for upon the lake alternately the sun made them lazy and the rain made them wet. Finally they ate the last bit of bacon and smoked and burned the last fearful and wonderful hoecake.

10 Immediately a little man volunteered to stay and hold the camp while the remaining three should go the Sullivan county miles to a farmhouse for supplies. They gazed at him dismally. "There's only one of you—the devil make a twin," they said in parting malediction, and disappeared down the hill in the 15 known direction of a distant cabin. When it came night and the hemlocks began to sob they had not returned. The little man sat close to his companion, the campfire, and encouraged it with logs. He puffed fiercely at a heavy built brier, and regarded a thousand shadows which were about to assault him. Suddenly 20 he heard the approach of the unknown, crackling the twigs and rustling the dead leaves. The little man arose slowly to his feet, his clothes refused to fit his back, his pipe dropped from his mouth, his knees smote each other.

"Hah!" he bellowed hoarsely in menace. A growl replied and a 25 bear paced into the light of the fire. The little man supported himself upon a sapling and regarded his visitor.

The bear was evidently a veteran and a fighter, for the black of his coat had become tawny with age. There was confidence in his gait and arrogance in his small, twinkling eye. He rolled 30 back his lips and disclosed his white teeth. The fire magnified the red of his mouth. The little man had never before confront-ed the terrible and he could not wrest it from his breast. "Hah!" he roared. The bear interpreted this as the challenge of a gladi-ator. He approached warily. As he came near, the boots of fear 35 were suddenly upon the little man's feet. He cried out and then darted around the campfire. "Ho!" said the bear to himself, "this thing won't fight—it runs. Well, suppose I catch it." So upon his features there fixed the animal look of going—some-where. He started intensely around the campfire. The little man 40 shrieked and ran furiously. Twice around they went.

The hand of heaven sometimes falls heavily upon the righteous. The bear gained.

In desperation the little man flew into the tent. The bear stopped and sniffed at the entrance. He scented the scent of
45 many men. Finally he ventured in.

The little man crouched in a distant corner. The bear advanced, creeping, his blood burning, his hair erect, his jowls dripping. The little man yelled and rustled clumsily under the flap at the end of the tent. The bear snarled awfully and made a jump and
50 a grab at his disappearing game. The little man, now without the tent, felt a tremendous paw grab his coat tails. He squirmed and wriggled out of his coat like a schoolboy in the hands of an avenger. The bear bowled triumphantly and jerked the coat into the tent and took two bites, a punch and a hug before he dis-
55 covered his man was not in it. Then he grew not very angry, for a bear on a spree is not a black-haired pirate.

He is merely a hoodlum. He lay down on his back, took the coat on his four paws and began to play uproariously with it. The most appalling, blood-curdling whoops and yells came to where
60 the little man was crying in a treetop and froze his blood. He moaned a little speech meant for a prayer and clung convul- sively to the bending branches. He gazed with tearful wistful- ness at where his comrade, the campfire, was giving dying flick- ers and crackles. Finally, there was a roar from the tent which
65 eclipsed all roars; a snarl which it seemed would shake the stol- id silence of the mountain and cause it to shrug its granite shoulders. The little man quaked and shriveled to a grip and a pair of eyes. In the glow of the embers he saw the white tent quiver and fall with a crash. The bear's merry play had dis-
70 turbed the center pole and brought a chaos of canvas upon his head.

Now the little man became the witness of a mighty scene. The tent began to flounder. It took flopping strides in the direction of the lake. Marvelous sounds came from within—rips and
75 tears, and great groans and pants. The little man went into gig- gling hysterics. The entangled monster failed to extricate him- self before he had walloped the tent frenziedly to the edge of the mountain. So it came to pass that three men, clambering up the hill with bundles and baskets, saw their tent approaching. It
80 seemed to them like a white-robed phantom pursued by hor- nets. Its moans riffled the hemlock twigs.

The three men dropped their bundles and scurried to one side, their eyes gleaming with fear. The canvas avalanche swept past them. They leaned, faint and dumb, against trees and listened,

85 their blood stagnant. Below them it struck the base of a great
    pine tree, where it writhed and struggled. The three watched its
    convolutions a moment and then started terrifically for the top
    of the hill. As they disappeared, the bear cut loose with a
    mighty effort. He cast one disheveled and agonized look at the
90 white thing, and then started wildly for the inner recesses of the
    forest.

    The three fear-stricken individuals ran to the rebuilt fire. The lit-
    tle man reposed by it calmly smoking. They sprang at him and
    overwhelmed him with interrogations. He contemplated dark-
95 ness and took a long, pompous puff. "There's only one of me—
    and the devil made a twin," he said.

15. In the context of the passage, "the devil make a twin" (line 13)
    most nearly means

    Ⓐ Twins are considered devilish.

    Ⓑ The only company you'll have is the devil.

    Ⓒ The devil will bring you someone to talk to.

    Ⓓ We're angry at you for staying behind.

    Ⓔ The devil comes out at night in these woods.

16. The phrase "a thousand shadows which were about to assault
    him" (line 19) is best read as

    Ⓐ literal

    Ⓑ irony

    Ⓒ hyperbole

    Ⓓ figurative

    Ⓔ sly

17. In line 30, the word "magnified" most nearly means

    Ⓐ emphasized

    Ⓑ enlarged

    Ⓒ glorified

    Ⓓ increased

    Ⓔ overstated

18. In writing of "the boots of fear" (line 34), the author implies that

    Ⓐ fear can paralyze the man who is afraid.

    Ⓑ you can't feel your feet when you're afraid.

    Ⓒ fear can be conquered by wearing boots.

    Ⓓ being afraid can make you run faster.

    Ⓔ the man in the story had magical boots.

19. Crane uses the expression "The hand of heaven sometimes falls heavily upon the righteous" (line 41) to mean that

   Ⓐ God punishes those who blaspheme.

   Ⓑ all creatures are treated equally by heaven.

   Ⓒ we can't know why something happens.

   Ⓓ bears do not attack righteous men.

   Ⓔ the good guys don't always win.

20. In line 49 the word "awfully" most nearly means

   Ⓐ unpleasantly

   Ⓑ poorly

   Ⓒ awe-inspiringly

   Ⓓ formidably

   Ⓔ badly

21. From lines 58 through 62 you can conclude that

   Ⓐ the little man thought he was about to die.

   Ⓑ bears are basically playful animals.

   Ⓒ everything is scarier in the dark.

   Ⓓ splitting a party in the woods is a bad idea.

   Ⓔ nature is harsh and unyielding.

22. The phrase "shrug its granite shoulders" (line 66) is used as

   Ⓐ a measure of the strength of the little man's quaking

   Ⓑ a metaphor for the ferocity of the bear

   Ⓒ a way to indicate how loud the bear's roar was

   Ⓓ an expression of excitement

   Ⓔ a transition between paragraphs

23. The author uses "overwhelmed him with interrogations" (line 94) to mean

   Ⓐ attacked him for scaring them

   Ⓑ demanded immediate answers

   Ⓒ needed his reassurance

   Ⓓ argued with him needlessly

   Ⓔ asked him many questions

24. Which of these proverbs most aptly summarizes the story in the passage?

    Ⓐ The cat in gloves catches no mice.

    Ⓑ A stitch in time saves nine.

    Ⓒ He that lives on hope will die fasting.

    Ⓓ He who laughs last, laughs best.

    Ⓔ Beware of little expenses; a small leak will sink a great ship.

STOP

If you finish before time is called, you may check your work on this section only. Do not turn to any other section in the test.

Section 2

1. Ⓐ Ⓑ Ⓒ Ⓓ Ⓔ	9. Ⓐ Ⓑ Ⓒ Ⓓ Ⓔ	17. Ⓐ Ⓑ Ⓒ Ⓓ Ⓔ
2. Ⓐ Ⓑ Ⓒ Ⓓ Ⓔ	10. Ⓐ Ⓑ Ⓒ Ⓓ Ⓔ	18. Ⓐ Ⓑ Ⓒ Ⓓ Ⓔ
3. Ⓐ Ⓑ Ⓒ Ⓓ Ⓔ	11. Ⓐ Ⓑ Ⓒ Ⓓ Ⓔ	19. Ⓐ Ⓑ Ⓒ Ⓓ Ⓔ
4. Ⓐ Ⓑ Ⓒ Ⓓ Ⓔ	12. Ⓐ Ⓑ Ⓒ Ⓓ Ⓔ	20. Ⓐ Ⓑ Ⓒ Ⓓ Ⓔ
5. Ⓐ Ⓑ Ⓒ Ⓓ Ⓔ	13. Ⓐ Ⓑ Ⓒ Ⓓ Ⓔ	21. Ⓐ Ⓑ Ⓒ Ⓓ Ⓔ
6. Ⓐ Ⓑ Ⓒ Ⓓ Ⓔ	14. Ⓐ Ⓑ Ⓒ Ⓓ Ⓔ	22. Ⓐ Ⓑ Ⓒ Ⓓ Ⓔ
7. Ⓐ Ⓑ Ⓒ Ⓓ Ⓔ	15. Ⓐ Ⓑ Ⓒ Ⓓ Ⓔ	23. Ⓐ Ⓑ Ⓒ Ⓓ Ⓔ
8. Ⓐ Ⓑ Ⓒ Ⓓ Ⓔ	16. Ⓐ Ⓑ Ⓒ Ⓓ Ⓔ	24. Ⓐ Ⓑ Ⓒ Ⓓ Ⓔ

SECTION 3

Time—25 minutes

18 Questions

Turn to Section 3 of your answer sheet to answer the questions in this section.

Directions: This section contains two types of questions. You have 25 minutes to complete both types. For questions 1–8, solve each problem and decide which is the best of the choices given. Fill in the corresponding circle on the answer sheet. You can use any available space for scratchwork.

Notes:

1. The use of a calculator is permitted.

2. All numbers used are real numbers.

3. Figures that accompany problems in the test are intended to provide information that is useful in solving the problems. They are drawn as accurately as possible EXCEPT when it is stated in a specific problem that the figure is not drawn to scale. All figures lie in a plane unless otherwise indicated.

4. Unless otherwise specified, the domain of any function f is assumed to be the set of real numbers x for which $f(x)$ is a real number.

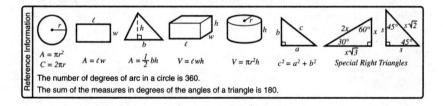

Reference Information

$A = \pi r^2$
$C = 2\pi r$ $A = \ell w$ $A = \frac{1}{2}bh$ $V = \ell wh$ $V = \pi r^2 h$ $c^2 = a^2 + b^2$ *Special Right Triangles*

The number of degrees of arc in a circle is 360.
The sum of the measures in degrees of the angles of a triangle is 180.

---

1. m is 250% of n, and 15% of n is 45. What is 12% of m?

    Ⓐ 12

    Ⓑ 30

    Ⓒ 90

    Ⓓ 120

    Ⓔ 450

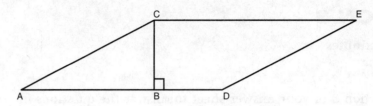

Note: Figure not drawn to scale.

2. In the figure above, $\overline{AC} \parallel \overline{DE}$ and $\overline{AD} \parallel \overline{CE}$ and $\angle ACB = 60°$. What is $\angle CED$?

Ⓐ 15°

Ⓑ 30°

Ⓒ 45°

Ⓓ 60°

Ⓔ 90°

3. A jar contains a mix of black beans and white beans. There are 16 white beans in the jar. When you reach into the jar and draw out a bean at random, the probability of drawing a black bean is 75%. How many total beans are in the jar?

Ⓐ 8

Ⓑ 12

Ⓒ 16

Ⓓ 32

Ⓔ 64

4. The greatest common factor of the integers a and b is 7, and the least common multiple of a and b is 210. The value of a is 14. What is the value of b?

Ⓐ 7

Ⓑ 14

Ⓒ 35

Ⓓ 105

Ⓔ 210

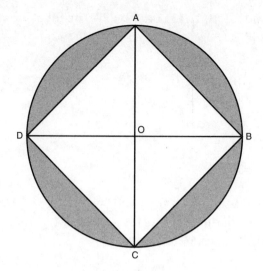

5. The figure above shows a circle with its center at O with four identical isosceles triangles inscribed in the circle. The distance AB is $2\sqrt{2}$ units. What is the area of the shaded region?

   Ⓐ 8

   Ⓑ $\frac{4}{\pi}$

   Ⓒ $4\sqrt{2}$

   Ⓓ $16\pi - 8$

   Ⓔ $4\pi - 8$

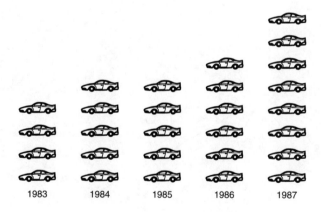

| 1983 | 1984 | 1985 | 1986 | 1987 |

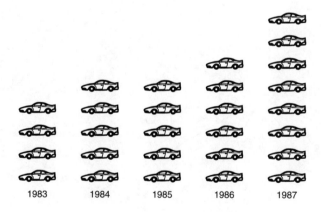 = 50,000 autos

6. Referring to the figure above, what was the average annual sales growth between 1985 and 1987?

   Ⓐ 75,000

   Ⓑ 50,000

   Ⓒ 40,000

   Ⓓ 25,000

   Ⓔ 10,000

7. The union of sets A and B is {1, 3, 7, 11, 14, 17, 22}. The intersection of sets A and B is {7, 11, 22}. Set A is {1, 3, 7, 11, 22}. What is set B?

   Ⓐ {7, 11, 22}

   Ⓑ {7, 11, 14, 17, 22}

   Ⓒ {14, 17, 22}

   Ⓓ {14, 17}

   Ⓔ {1, 3, 7, 22}

8. Lines *l* and *m* are parallel and intersect the y axis two units apart from each other. The equation of line *l* is $y = -2x + 4$. Which of these could be the equation of line *m*?

   Ⓐ $y = -\frac{1}{2}x + 4$

   Ⓑ $y = \frac{1}{2}x + 4$

   Ⓒ $y = 2x + 2$

   Ⓓ $y = 2x - 2$

   Ⓔ $y = x + 4$

9. If $a^2 + b^2 = 75$ and $a^2 - b^2 = -25$ then what is one possible value of *a*?

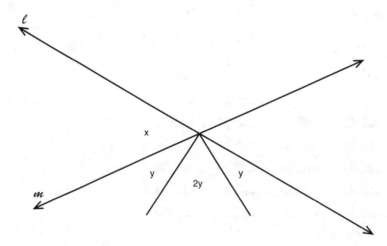

Note: Figure not drawn to scale.

10. In the figure above, *l* and *m* are straight lines. Angle y is 17°. What is angle x?

11. Two successive measurements of the number of elk in a game reserve are 52 and 68. What percent change is this?

12. $f(x) = \dfrac{14}{(x - 7)}$. What integer is not in the domain of *f*?

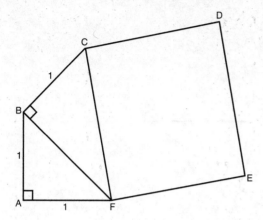

13. What is the area of square CDEF?

14. What is the difference between the median and the mode of the set of numbers 4, 17, 11, 14, 3, 2, 8, 22, 18?

15. Define a><b as 2a + 2b. What is (3><4)><.5?

16. Thirty percent of the students in a school are juniors, and 12% of the students in the same school have red hair. What is the probability that a student selected at random from this school will be a junior with red hair?

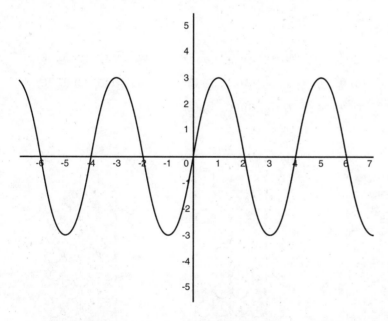

17. The figure above shows a portion of the graph of $g(x)$. What is the first positive zero of the function $g(x + 3)$?

18. How many axes of reflective symmetry are present in the figure above?

STOP

If you finish before time is called, you may check your work on this section only. Do not turn to any other section in the test.

Section 3

1. Ⓐ Ⓑ Ⓒ Ⓓ Ⓔ   4. Ⓐ Ⓑ Ⓒ Ⓓ Ⓔ   7. Ⓐ Ⓑ Ⓒ Ⓓ Ⓔ

2. Ⓐ Ⓑ Ⓒ Ⓓ Ⓔ   5. Ⓐ Ⓑ Ⓒ Ⓓ Ⓔ   8. Ⓐ Ⓑ Ⓒ Ⓓ Ⓔ

3. Ⓐ Ⓑ Ⓒ Ⓓ Ⓔ   6. Ⓐ Ⓑ Ⓒ Ⓓ Ⓔ

9.   10.   11.

   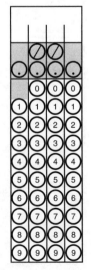   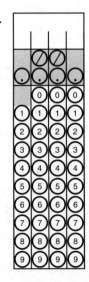

12.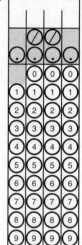

13.

14.

15.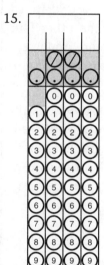

16.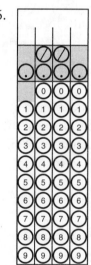

17.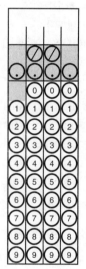

18.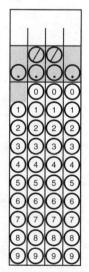

SECTION 4

Time—25 minutes

35 Questions

Turn to Section 4 of your answer sheet to answer the questions in this section.

Directions: For each question in this section, select the best answer from among the choices given and fill in the corresponding circle on the answer sheet.

The following sentences test correctness and effectiveness of expression. Part of each sentence or the entire sentence is underlined; beneath each sentence are five ways of phrasing the underlined material. Choice A repeats the original phrasing; the other four choices are different. If you think the original phrasing produces a better sentence than any of the alternatives, select choice A; if not, select one of the other choices.

In making your selection, follow the requirements of standard written English; that is, pay attention to grammar, choice of words, sentence construction, and punctuation. Your selection should result in the most effective sentence—clear and precise, without awkwardness or ambiguity.

EXAMPLE:

The weather that winter was <u>worse than for at least five decades</u>.

- **A** worse than for at least five decades
- **B** the worse it was for at least five decades
- **C** worse. Than it had been for at least five decades.
- **D** the worst that it had been for at least five decades
- **E** the worst it was for at least five decades.

Answer: **D**

1. Geography, in addition to World History, <u>are offered to</u> the lower classmen.

   Ⓐ are offered to

   Ⓑ are not offered to

   Ⓒ are offered for

   Ⓓ is offered to

   Ⓔ is offered for

2. By the time <u>we return to class</u>, the teacher had already handed out the exam papers.

   Ⓐ we return to class

   Ⓑ we returned to class

   Ⓒ he return to class

   Ⓓ they return to class

   Ⓔ we got to class

3. She identified the tall man in lineup as <u>the man that</u> stole her purse.

   Ⓐ the man that

   Ⓑ the thief that

   Ⓒ the man who

   Ⓓ that man that

   Ⓔ the thief who

4. <u>Vaporization is when</u> a substance changes from a liquid into a gas.

   Ⓐ Vaporization is when

   Ⓑ Vaporization is

   Ⓒ Vaporization is that which occurs when

   Ⓓ Vaporization occurs when

   Ⓔ Vaporization is what happens when

5. The pilot turned the gas valve, and the balloon <u>rose up into</u> the sky.

   Ⓐ rose up into

   Ⓑ rose into

   Ⓒ rose up to

   Ⓓ climbed into

   Ⓔ climbed up to

6. Unfortunately, Marilyn was <u>more concerned with her</u> social life than her grades.

   - Ⓐ more concerned with her
   - Ⓑ concerned with her
   - Ⓒ less concerned with her
   - Ⓓ less concerned with
   - Ⓔ more concerned about her

7. She <u>feels badly about</u> flunking her midterms.

   - Ⓐ feels badly about
   - Ⓑ feels bad about
   - Ⓒ felt badly about
   - Ⓓ feels badly in regards to
   - Ⓔ feels bad because she's

8. After listening to last night's forecast, I expected it to <u>be more cold this morning</u>.

   - Ⓐ be more cold this morning
   - Ⓑ be more colder this morning
   - Ⓒ be more cold
   - Ⓓ be colder than yesterday this morning
   - Ⓔ be colder this morning

9. Though nonsectarian in theory, <u>in reality, many community clubs were havens from</u> social discrimination.

   - Ⓐ in reality, many community clubs were havens from
   - Ⓑ many community clubs were havens from
   - Ⓒ many community clubs were, in reality, havens from
   - Ⓓ many community clubs were havens of
   - Ⓔ in reality, many community clubs were havens for

10. The desert community seems to offer little diversity at first, offering <u>little but scrub, dry lakebeds, and ugly Joshua trees</u>.

    - Ⓐ little but scrub, dry lakebeds, and ugly Joshua trees
    - Ⓑ little but low scrub, dry lakebeds, and ugly Joshua trees
    - Ⓒ little more than scrub, dry lakebeds, and ugly Joshua trees
    - Ⓓ little less than scrub, dry lakebeds, and ugly Joshua trees
    - Ⓔ nothing but scrub, dry lakebeds, and ugly Joshua trees

11. Chuck Yeager started life <u>in a small town on the Mud River in Virginia, named Myra</u>.

   Ⓐ in a small town on the Mud River in Virginia, named Myra.

   Ⓑ in Myra, Virginia, a small town on the Mud River

   Ⓒ in Myra, a small town on the Mud River in Virginia

   Ⓓ in a small town on the Mud River in Virginia

   Ⓔ in a small town on the Mud River, named Myra

The following sentences test your ability to recognize grammar and usage errors. Each sentence contains either a single error or no error at all. No sentence contains more than one error. The error, if there is one, is underlined and lettered. If the sentence contains an error, select the one underlined part that must be changed to make the sentence correct. If the sentence is correct, select choice E. In choosing answers, follow the requirements of standard written English.

EXAMPLE:

The modern personal computer is <u>a revolutionary</u>

                                              A

<u>instrument</u> <u>that can be used</u> for composing a sonnet,

     B

planning a bridge, or <u>to create digital movies</u>, but

                          C

<u>at the most basic level</u> it is still just a

        D

collection of digital impulses. <u>No error</u>

                                    E

Answer: Ⓒ

---

12. The park is usually <u>more crowded and noisier</u>

                              A

<u>on nice days</u> <u>when everyone shows up</u> <u>with their kids and dogs</u>.

       B   C   D

<u>No Error</u>

   E

13. We thought the birds might reject this new seed,
      A   B

but they are eating us out of house and home and
                          C

none of the seed is left. No Error
        D   E

14. Lincoln Steffens was the pioneer investigative
                          A

reporter, he wrote fearlessly on the abuses
        B   C

of government. No Error
      D   E

15. Until Woodrow Wilson was elected President, the
      A   B

United States was in the habit of recognizing de
                C   D

facto governments. No Error
              E

16. The new family home was only one story,
                        A

not terribly large, and run down, but had a nice view.
        B   C   D

No Error
  E

17. Success in business, any business, no matter how small,
                      A   B

played a more important role in the immigrant's daily life
             C   D

than education. No Error
          E

18. Gems are priceless in her culture, but she kept none
                  A   B

of them for herself. No Error
     C   D   E

19. She <u>is to be</u> inducted <u>as an initiate</u> <u>at noon</u>
        A   B   C

   <u>on the first Sunday</u> of March. <u>No Error</u>
       D   E

20. <u>In conclusion</u>, Bertha von Suttner <u>profoundly influenced</u>
      A   B

   Alfred Nobel, <u>despite the fact</u> that
             C

   she married <u>someone else</u>. <u>No Error</u>
           D   E

21. In 1888, Massachusetts became the first state
   <u>to use ballots</u> that contained the names <u>of all the candidates</u>
       A   B

   <u>on each ballot</u> instead of using different
       C

   colored ballots <u>for each candidate</u>. <u>No Error</u>
           D   E

22. <u>Running madly through the forest,</u>
         A

   <u>the thunder shook the earth</u> and <u>the lightning pierced</u>
        B   C

   <u>the night sky</u>. <u>No Error</u>
     D   E

23. <u>Before you say something you'll regret,</u> <u>take a deep breathe,</u>
          A   B

   <u>calmly clear your mind,</u> <u>and count to 10</u>. <u>No Error</u>
        C   D   E

24. Cinderella <u>looked at the clock</u> <u>but didn't realize</u>
         A   B

   it was midnight <u>until</u> she <u>heard it chime</u>.
           C   D

   <u>No Error</u>
    E

25. Sam and Tom raced to <u>the frozen Mississippi</u>
                                         A

    <u>where they scrambled</u> to be the first <u>to don his skates</u>
              B   C

    and <u>meet the ice</u>. <u>No Error</u>
              D   E

26. The excitement <u>of the new baby's arrival</u>
                               A

    <u>was challenged by</u> the fear <u>that the small and weak child</u>
              B   C

    <u>might not</u> survive the night. <u>No Error</u>
         D   E

27. John had <u>a talent</u> for business and
                   A

    <u>subsequently met</u> <u>with great financial success</u>,
              B   C

    <u>but he had little patience</u> for family. <u>No Error</u>
              D   E

28. Samuel Clemens <u>wrote under the pen name</u>
                                A

    Mark Twain, <u>which was</u> a <u>river-piloting term</u>
                      B   C

    <u>for deep, safe water</u>. <u>No Error</u>
              D   E

29. The United States Constitution <u>requires the Senate</u>
                                              A

    <u>to confirm</u> any presidential nominations
         B

    <u>to the Supreme Court</u> before <u>he can</u> actually be sworn
              C   D

    into office. <u>No Error</u>
                      E

Directions: The following passage is an early draft of an essay. Some parts of the passage need to be rewritten.

Read the passage and select the best answers for the questions that follow. Some questions are about particular sentences or parts of sentences and ask you to improve sentence structure and word choice. Other questions ask you to consider organization and development. In choosing answers, follow the requirements of standard written English.

Questions 30–35 are based on the following passage.

(1)The saying that we're only as strong as our weakest link may be provincial, but it's remarkably true. (2)Life is such a toe-shoe precision dance that breaking just one cog in the machinery often has unintended consequences.

(3)By 1911, the playful and elusive sea otter had been hunted to the brink of extinction for its soft, dense fur. (4)Almost too late, the United States, Great Britain, Russia, and Japan established a treaty that banned hunting the sea otter.

(5)The sea otter was slow to rebound. (6)As their populations plummeted, so did their habitats and primary food source. (7)Sea otters rest, nest and feed in floating beds of kelp where sea urchins, their main food source, also live.

(8)Sea urchins eat kelp. (9)As the sea otters disappeared, the population of sea urchins grew uncontrolled, eating the forests of kelp as their populations exploded. (10)In order to sustain their growing colonies, the sea urchins devoured their habitats— the kelp forests.

(11)Without the kelp forests, there were no sea urchins. (12)Without the sea urchins, the sea otters had no food. (13)Ban or no ban, the sea otters were in serious trouble.

30. Sentence 2 doesn't really work. What's the problem with it?
    Ⓐ It's redundant of the first.
    Ⓑ The two subjects don't match: Broken machinery doesn't support or develop the ballerina imagery created in the first phrase.
    Ⓒ It's too wordy.
    Ⓓ It's a bit dire for the opening sentence.
    Ⓔ It would work better as a closing statement.

31. There's a problem between the first and second paragraphs. Can you spot it?

    Ⓐ There should be no paragraph break between sentence 2 and 3.

    Ⓑ It's bad style to start a paragraph with the phrase "By ...,."

    Ⓒ Move sentence 7 to the end of the first paragraph.

    Ⓓ Move sentence 8 to the end of the first paragraph.

    Ⓔ There's no transition from the thesis to the supporting example.

32. Sentence 6 doesn't seem to make sense. It takes four sentences to develop and clarify this statement. What would help?

    Ⓐ Delete the sentence. It isn't needed.

    Ⓑ Replace the first pronoun, their, with a definite noun.

    Ⓒ Move sentences 4 and 5 to a new paragraph following sentence 12.

    Ⓓ Add a transitional sentence between sentences 6 and 7.

    Ⓔ Replace the second phrase with "their habitats and primary food source disappeared."

33. How would you improve sentence 7?

    Ⓐ Insert a comma after nest.

    Ⓑ It might work better as two sentences: one that discusses habitat and a second that discusses their food source, the sea urchin.

    Ⓒ The word "feed" is unnecessary. Remove it and update the "rest, nest" series appropriately by inserting the word "and."

    Ⓓ Replace the sea urchin reference with the following phrase: , which they share with their primary food source, the sea urchin.

    Ⓔ A combination of Ⓐ and Ⓓ.

34. Sentences 8 and 9 are a bit awkward. What would you do to improve the movement?

    Ⓐ Change sentence 8 to the following: Kelp is the primary food source for both sea urchins and sea otters, and with the proper balance, there's enough for all.

    Ⓑ Combine sentences 8 and 9.

    Ⓒ Reposition sentence 8 between sentences 9 and 10.

    Ⓓ Change sentence 8 to the following: Both sea others and sea urchins eat kelp.

    Ⓔ Delete sentence 8. Sentence 9 makes it clear that sea urchins eat kelp.

35. What would you do to improve the end of the passage?

    Ⓐ Nothing, it ends well.

    Ⓑ Add a conclusion that tells the fate of the sea otter after the ban.

    Ⓒ Add a conclusion that stresses how the ban returned the ecosystem's balance so the sea otters' population can grow while protected by the ban.

    Ⓓ Move sentences 4 and 5 between sentences 12 and 13. Then, add a conclusion that stresses how the ban returned the ecosystem's balance so the sea otters' population can grow while protected by the ban.

    Ⓔ Move sentences 4 and 5 to the end of the passage and then delete sentence 13.

STOP

If you finish before time is called, you may check your work on this section only. Do not turn to any other section in the test.

Section 4

1. Ⓐ Ⓑ Ⓒ Ⓓ Ⓔ   13. Ⓐ Ⓑ Ⓒ Ⓓ Ⓔ   25. Ⓐ Ⓑ Ⓒ Ⓓ Ⓔ

2. Ⓐ Ⓑ Ⓒ Ⓓ Ⓔ   14. Ⓐ Ⓑ Ⓒ Ⓓ Ⓔ   26. Ⓐ Ⓑ Ⓒ Ⓓ Ⓔ

3. Ⓐ Ⓑ Ⓒ Ⓓ Ⓔ   15. Ⓐ Ⓑ Ⓒ Ⓓ Ⓔ   27. Ⓐ Ⓑ Ⓒ Ⓓ Ⓔ

4. Ⓐ Ⓑ Ⓒ Ⓓ Ⓔ   16. Ⓐ Ⓑ Ⓒ Ⓓ Ⓔ   28. Ⓐ Ⓑ Ⓒ Ⓓ Ⓔ

5. Ⓐ Ⓑ Ⓒ Ⓓ Ⓔ   17. Ⓐ Ⓑ Ⓒ Ⓓ Ⓔ   29. Ⓐ Ⓑ Ⓒ Ⓓ Ⓔ

6. Ⓐ Ⓑ Ⓒ Ⓓ Ⓔ   18. Ⓐ Ⓑ Ⓒ Ⓓ Ⓔ   30. Ⓐ Ⓑ Ⓒ Ⓓ Ⓔ

7. Ⓐ Ⓑ Ⓒ Ⓓ Ⓔ   19. Ⓐ Ⓑ Ⓒ Ⓓ Ⓔ   31. Ⓐ Ⓑ Ⓒ Ⓓ Ⓔ

8. Ⓐ Ⓑ Ⓒ Ⓓ Ⓔ   20. Ⓐ Ⓑ Ⓒ Ⓓ Ⓔ   32. Ⓐ Ⓑ Ⓒ Ⓓ Ⓔ

9. Ⓐ Ⓑ Ⓒ Ⓓ Ⓔ   21. Ⓐ Ⓑ Ⓒ Ⓓ Ⓔ   33. Ⓐ Ⓑ Ⓒ Ⓓ Ⓔ

10. Ⓐ Ⓑ Ⓒ Ⓓ Ⓔ   22. Ⓐ Ⓑ Ⓒ Ⓓ Ⓔ   34. Ⓐ Ⓑ Ⓒ Ⓓ Ⓔ

11. Ⓐ Ⓑ Ⓒ Ⓓ Ⓔ   23. Ⓐ Ⓑ Ⓒ Ⓓ Ⓔ   35. Ⓐ Ⓑ Ⓒ Ⓓ Ⓔ

12. Ⓐ Ⓑ Ⓒ Ⓓ Ⓔ   24. Ⓐ Ⓑ Ⓒ Ⓓ Ⓔ

SECTION 5

Time—25 minutes

24 Questions

Turn to Section 5 of your answer sheet to answer the questions in this section.

Directions: For each question in this section, select the best answer from among the choices given and fill in the corresponding circle on the answer sheet.

Each sentence below has one or two blanks, each blank indicating that something has been omitted. Beneath the sentence are five words or sets of words labeled A through E. Choose the word or set of words that, when inserted in the sentence, <u>best</u> fits the meaning of the sentence as a whole.

EXAMPLE:

The Internet is _____ now, being available in 78% of all American households.

- **A** unimportant
- **B** transitory
- **C** migrating
- **D** negligible
- **E** ubiquitous

Answer: **E**

---

1. The teacher makes no _____ for tardiness and sends all late arrivals to the office.
   - **A** reception
   - **B** exception
   - **C** expectations
   - **D** exemption
   - **E** omission

2. Tax reform is an often-heard _____ that is seldom _____.
   - **A** pledge . . honored
   - **B** oath . . guaranteed
   - **C** quote . . remembered
   - **D** vow . . broken
   - **E** guarantee . . fulfilled

3. At age 54, Mikhail Gorbachev _____ Chernenko in 1985, becoming the youngest _____ of the USSR since Josef Stalin.

    Ⓐ assassinated . . chairman

    Ⓑ inaugurated . . President

    Ⓒ succeeded . . leader

    Ⓓ preceded . . dictator

    Ⓔ followed . . Prime Minister

4. The 1980s were a(n) _____ of dramatic and stunning change, more so than any other decade in that century.

    Ⓐ epoch

    Ⓑ bounty

    Ⓒ boon

    Ⓓ windfall

    Ⓔ respite

5. The subject of congressional salaries has been hotly _____ for years, and the _____ isn't likely to end anytime soon.

    Ⓐ discussed . . argument

    Ⓑ argued . . problem

    Ⓒ pondered . . disagreement

    Ⓓ deliberated . . hullabaloo

    Ⓔ debated . . controversy

6. Tahiti, a tropical paradise under French _____, attracts many vacationers each year.

    Ⓐ power

    Ⓑ rule

    Ⓒ command

    Ⓓ dominion

    Ⓔ dominance

7. Magellan was the first to _____ the many continents to _____ the globe.

    Ⓐ avoid . . orbit

    Ⓑ bypass . . circumnavigate

    Ⓒ dodge . . encircle

    Ⓓ evade . . traverse

    Ⓔ circumnavigate . . map

8. The Fourteenth and Fifteenth amendments are said to be the
   _____ of equal rights, safeguarding the rights of all citizens, not
   just some citizens.

   Ⓐ beginning

   Ⓑ defense

   Ⓒ bulwark

   Ⓓ foundation

   Ⓔ objective

The passages below are followed by questions based on their content; questions following a pair of related passages may also be
based on the relationship between the paired passages. Answer the
questions on the basis of what is <u>stated</u> or <u>implied</u> in the passages
and in any introductory material that may be provided.

Questions 9–10 are based on the following passage.

By the time of the Civil War, more than two centuries after the
first colonist arrived in New England, half the nation's land was
still nearly empty. The frontier—a ragged line of settlements
Line from the East—ran through part of Minnesota, along the border
5 of Iowa, Missouri, and Arkansas and then swung westward into
Texas. Reaching in from the West Coast there was also a thin
line of settlements in California, Oregon, and Washington.
Between these two frontiers there were only a few islands of set-
tlers, such as the Mormons in Utah, the miners in Colorado, and
10 the Mexican Americans in New Mexico. Even in the "settled"
areas on the edge of the open land, it was often a long way
between neighbors.

9. By 1860, there were two frontiers. List their border states.

   Ⓐ New England and New Mexico

   Ⓑ Minnesota, Iowa, Missouri, and Arkansas; California,
      Oregon, and Washington

   Ⓒ Minnesota, Iowa, Missouri, and Texas; California, Oregon,
      and Washington

   Ⓓ Utah, Colorado, and New Mexico

   Ⓔ Minnesota, Iowa, Missouri, Arkansas and Texas; California,
      Oregon, and Washington

10. This passage would make a good introduction into the discussion of what topic?

   Ⓐ settling the great plains between the two 1860 frontiers

   Ⓑ westward expansion

   Ⓒ the hardships faced by pioneers

   Ⓓ how Mormons, miners, and Mexicans settled the great plains

   Ⓔ discovering the western half of the United States

Questions 11–12 are based on the following passage.

AIDS is most often transmitted through physical sexual relations and through the shared needles of drug users. Those most at risk from the disease were homosexuals and certain drug addicts.
Line Scientists feared that it might spread through the whole population.
5 Suddenly, sexual license, a popular idea in the 1960s was found to be dangerous to the health of all. Since there was no known cure, education and sexual abstinence became the only ways to slow the spread of AIDS. Dr. C. Everett Koop, Surgeon General under Ronald Reagan, set a wise example by urging that grade
10 school students be taught about the disease. AIDS, the shocking discovery of the early 1980s, threatened to become a worldwide catastrophe. Between 2000 and 2020, it is estimated that 68 million people will die prematurely as a result of AIDS.

11. What does the author mean by the phrase "sexual license?"

   Ⓐ permission to engage in sexual activities

   Ⓑ complete sexual freedom without consideration of consequences

   Ⓒ the freedom to participate in sexual activities without social or religious restrictions

   Ⓓ protected sexual activity

   Ⓔ prostitution

12. Why did Dr. C. Everett Koop, Surgeon General, incorporate AIDS into grade school curriculum?

   Ⓐ to protect the next generation from AIDS.

   Ⓑ to further his sexually repressive agenda.

   Ⓒ It was an excuse to finally introduce sex education into the classroom in communities that still objected.

   Ⓓ to educate the next generation in the hopes of slowing the spread of AIDS.

   Ⓔ to slow the spread of AIDS.

Questions 13–24 are based on the following passages.

These two passages are taken from biographies of George Washington that were published about 25 years apart. Though both authors rely on many of the same sources, they choose to emphasize different aspects of their subject.

Passage 1:

In the House of Burgesses Washington was a taciturn member, yet he seemed to have got a great deal of political knowledge and wisdom so that his colleagues thought of him as the solid man of the House and they referred many matters to him as if
Line
5   for final decision. He followed political affairs in the newspapers. Above all, at Mount Vernon he heard all sides from the guests who passed his domain and enjoyed his hospitality. From the moment that the irritation between Great Britain and the Colonies became bitter he seems to have made up his mind that
10 the contention of the Colonists was just. After that he never wavered, but he was not a sudden or a shallow clamorer for Independence. He believed that the sober second sense of the British would lead them to perceive that they had made a mistake. When at length the Colonies had to provide themselves with an
15 army and to undertake a war, he was the only candidate seriously considered for General, although John Hancock, who had made his peacock way so successfully in many walks of life, thought that he alone was worthy of the position. Who shall describe Washington's life as Commander-in-Chief of the Colonial forces
20 during the Revolutionary War? What other commander ever had a task like his? For a few weeks the troops led by Napoleon—the barefooted and ragged heroes of Lodi and Arcola and Marengo—were equally destitute, but victory brought them food and clothes and prosperity. Whereas Washington's men had no
25 comfort before victory and none after it.

Some of the military critics to-day deny Washington's right to be ranked among the great military commanders of the world, but the truth is that he commanded during nearly eight years and won one of the supreme crucial wars of history against far superior
30 forces. The General who did that was no understrapper. The man whose courage diffused itself among the ten thousand starving soldiers at Valley Forge, and enabled them to endure against the starvation and distress of a winter, may very well fail to be classified among the Prince Ruperts and the Marshal
35 Neys of battle, but he ranks first in a higher class. His Fabian[1] policy, which troubled so many of his contemporaries, saved the American Revolution. His title as General is secure. Nor should we forget that it was his scrupulous patriotism which prevented the cropping out of militarism in this country.

40 Finally, a country which owed its existence to him chose him to
be for eight years its first President. He saw the planting of the
roots of the chief organs of its government. In every act he
looked far forward into the future. He shunned making or following evil precedents. He endured the most virulent personal

45 abuse that has ever been poured out on American public men,
preferring that to using the power which his position gave him,
and denaturing the President into a tyrant. Nor should we fail
to honor him for his insistence on dignity and a proper respect
for his office. His enemies sneered at him for that, but we see

50 plainly how much it meant to this new Nation to have such
qualities exemplified. Had Thomas Jefferson been our first
President in his *sans-culotte*[2] days, our Government might not
have outlasted the *sans-culottist* enthusiasts in France. A man is
known by his friends. The chosen friends of Washington were

55 among the best of his time in America. Hamilton, Henry Knox,
Nathanael Greene, John Jay, John Marshall—these were some.

Although Washington was less learned than many of the men
of his time in political theory and history, he excelled them all
in a concrete application of principles. He had the widest

60 acquaintance among men of different sorts. He heard all opinions,
but never sacrificed his own. As I have said earlier, he was the
most *actual* statesman of his time; the people in Virginia came
very early to regard him as a man apart; this was true of the
later days when the Government sat in New York and Philadelphia.

65 If they sought a reason, they usually agreed that Washington
excelled by his character, and if you analyze most closely you
will never get deeper than that. Reserved he was, and not a loose
or glib talker, but he always showed his interest and gave close
attention. After Yorktown, when the United States proclaimed to

70 the world that they were an independent Republic, Europe rec-
ognized that this was indeed a Republic unlike all those which
had preceded it during antiquity and the Middle Age. Foreigners
doubted that it could exist. They doubted that Democracy could
ever govern a nation. They knew despots, like the Prussian King,

75 Frederic, who walked about the streets of Berlin and used his
walking-stick on the cringing persons whom he passed on the
sidewalk and did not like the looks of. They remembered the crazy
Czar, Peter, and they knew about the insane tendencies of the
British sovereign, George. The world argued from these and other

80 examples that monarchy was safe; it could not doubt that the
supply of monarchs would never give out; but it had no hope of
a Republic governed by a President. It was George Washington
more than any other agency who made the world change its
mind and conclude that the best President was the best kind of

85 monarch.

It is reported that after he died many persons who had been his neighbors and acquaintances confessed that they had always felt a peculiar sense of being with a higher sort of person in his presence: a being not superhuman, but far above common men.
90 That feeling will revive in the heart of any one to-day who reads wisely in the fourteen volumes of "Washington's Correspondence," in which, as in a mine, are buried the passions and emotions from which sprang the American Revolution and the American Constitution. That George Washington lived and achieved is the
95 justification and hope of the United States.

Passage 2:

There must have been something very impressive about a man who, with no pretensions to the art of the orator and with no touch of the charlatan, could so move and affect vast bodies of men by his presence alone. But the people, with the keen eye of
100 affection, looked beyond the mere outward nobility of form. They saw the soldier who had given them victory, the great statesman who had led them out of confusion and faction to order and good government. Party newspapers might rave, but the instinct of the people was never at fault. They loved, trusted and well-nigh
105 worshiped Washington living, and they have honored and reverenced him with an unchanging fidelity since his death, nearly a century ago.

But little more remains to be said. Washington had his faults, for he was human; but they are not easy to point out, so perfect
110 was his mastery of himself. He was intensely reserved and very silent, and these are the qualities which gave him the reputation in history of being distant and unsympathetic. In truth, he had not only warm affections and a generous heart, but there was a strong vein of sentiment in his composition. At the same time he
115 was in no wise romantic, and the ruling element in his make-up was prose, good solid prose, and not poetry. He did not have the poetical and imaginative quality so strongly developed in Lincoln. Yet he was not devoid of imagination, although it was here that he was lacking, if anywhere. He saw facts, knew them, mastered
120 and used them, and never gave much play to fancy; but as his business in life was with men and facts, this deficiency, if it was one, was of little moment. He was also a man of the strongest passions in every way, but he dominated them; they never ruled him. Vigorous animal passions were inevitable, of course, in a
125 man of such a physical make-up as his. How far he gave way to them in his youth no one knows, but the scandals which many persons now desire to have printed, ostensibly for the sake of truth, are, so far as I have been able to learn, with one or two dubious exceptions, of entirely modern parentage. I have run

130 many of them to earth; nearly all are destitute of contemporary authority, and they may be relegated to the dust-heaps. If he gave way to these propensities in his youth, the only conclusion that I have been able to come to is that he mastered them when he reached man's estate.

135 He had, too, a fierce temper, and although he gradually subdued it, he would sometimes lose control of himself and burst out into a tempest of rage. When he did so he would use strong and even violent language, as he did at Kip's Landing and at Monmouth. Well-intentioned persons in their desire to make him a faultless

140 being have argued at great length that Washington never swore, and but for their argument the matter would never have attracted much attention. He was anything but a profane man, but the evidence is beyond question that if deeply angered he would use a hearty English oath; and not seldom the action accompanied

145 the word, as when he rode among the fleeing soldiers at Kip's Landing, striking them with his sword, and almost beside himself at their cowardice. Judge Marshall used to tell also of an occasion when Washington sent out an officer to cross a river and bring back some information about the enemy, on which the action

150 of the morrow would depend. The officer was gone some time, came back, and found the general impatiently pacing his tent. On being asked what he had learned, he replied that the night was dark and stormy, the river full of ice, and that he had not been able to cross. Washington glared at him a moment, seized a

155 large leaden inkstand from the table, hurled it at the offender's head, and said with a fierce oath, "Be off, and send me a *man!*" The officer went, crossed the river, and brought back the information.

But although he would now and then give way to these tremendous
160 bursts of anger, Washington was never unjust. As he said to one officer, "I never judge the propriety of actions by after events;" and in that sound philosophy is found the secret not only of much of his own success, but of the devotion of his officers and men. He might be angry with them, but he was never unfair. In

165 truth, he was too generous to be unjust or even over-severe to any one, and there is not a line in all his writings which even suggests that he ever envied any man. So long as the work in hand was done, he cared not who had the glory, and he was perfectly magnanimous and perfectly at ease about his own

170 reputation. He never showed the slightest anxiety to write his own memoirs, and he was not in the least alarmed when it was proposed to publish the memoirs of other people, like General Charles Lee, which would probably reflect upon him.

He had the same confidence in the judgment of posterity that
175 he had in the future beyond the grave. He regarded death with
entire calmness and even indifference not only when it came to
him, but when in previous years it had threatened him. He
loved life and tasted of it deeply, but the courage which never
forsook him made him ready to face the inevitable at any
180 moment with an unruffled spirit. In this he was helped by his
religious faith, which was as simple as it was profound. He had
been brought up in the Protestant Episcopal Church, and to
that church he always adhered; for its splendid liturgy and
stately forms appealed to him and satisfied him. He loved it too
185 as the church of his home and his childhood. Yet he was as far
as possible from being sectarian, and there is not a word of his
which shows anything but the most entire liberality and toleration.
He made no parade of his religion, for in this as in other things
he was perfectly simple and sincere. He was tortured by no doubts
190 or questionings, but believed always in an overruling Providence
and in a merciful God, to whom he knelt and prayed in the day of
darkness or in the hour of triumph with a supreme and childlike
confidence.

[1] Slow and cautions, after the Roman general Quintus Fabius Maximus Verrucosus
who preferred to avoid a decisive contest.

[2] Sans-culotte (literally, "without breeches"): the common people who rose up in the
French Revolution, and, by extension, any political movement consisting mainly of
artisans, farmers, and workers.

13. In lines 7-13, the author of passage 1 states that

   Ⓐ Washington was in favor of independence as soon as
   relations with Great Britain turned bitter.

   Ⓑ Washington began to prepare to lead the colonial army
   after talking to Mount Vernon visitors.

   Ⓒ Washington thought from his earliest days that the
   colonies should be independent.

   Ⓓ Washington supported the colonists, but hoped that war
   could be avoided.

   Ⓔ Washington thought that the drive for independence was a
   mistake.

14. The phrase "it was his scrupulous patriotism which prevented
the cropping out of militarism" (lines 38 and 39) most nearly
means

   Ⓐ His vigorous action prevented the loss of the war.

   Ⓑ Winning the war enabled farmers to leave the military
   ranks and go back to their fields.

C His love of country caused him to decline the chance of military rule.

D His outstanding leadership prevented the colonists from being crushed by a British military.

E His strong character kept local militias from acting precipitously on their own.

15. In mentioning Thomas Jefferson in the third paragraph, the author of passage 1 implies that

A Washington, unlike Jefferson, was careful to keep the nation at a fitting distance from the French government.

B Jefferson would not have used the power of the presidency as wisely as Washington did.

C having a different first president would have had a lasting impression on the way that we perceive the presidency.

D Jefferson was not in the habit of looking far into the future, but preferred to react to circumstances instead.

E The office of the presidency was more important to the new nation than the particular man holding the office.

16. In stating that "the world argued from these and other examples that monarchy was safe" (line 79), the author of passage 1

A suggests that monarchy was a better form of government than a Republic.

B is sarcastically attacking advocates of monarchy.

C holds up a few monarchs as examples of rulers who were Washington's equal.

D shows that Washington was comparable to other heads of state of his day.

E dismisses the idea that a Republic is a viable form of government.

17. In speaking of "this deficiency" (line 121), the author of passage 2 refers to

A a tendency towards silence

B a lack of imagination

C vigorous animal passions

D an inability to write poetry

E a lack of success in love

18. Which of these conclusions can be drawn from the sentence beginning "Well-intentioned persons" in lines 139-142?

    Ⓐ Washington never swore.

    Ⓑ Washington argued at great length.

    Ⓒ Washington never attracted much attention.

    Ⓓ Washington was not a faultless person.

    Ⓔ Washington desired to be well-intentioned.

19. The sentence "I never judge the propriety of actions by after events" (line 161) most nearly means

    Ⓐ I never decide whether something is right by considering its actual effects.

    Ⓑ I never question the politeness of men based on what I read in the papers.

    Ⓒ I never evaluate when to act from knowledge of the enemy's actions.

    Ⓓ I never fit my own actions to someone else's ideas of right and wrong.

    Ⓔ I never hold back when it is better to be generous.

20. The first three sentences of the last paragraph of passage 2 suggest that

    Ⓐ regarding death with utter calmness makes it difficult to enjoy life.

    Ⓑ courage to face death comes from a deep love and appreciation of life.

    Ⓒ confidence in the judgment of posterity is a source of deep courage.

    Ⓓ loving life without a faith in the afterlife leaves one with a ruffled spirit.

    Ⓔ death is a matter that should be regarded with entire calmness and even indifference.

21. Passage 2 as a whole suggests that its author would most likely evaluate the final paragraph of passage 1 as

    Ⓐ truthful

    Ⓑ understated

    Ⓒ humorous

    Ⓓ prescient

    Ⓔ overblown

22. Which of the following statements would both authors likely agree on, based on the material in the passages?

    Ⓐ Washington's bursts of bad temper were well-known.

    Ⓑ Washington's courage shored up the soldiers at Valley Forge.

    Ⓒ Washington had a deep religious faith.

    Ⓓ Washington was by nature silent.

    Ⓔ Washington viewed the presidency as an office that ought to be dignified.

23. Compared to passage 1, passage 2

    Ⓐ is more concerned with the personal side of Washington.

    Ⓑ tries to judge Washington by acts rather than words.

    Ⓒ is skeptical of Washington's military prowess.

    Ⓓ credits Washington more plainly with setting the spirit of the presidency.

    Ⓔ compares Washington more with other heads of state.

24. The author of passage 1 would most likely regard the scandals mentioned at line 126 in passage 2 as

    Ⓐ likely to be true but not important in the grand scheme of things.

    Ⓑ impossible to prove or disprove and therefore not to be considered.

    Ⓒ incompatible with what we know of Washington from other sources.

    Ⓓ slurs dreamed up by Washington's political opponents.

    Ⓔ well-documented in Washington's own correspondence.

STOP

If you finish before time is called, you may check your work on this section only. Do not turn to any other section in the test.

Section 5

1. Ⓐ Ⓑ Ⓒ Ⓓ Ⓔ	9. Ⓐ Ⓑ Ⓒ Ⓓ Ⓔ	17. Ⓐ Ⓑ Ⓒ Ⓓ Ⓔ
2. Ⓐ Ⓑ Ⓒ Ⓓ Ⓔ	10. Ⓐ Ⓑ Ⓒ Ⓓ Ⓔ	18. Ⓐ Ⓑ Ⓒ Ⓓ Ⓔ
3. Ⓐ Ⓑ Ⓒ Ⓓ Ⓔ	11. Ⓐ Ⓑ Ⓒ Ⓓ Ⓔ	19. Ⓐ Ⓑ Ⓒ Ⓓ Ⓔ
4. Ⓐ Ⓑ Ⓒ Ⓓ Ⓔ	12. Ⓐ Ⓑ Ⓒ Ⓓ Ⓔ	20. Ⓐ Ⓑ Ⓒ Ⓓ Ⓔ
5. Ⓐ Ⓑ Ⓒ Ⓓ Ⓔ	13. Ⓐ Ⓑ Ⓒ Ⓓ Ⓔ	21. Ⓐ Ⓑ Ⓒ Ⓓ Ⓔ
6. Ⓐ Ⓑ Ⓒ Ⓓ Ⓔ	14. Ⓐ Ⓑ Ⓒ Ⓓ Ⓔ	22. Ⓐ Ⓑ Ⓒ Ⓓ Ⓔ
7. Ⓐ Ⓑ Ⓒ Ⓓ Ⓔ	15. Ⓐ Ⓑ Ⓒ Ⓓ Ⓔ	23. Ⓐ Ⓑ Ⓒ Ⓓ Ⓔ
8. Ⓐ Ⓑ Ⓒ Ⓓ Ⓔ	16. Ⓐ Ⓑ Ⓒ Ⓓ Ⓔ	24. Ⓐ Ⓑ Ⓒ Ⓓ Ⓔ

SECTION 6

Time—25 minutes

20 Questions

Turn to Section 6 of your answer sheet to answer the questions in this section.

Directions: For this section, solve each problem and decide which is the best of the choices given. Fill in the corresponding circle on the answer sheet. You can use any available space for scratchwork.

Notes:

1. The use of a calculator is permitted.

2. All numbers used are real numbers.

3. Figures that accompany problems in the test are intended to provide information that is useful in solving the problems. They are drawn as accurately as possible EXCEPT when it is stated in a specific problem that the figure is not drawn to scale. All figures lie in a plane unless otherwise indicated.

4. Unless otherwise specified, the domain of any function f is assumed to be the set of real numbers x for which $f(x)$ is a real number.

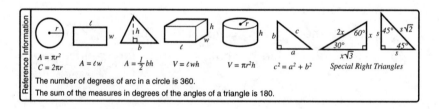

Reference Information

$A = \pi r^2$
$C = 2\pi r$ $A = \ell w$ $A = \frac{1}{2}bh$ $V = \ell wh$ $V = \pi r^2 h$ $c^2 = a^2 + b^2$ *Special Right Triangles*

The number of degrees of arc in a circle is 360.
The sum of the measures in degrees of the angles of a triangle is 180.

1. If $2x + y = 19$ and $x - y = 5$, what is y?

   Ⓐ 3

   Ⓑ 5

   Ⓒ 8

   Ⓓ 13

   Ⓔ 19

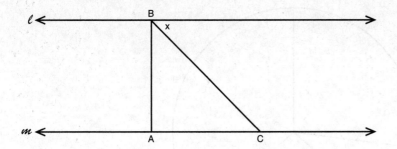

2. In the figure above, $l \| m$ and $\triangle ABC$ is an isosceles right triangle. What is $\angle x$?

    Ⓐ 15°

    Ⓑ 30°

    Ⓒ 45°

    Ⓓ 60°

    Ⓔ 90°

3. Which of these expressions gives the largest result?

    Ⓐ 3 + 3 + 3

    Ⓑ 3 × 3 × 3

    Ⓒ $3^3 + 3^3$

    Ⓓ 3^{3^3}

    Ⓔ 333

4. Point P is at (–5, 17) and point Q is at ($4\sqrt{3}$, 6). How many lines can you draw that pass through both point P and point Q?

    Ⓐ 0

    Ⓑ 1

    Ⓒ 2

    Ⓓ 3

    Ⓔ 4

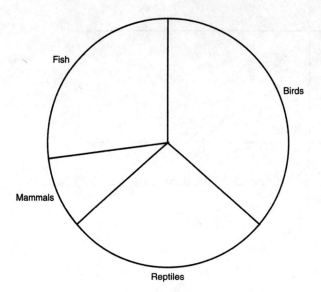

5. The figure above shows the overall holdings of a zoo. The zoo has the same number of reptiles and fish, 20 mammals, and four times as many birds as mammals. If the number of reptiles is $\frac{3}{4}$ the number of birds, how many fish are in the zoo?

   Ⓐ 20

   Ⓑ 40

   Ⓒ 60

   Ⓓ 80

   Ⓔ 100

6. The sum of four consecutive prime numbers is 72. What is the smallest of these numbers?

   Ⓐ 2

   Ⓑ 11

   Ⓒ 13

   Ⓓ 19

   Ⓔ 23

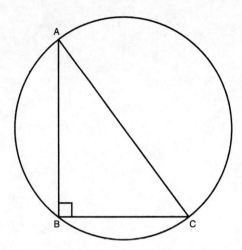

7. In the figure above, AB = 4 and BC = 3. The center of the circle lies on line AC. What is the circumference of the circle?

   Ⓐ 3π

   Ⓑ 3π²

   Ⓒ 4π

   Ⓓ 5π

   Ⓔ 5π²

8. The mean of a set of 10 numbers is 18. When you remove the smallest 3 of these numbers, the mean of the remaining numbers is 22. What is the sum of the smallest 3 numbers?

   Ⓐ 9

   Ⓑ 10

   Ⓒ 18

   Ⓓ 22

   Ⓔ 26

9. Define $f(x,y) = x^2 - xy$. For which of the below values of x and y is $f(x,y)$ the largest?

   Ⓐ x = 3, y = −3

   Ⓑ x = 3, y = 3

   Ⓒ x = −3, y = 0

   Ⓓ x = −3, y = −3

   Ⓔ x = 0, y = 3

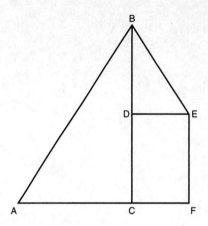

<u>Note:</u> Figure not drawn to scale.

10. In the figure above, ΔABC and ΔEBD are similar triangles. BD = CD = 1 and AC = 1.5. What is the area of rectangle CDEF?

    Ⓐ .5

    Ⓑ .75

    Ⓒ 1

    Ⓓ 1.5

    Ⓔ 2.25

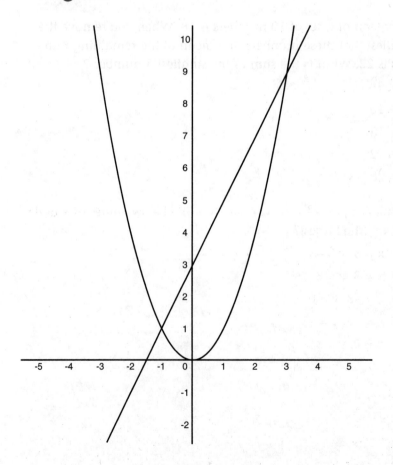

11. The figure above shows the graphs of $y = x^2$ and $y = ax + b$. The two graphs intersect at $x = -1$ and $x = 3$. What is a?

    Ⓐ -2

    Ⓑ -1.5

    Ⓒ 0

    Ⓓ 2

    Ⓔ 3

12. Define 🍎 as follows: x 🍎 $y = |x - y|$. If 3 🍎 $z = 5$ and z 🍎 $w = 2$, which of these is a possible value for w?

    Ⓐ -5

    Ⓑ -4

    Ⓒ -2

    Ⓓ 5

    Ⓔ 8

13. Let $f(x) = x^2 + ax + b$. If the zeroes of this polynomial are at -4 and -2, what is $f(9)$?

    Ⓐ 35

    Ⓑ 81

    Ⓒ 90

    Ⓓ 143

    Ⓔ 181

14. A fair coin is tossed eight times. What is the probability that only one of the tosses will come up heads?

    Ⓐ $\frac{1}{256}$

    Ⓑ $\frac{1}{64}$

    Ⓒ $\frac{1}{32}$

    Ⓓ $\frac{1}{16}$

    Ⓔ $\frac{1}{8}$

15. A right circular cone with diameter 2 and height 2 and a cube have the same volume. What is the length of the side of the cube?

    Ⓐ $\sqrt{2\pi}$

    Ⓑ $2\sqrt[3]{2\pi}$

    Ⓒ $2\pi^3$

    Ⓓ $\sqrt{2\pi}$

    Ⓔ 2π

16. Two opposite faces of a cube are colored white, and the other four faces are colored black. Which of the figures below could *not* be produced by cutting along the edges of the cube and flattening the results into the plane?

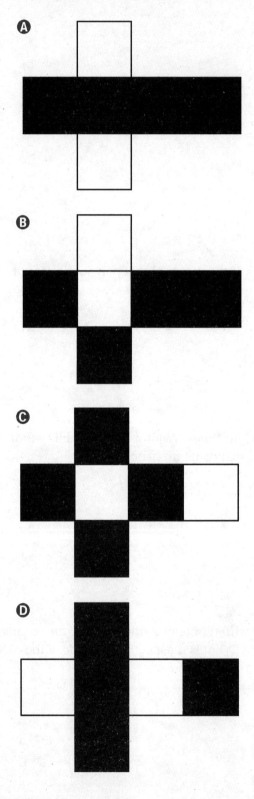

E

17. If m and n are both even integers, which of these could be an odd integer:

    I. m + n

    II. m − n

    III. $^{(m+n}$

    Ⓐ I only

    Ⓑ II only

    Ⓒ III only

    Ⓓ I and II

    Ⓔ II and III

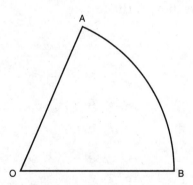

<u>Note:</u> Figure not drawn to scale.

18. In the figure above, OA = 5 and the area of the sector OAB is 5π. What is the length of the arc AB?

    Ⓐ 2

    Ⓑ 2π

    Ⓒ 4

    Ⓓ 4π

    Ⓔ 5π

19. The summer reading shelf at the library contains 30 books. A student must select three books to read over the summer. How many different sets of three books could the student select?

    Ⓐ 6

    Ⓑ 812

    Ⓒ 4,060

    Ⓓ 8,120

    Ⓔ 24,360

20. A circle has a diameter that is a positive integer, and an area that is less than 10 units. How many different circles fulfill this condition?

    Ⓐ One

    Ⓑ Two

    Ⓒ Three

    Ⓓ Four

    Ⓔ Five

STOP

If you finish before time is called, you may check your work on this section only. Do not turn to any other section in the test.

Section 6

1. Ⓐ Ⓑ Ⓒ Ⓓ Ⓔ   8. Ⓐ Ⓑ Ⓒ Ⓓ Ⓔ   15. Ⓐ Ⓑ Ⓒ Ⓓ Ⓔ

2. Ⓐ Ⓑ Ⓒ Ⓓ Ⓔ   9. Ⓐ Ⓑ Ⓒ Ⓓ Ⓔ   16. Ⓐ Ⓑ Ⓒ Ⓓ Ⓔ

3. Ⓐ Ⓑ Ⓒ Ⓓ Ⓔ   10. Ⓐ Ⓑ Ⓒ Ⓓ Ⓔ   17. Ⓐ Ⓑ Ⓒ Ⓓ Ⓔ

4. Ⓐ Ⓑ Ⓒ Ⓓ Ⓔ   11. Ⓐ Ⓑ Ⓒ Ⓓ Ⓔ   18. Ⓐ Ⓑ Ⓒ Ⓓ Ⓔ

5. Ⓐ Ⓑ Ⓒ Ⓓ Ⓔ   12. Ⓐ Ⓑ Ⓒ Ⓓ Ⓔ   19. Ⓐ Ⓑ Ⓒ Ⓓ Ⓔ

6. Ⓐ Ⓑ Ⓒ Ⓓ Ⓔ   13. Ⓐ Ⓑ Ⓒ Ⓓ Ⓔ   20. Ⓐ Ⓑ Ⓒ Ⓓ Ⓔ

7. Ⓐ Ⓑ Ⓒ Ⓓ Ⓔ   14. Ⓐ Ⓑ Ⓒ Ⓓ Ⓔ

SECTION 7

Time—20 minutes

19 Questions

Turn to Section 7 of your answer sheet to answer the questions in this section.

Directions: For each question in this section, select the best answer from among the choices given and fill in the corresponding circle on the answer sheet.

Each sentence below has one or two blanks, each blank indicating that something has been omitted. Beneath the sentence are five words or sets of words labeled A through E. Choose the word or set of words that, when inserted in the sentence, <u>best</u> fits the meaning of the sentence as a whole.

EXAMPLE:

The Internet is _____ now, being available in 78% of all American households.

- **A** unimportant
- **B** transitory
- **C** migrating
- **D** negligible
- **E** ubiquitous

Answer: **E**

---

1. You should always wear a protective apron, gloves, and goggles when working with _____ chemicals.
    - **A** sarcastic
    - **B** corrosive
    - **C** caudated
    - **D** cauterized
    - **E** acrid

2. After the last administration's scandal, the public was _____ of his predecessor's promises.
    - **A** wary
    - **B** careless
    - **C** trusting
    - **D** reticent
    - **E** unsuspecting

3. The clerk complained that proofreading the long columns of
   _____ symbols was _____ work.

   Ⓐ archaic . . relaxing

   Ⓑ illegible . . dangerous

   Ⓒ impenetrable . . boring

   Ⓓ ancient . . interesting

   Ⓔ unintelligible . . tedious

4. Growing up with a(n) _____ nana was an adventure—we never
   knew what to expect, and she sure did open our young minds to
   a world of possibilities.

   Ⓐ eccentric

   Ⓑ eclectic

   Ⓒ erratic

   Ⓓ temperamental

   Ⓔ menacing

5. Being familiar only with her _____ business persona, we were
   unprepared for the _____ personality we met at the office party.

   Ⓐ reclusive . . optimistic

   Ⓑ aloof . . reticent

   Ⓒ malicious . . gregarious

   Ⓓ sanguine . . diffident

   Ⓔ benevolent . . assertive

6. Her _____ mindset was so _____; she was difficult to
   work with.

   Ⓐ notorious . . odious

   Ⓑ cantankerous . . amiable

   Ⓒ congenial . . amusing

   Ⓓ affable . . intolerable

   Ⓔ dogmatic . . invidious

The passage below is followed by questions based on its content.
Answer the questions on the basis of what is <u>stated</u> or <u>implied</u> in the
passages and in any introductory material that may be provided.

Questions 7–19 are based on the following passage.

*The following passage is from a novel set on Santa Catalina island off
California in 1920.*

It was now something over two years since Harrison Blair, then fresh from Yale, had astonished both those who wished him well and those who, for various envious reasons, did not, with
Line the wholly unreasonable success of his first book. For, to those
5 who did not understand, his sudden fame had seemed all the more surprising in that it rested upon nothing more substantial than a slender volume of Indian verse. So unusual, however, had been his treatment of this well-worn subject as to call forth more than a little comment from even the most conservative of
10 critics. The Brush and Pen had hastened to confer upon him an honorary membership. Cadmon, magic weaver of Indian music, had written a warm letter of appreciation. And, most precious tribute of all, the Atlantic Monthly had become interested in his career.

15 To be sure, it was nothing more than might have been expected of a man whose undergraduate work in English had aroused the reluctant wonder of more than one instructor. Nevertheless, the fact that he pulled stroke on the varsity crew had somewhat blinded other contemporaries to his more scholarly attainments.
20 Nor had anyone thought it probable, because of his father's wealth, that Blair, in any event, would feel called upon to do much more than make a frolic of life. No one, indeed, had been more taken aback than had his father to find him, a year after graduation, drudging over the assistant editor's desk of a struggling
25 magazine the payroll of which, to put it mildly, offered no financial inducements.

"It's good practice for me, though—quickest way to learn," was all he vouchsafed when the older man remonstrated.

Yet, had that same father, shrewd capitalist that he was, but
30 taken the trouble to reason back from premises evident enough, he might have been the first to realize that this tall son of his, with the keen gray eyes and a face the strength of which was but increased by the high cheek bones and squarely molded chin, was scarcely the type of man to sit idly by enjoying the
35 fruits of another's labor.

And now, after two years more of grinding apprenticeship, he had in mind something much bigger than the slender volume of verse—an adventure into authorship more suited to his metal—a story of which an intense personal sympathy would furnish fitting
40 atmosphere, with the final spur to his ambition a letter from the Atlantic even at the moment stowed safely away in his pocket.

Some two hours later, after an unexpectedly excellent dinner in the luxurious dining room, he sauntered over to the hotel desk. There was no more than the faintest probability that a clerk of
45 the St. Catherine would be able to tell him how to reach a secret

cavern bower above the Bay of Moons; still, he had to enter an opening wedge somewhere. The one man on duty was for the moment occupied with another guest, and Blair, lighting his after-dinner cigar, prepared with leisurely patience to await his turn.

50 The guest happened to be a young woman, rather pretty, he casually decided, although her greatest claim to beauty lay more, perhaps, in the swift changes in expression of which her face was capable, than in any actual regularity of line. For lack of anything better to do, Blair watched idly her encounter with
55 the clerk. There appeared to be some kind of misunderstanding.

"Awfully sorry it's happened that way, Miss Hastings," the man behind the desk was saying. He lifted with genuine reluctance the key she had just laid down. "We'd be mighty sorry to interfere with your work, but those small rooms always do go first. You
60 know that yourself."

"I hadn't heard about it, though. I didn't know they were all gone." Her voice quivered with disappointment.

Blair, whose vocation taught him a certain technical sympathy, shot a swift glance at her. She couldn't be more than twenty-two
65 or thereabouts, he decided less casually, and went on to observe her still further. She wore a shabby, broad-brimmed hat much faded as if from constant exposure to the sun, but the shadows in the coil of hair beneath were warmly golden.

"Couldn't you find a room down in the village somewhere, at
70 Mrs. Merrill's perhaps?" suggested the clerk.

"But Mrs. Merrill isn't here this spring." In spite of its quiver the voice was very sweet.

"No," she started to turn away, "I'll have to put it off again, I suppose. I've looked everywhere."

75 She took a step or two, hesitated, then returned to the desk.

"You're positive there isn't a single one of the small rooms left?" she pleaded. "I wouldn't care how far back it was,—anything would do. You can't think how I hate to give up. I had so hoped to finish it this time!"

80 The man shook his head.

"No, we're absolutely full just now. Later on there might be something, after the season is over."

"But that will be after school begins," answered the girl bitterly. "I can't work at all then!" and catching up a bag fully as shabby
85 as the hat, she hurried away.

"Who is she?" asked Blair abruptly, overlooking for the moment his original purpose in seeking the man.

"School-teacher from Pasadena," replied the clerk briefly. "Teaches art in some private school over there, I believe." He
90 eyed Blair amusedly. "Think you've met her before somewhere?"

Blair allowed his annoyance to show. "No, never laid eyes on her till just now. But I couldn't help feeling a bit sorry for her," he persisted. "She seemed so sort of cut up. What's the trouble?"

"I'm sorry for her myself," declared the man on the other side
95 as he hung the returned key on its board. "This is the third time that poor little woman's had to leave before she could finish what she came for on account of the expense. But what can we do?" He shrugged his shoulders. "The St. Catherine isn't exactly a Y. W. C. A."

100 "What is it she's trying to do?"

Amusement deepened in the man's eyes.

"She's supposed to be painting Indians."

"Indians!" To the amazement of the other man Blair suddenly leaned forward, his eyes agleam with interest.

105 "But I didn't know there were any around here."

"There aren't."

"Then how—?"

"Makes 'em up out of her head, I guess. I never heard that she had even a model."

7. The first paragraph of the passage portrays Harrison Blair as

   Ⓐ a man with many enemies

   Ⓑ a lover of leisure and women

   Ⓒ a man driven by envy

   Ⓓ someone with little imagination

   Ⓔ a promising young author

8. In line 4, "unreasonable" most nearly means

   Ⓐ immoderate

   Ⓑ excessive

   Ⓒ irrational

   Ⓓ unexpected

   Ⓔ inordinate

9. The phrase "the reluctant wonder of more than one instructor" (line 17) indicates that

   Ⓐ Blair's teachers wondered how he was able to complete his assignments.

   Ⓑ Blair's writing impressed teachers who expected he would do poorly.

   Ⓒ Blair's teachers did not understand how he could be reluctant about writing.

   Ⓓ Blair's teachers wondered whether he was cheating in their courses.

   Ⓔ Blair's instructors were angry at his attitude toward assignments.

10. The phrase "he vouchsafed when the older man remonstrated" (line 28) most nearly means

    Ⓐ He promised when the older man asked.

    Ⓑ He objected when the older man questioned.

    Ⓒ He explained when the older man offered.

    Ⓓ He stated when the older man raged.

    Ⓔ He deigned to reply when the older man objected.

11. The overall impression of Blair that the author of the passage gives is that he is

    Ⓐ extraordinary

    Ⓑ extravagant

    Ⓒ dilatory

    Ⓓ spoiled

    Ⓔ unsympathetic

12. In saying that Blair has "a certain technical sympathy" (line 63), the author implies that

    Ⓐ he preferred machines to people.

    Ⓑ he was extremely attractive to women.

    Ⓒ he spent time worrying about those with less money than himself.

    Ⓓ his powers of observation were unusual.

    Ⓔ he has developed the power of sharing the feelings of another.

13. The young woman wants one of the small rooms at the hotel because

    Ⓐ they have better light for painting.

    Ⓑ she can't afford a larger room.

    Ⓒ she doesn't need more space for her things.

    Ⓓ the intimate surroundings help her concentrate.

    Ⓔ she has no companion on this trip.

14. Blair's "annoyance" (line 91) arises from the clerk's

   Ⓐ insolence

   Ⓑ humor

   Ⓒ familiarity

   Ⓓ caginess

   Ⓔ abruptness

15. Why were Blair's eyes suddenly "agleam with interest" (line 104)?

   Ⓐ Because he saw an opportunity to ask the young lady out on a date

   Ⓑ Because he was worried that his own room at the hotel would not be available

   Ⓒ Because he didn't know it was possible to paint without a model

   Ⓓ Because of the coincidence between his own work about Indians and the young lady's paintings of Indians

   Ⓔ Because he had found a worthwhile cause on which to spend some of his money

16. The passage suggests that Blair's main strength is

   Ⓐ his unusual writing ability

   Ⓑ his attractiveness to the fair sex

   Ⓒ his ability to spend money wisely

   Ⓓ his dogged attention to detail

   Ⓔ his athletic ability

17. The major purpose of this passage is to

   Ⓐ provide background detail on the locale of the story.

   Ⓑ give a purpose for Blair's research into Indians.

   Ⓒ introduce some of the characters in the story.

   Ⓓ regale the reader with luxurious details of the fine life.

   Ⓔ show what life was like on Catalina in the 1920s.

18. The author is apparently most concerned to counteract which of these theories that she considers her audience is likely to have?

   Ⓐ School teachers are not paid much money.

   Ⓑ Vacation spots are all exotic.

   Ⓒ Inherited wealth acts as a bar to hard work.

   Ⓓ Hotel clerks are difficult to reason with.

   Ⓔ Good looks and intelligence go hand in hand.

19. Blair's father appears in this passage

A to show that "like father, like son" holds true in this case.

B as a device to introduce important facts about Blair's character.

C because he owns the St. Catherine.

D as a miser who is in stark contrast with his son.

E to indicate that family will play an important role in the story.

STOP

If you finish before time is called, you may check your work on this section only. Do not turn to any other section in the test.

Section 7

1. Ⓐ Ⓑ Ⓒ Ⓓ Ⓔ   8. Ⓐ Ⓑ Ⓒ Ⓓ Ⓔ   15. Ⓐ Ⓑ Ⓒ Ⓓ Ⓔ

2. Ⓐ Ⓑ Ⓒ Ⓓ Ⓔ   9. Ⓐ Ⓑ Ⓒ Ⓓ Ⓔ   16. Ⓐ Ⓑ Ⓒ Ⓓ Ⓔ

3. Ⓐ Ⓑ Ⓒ Ⓓ Ⓔ   10. Ⓐ Ⓑ Ⓒ Ⓓ Ⓔ   17. Ⓐ Ⓑ Ⓒ Ⓓ Ⓔ

4. Ⓐ Ⓑ Ⓒ Ⓓ Ⓔ   11. Ⓐ Ⓑ Ⓒ Ⓓ Ⓔ   18. Ⓐ Ⓑ Ⓒ Ⓓ Ⓔ

5. Ⓐ Ⓑ Ⓒ Ⓓ Ⓔ   12. Ⓐ Ⓑ Ⓒ Ⓓ Ⓔ   19. Ⓐ Ⓑ Ⓒ Ⓓ Ⓔ

6. Ⓐ Ⓑ Ⓒ Ⓓ Ⓔ   13. Ⓐ Ⓑ Ⓒ Ⓓ Ⓔ

7. Ⓐ Ⓑ Ⓒ Ⓓ Ⓔ   14. Ⓐ Ⓑ Ⓒ Ⓓ Ⓔ

SECTION 8

Time—20 minutes

16 Questions

Turn to Section 8 of your answer sheet to answer the questions in this section.

Directions: For this section, solve each problem and decide which is the best of the choices given. Fill in the corresponding circle on the answer sheet. You can use any available space for scratchwork.

Notes:

1. The use of a calculator is permitted.

2. All numbers used are real numbers.

3. Figures that accompany problems in the test are intended to provide information that is useful in solving the problems. They are drawn as accurately as possible EXCEPT when it is stated in a specific problem that the figure is not drawn to scale. All figures lie in a plane unless otherwise indicated.

4. Unless otherwise specified, the domain of any function f is assumed to be the set of real numbers x for which $f(x)$ is a real number.

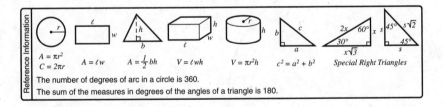

Reference Information

$A = \pi r^2$
$C = 2\pi r$
$A = \ell w$
$A = \frac{1}{2}bh$
$V = \ell wh$
$V = \pi r^2 h$
$c^2 = a^2 + b^2$
Special Right Triangles

The number of degrees of arc in a circle is 360.
The sum of the measures in degrees of the angles of a triangle is 180.

---

1. If 40% of x is 10, what is 3x + 7?

   (A) 37

   (B) 47

   (C) 72

   (D) 82

   (E) 407

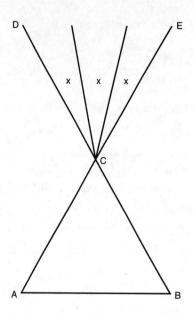

2. In the figure above, ACE and BCD are straight lines, and ∠CAB = ∠CBA = 60°. What is ∠x?

    Ⓐ 15°

    Ⓑ 20°

    Ⓒ 25°

    Ⓓ 30°

    Ⓔ 35°

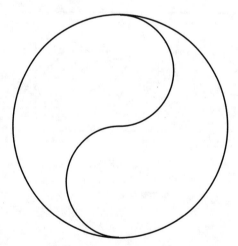

3. What type of symmetry does the figure above possess?

    Ⓐ reflective symmetry across one axis only

    Ⓑ reflective symmetry across two axes only

    Ⓒ rotational symmetry only

    Ⓓ both reflective symmetry and rotational symmetry

    Ⓔ neither reflective symmetry nor rotational symmetry

4. Given that –4x + 12 < 16, which of these statements is true?

   Ⓐ x > 1

   Ⓑ x < 1

   Ⓒ x < –1

   Ⓓ x > –1

   Ⓔ There is not enough information to solve the problem.

5. A class includes three quizzes and a final exam that counts for as much as two quizzes. A student has an average score of 88 before taking the final exam. What must she score on the final exam to raise her average to 90?

   Ⓐ 90

   Ⓑ 91

   Ⓒ 92

   Ⓓ 93

   Ⓔ 94

6. The price of a widget is originally $90. The manufacturer increases the price by 10% and then decreases the price by 10%. What is the final price of the widget?

   Ⓐ $89.00

   Ⓑ $89.10

   Ⓒ $90.00

   Ⓓ $90.10

   Ⓔ $91.00

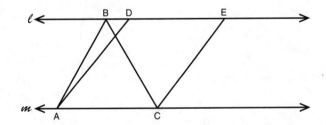

7. In the figure above, $l \parallel m$. The area of the equilateral triangle ABC is 6. What is the area of parallelogram ADEC?

   Ⓐ $6\sqrt{2}$

   Ⓑ $6\sqrt{3}$

   Ⓒ 10

   Ⓓ 12

   Ⓔ 14

Transistor price

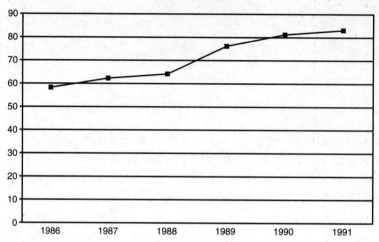

8. According to the graph above, between which two years did the price of transistors increase by the highest percentage?

Ⓐ 1986 and 1987

Ⓑ 1987 and 1988

Ⓒ 1988 and 1989

Ⓓ 1989 and 1990

Ⓔ 1990 and 1991

9. You have an unlimited supply of blocks that are rectangular solids with sides 1 inch, 1 inch, and [bf]1/2 inch. How many of these blocks will you need to fill a cubical box with each side equal to 12 inches?

Ⓐ 72

Ⓑ 144

Ⓒ 288

Ⓓ 1,728

Ⓔ 3,456

10. a, b, c, d, and e are consecutive integers. Which of the following can *not* be the sum of these five integers?

Ⓐ –8,405

Ⓑ –100

Ⓒ 0

Ⓓ 227

Ⓔ 9,810

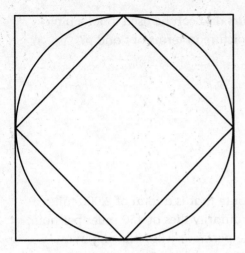

11. The figure shows a circle inscribed in a square, with the circle exactly tangent to the four sides of the square. A second square is inscribed in the circle so that its corners all lie on the circle. If the area of the outer square is 4, what is the area of the inner square?

    Ⓐ $\sqrt{2}$

    Ⓑ 2

    Ⓒ $\frac{5}{2}$

    Ⓓ 2π

    Ⓔ $\frac{3}{2}$

12. The first three terms of an arithmetic sequence are 2, 6, and 10. What is the sum of the 49th and 50th terms of the sequence?

    Ⓐ 388

    Ⓑ 392

    Ⓒ 396

    Ⓓ 398

    Ⓔ 400

13. One square has an area of 4, and a second square has an area of 16. What is the ratio of the perimeter of the first square to the perimeter of the second square?

    Ⓐ 16:1

    Ⓑ 16:4

    Ⓒ 2:1

    Ⓓ 1:1

    Ⓔ 1:2

14. One roll of film costs f dollars and can be used to take p pictures. What is the cost per picture in terms of f and p?

   Ⓐ fp

   Ⓑ $\frac{p}{f}$

   Ⓒ $\frac{f}{p}$

   Ⓓ f + p

   Ⓔ p − f

15. A plane flies a round-trip route that is a total of 2,000 miles each way. The plan itself ordinarily flies at 450 miles per hour, but there is a steady 50 mile per hour wind blowing in one direction. The net effect is that the plane flies at 400 miles per hour in one direction, and 500 miles per hour in the other. What is the average (arithmetical mean) speed of the plane over the entire route?

   Ⓐ 425

   Ⓑ 444 $\frac{4}{9}$

   Ⓒ 450

   Ⓓ 463 $\frac{2}{9}$

   Ⓔ 475

16. All of the line segments in the figure are one unit long, and the central quadrilateral is a square. What is the distance AB?

   Ⓐ 1 + √3

   Ⓑ 1 + √3/2

    Ⓒ 2.5

    Ⓓ 3

    Ⓔ $1 + \pi$

STOP

If you finish before time is called, you may check your work on this section only. Do not turn to any other section in the test.

Section 8

1. Ⓐ Ⓑ Ⓒ Ⓓ Ⓔ   7. Ⓐ Ⓑ Ⓒ Ⓓ Ⓔ   13. Ⓐ Ⓑ Ⓒ Ⓓ Ⓔ

2. Ⓐ Ⓑ Ⓒ Ⓓ Ⓔ   8. Ⓐ Ⓑ Ⓒ Ⓓ Ⓔ   14. Ⓐ Ⓑ Ⓒ Ⓓ Ⓔ

3. Ⓐ Ⓑ Ⓒ Ⓓ Ⓔ   9. Ⓐ Ⓑ Ⓒ Ⓓ Ⓔ   15. Ⓐ Ⓑ Ⓒ Ⓓ Ⓔ

4. Ⓐ Ⓑ Ⓒ Ⓓ Ⓔ   10. Ⓐ Ⓑ Ⓒ Ⓓ Ⓔ   16. Ⓐ Ⓑ Ⓒ Ⓓ Ⓔ

5. Ⓐ Ⓑ Ⓒ Ⓓ Ⓔ   11. Ⓐ Ⓑ Ⓒ Ⓓ Ⓔ

6. Ⓐ Ⓑ Ⓒ Ⓓ Ⓔ   12. Ⓐ Ⓑ Ⓒ Ⓓ Ⓔ

SECTION 9

Time—10 minutes

14 Questions

Turn to Section 9 of your answer sheet to answer the questions in this section.

> **Directions:** For each question in this section, select the best answer from among the choices given and fill in the corresponding circle on the answer sheet.

The following sentences test correctness and effectiveness of expression. Part of each sentence or the entire sentence is underlined; beneath each sentence are five ways of phrasing the underlined material. Choice A repeats the original phrasing; the other four choices are different. If you think the original phrasing produces a better sentence than any of the alternatives, select choice A; if not, select one of the other choices.

In making your selection, follow the requirements of standard written English; that is, pay attention to grammar, choice of words, sentence construction, and punctuation. Your selection should result in the most effective sentence—clear and precise, without awkwardness or ambiguity.

EXAMPLE:

The weather that winter was <u>worse than for at least five decades</u>.

- **A** worse than for at least five decades
- **B** the worse it was for at least five decades
- **C** worse. Than it had been for at least five decades.
- **D** the worst that it had been for at least five decades
- **E** the worst is was for at least five decades.

Answer: **D**

1. You may find it difficult to comprehend <u>that which you</u> read if you don't know the underlying grammar rules.
   - **A** that which you
   - **B** what
   - **C** what you
   - **D** what is
   - **E** that what is

2. First identify the error, and then correct <u>the error</u>.
   - **A** the error
   - **B** what's wrong
   - **C** the mistake
   - **D** it
   - **E** your mistake

3. The band, in addition to the cheerleaders, <u>is already on their way</u> to the game.

    Ⓐ is already on their way

    Ⓑ is already on its way

    Ⓒ is already gone

    Ⓓ has left

    Ⓔ is going

4. After two weeks, the children were still unmanageable <u>so the teacher</u> asked for a transfer.

    Ⓐ so the teacher

    Ⓑ and their teacher

    Ⓒ ; the teacher

    Ⓓ so she

    Ⓔ so their teacher

5. <u>Neither of the girls</u> is going to the prom, although all were invited.

    Ⓐ Neither of the girls

    Ⓑ Neither girl

    Ⓒ None of the girls

    Ⓓ None of them

    Ⓔ Neither Susan nor Betty

6. <u>Neither the dog nor the cows</u> has been attended to yet.

    Ⓐ Neither the dog nor the cows

    Ⓑ None of the animals

    Ⓒ Neither the cows nor the dog

    Ⓓ Either the dog or the cows

    Ⓔ Neither the dog nor the cow

7. Cities began <u>to sprout up</u> in the shadow of the virgin forest.

    Ⓐ to sprout up

    Ⓑ to grow

    Ⓒ to take sprout

    Ⓓ to sprout

    Ⓔ to appear

8. The South is a diverse land of <u>different climates, different soils, and societies</u>.

    Ⓐ different climates, different soils, and societies

    Ⓑ climates, soils, and societies

    Ⓒ different climates, soils and societies

    Ⓓ different climates, soils, and societies

    Ⓔ different climates, and different soils, and different societies

9. Henry David Thoreau, a transcendentalist, <u>believed that God was an oversoul</u>, whose presence shows us good and evil.

    Ⓐ believed that God was an oversoul

    Ⓑ believes that God is an oversoul

    Ⓒ believed that God is an oversoul

    Ⓓ believes that God has an oversoul

    Ⓔ believes God was an oversoul

10. By 1929, U.S. businesses <u>had been spending</u> $3 billion a year for advertising through newspapers, magazines, billboards, direct mail, and the new medium of radio.

    Ⓐ had been spending

    Ⓑ has spent

    Ⓒ were spent

    Ⓓ were spending

    Ⓔ will spent

11. Returning to America a national hero, <u>we were unsure about which political party he belonged to</u>.

    Ⓐ we were unsure about which political party he belonged to.

    Ⓑ he was unsure about which political party he belonged to

    Ⓒ we were unsure about which political party he belonged

    Ⓓ we were unsure about which political party we belonged to

    Ⓔ he was unsure about which political party we belonged to

12. Foreigners could no longer afford <u>to buy up American goods</u>.

    Ⓐ to buy up American goods

    Ⓑ to buy up American products

    Ⓒ to buy American goods

    Ⓓ American goods

    Ⓔ American products

13. <u>The sagging economies of post-war Europe</u> contributed to America's Great Depression.

    Ⓐ The sagging economies of post-war Europe

    Ⓑ Post-war Europe's sagging economies

    Ⓒ Europe's post-war sagging economies

    Ⓓ The sagging economy of post-war Europe

    Ⓔ Europe's sagging post-war economy

14. Because of America's diverse communities, immigrants <u>were likelier to feel</u> at home here than anywhere else except home.

    Ⓐ were likelier to feel

    Ⓑ was likelier to feel

    Ⓒ were more likely to feel

    Ⓓ were most likely to feel

    Ⓔ was most likely to feel

STOP

If you finish before time is called, you may check your work on this section only. Do not turn to any other section in the test.

Section 9

1. Ⓐ Ⓑ Ⓒ Ⓓ Ⓔ	6. Ⓐ Ⓑ Ⓒ Ⓓ Ⓔ	
2. Ⓐ Ⓑ Ⓒ Ⓓ Ⓔ	7. Ⓐ Ⓑ Ⓒ Ⓓ Ⓔ	11. Ⓐ Ⓑ Ⓒ Ⓓ Ⓔ
3. Ⓐ Ⓑ Ⓒ Ⓓ Ⓔ	8. Ⓐ Ⓑ Ⓒ Ⓓ Ⓔ	12. Ⓐ Ⓑ Ⓒ Ⓓ Ⓔ
4. Ⓐ Ⓑ Ⓒ Ⓓ Ⓔ	9. Ⓐ Ⓑ Ⓒ Ⓓ Ⓔ	13. Ⓐ Ⓑ Ⓒ Ⓓ Ⓔ
5. Ⓐ Ⓑ Ⓒ Ⓓ Ⓔ	10. Ⓐ Ⓑ Ⓒ Ⓓ Ⓔ	14. Ⓐ Ⓑ Ⓒ Ⓓ Ⓔ

Check your work!

Quick-check answer key and detailed explanations of correct *and* incorrect answers

Section 1

Grading the essay is subjective, so there's no way we can help you through this process. Our best advice is to ask someone you trust who has the expertise to actually grade your essay to help you. If you have to go it alone, be sure to check for the following:

- Is the thesis well developed, insightful, and focused?
- Did you use clear and appropriate examples, anecdotes, and reasons to support your position?
- Are your thoughts organized logically?
- Did you use a variety of writing techniques, such as varied sentence structure and length?
- Did you use appropriate words?
- Is the essay free of grammatical and spelling errors?

If possible, put a few days between test day and the day you try to grade your own work. Proofing your own work is very difficult—give your mind a chance to forget a bit. A few days later, you'll get a fresher, more objective look at the essay.

Don't try to assign an actual score to your essay. Instead, find your weak points and continue to practice in order to build your skills in that area.

Section 2

1. D	7. A	13. C	19. E
2. E	8. C	14. B	20. D
3. B	9. E	15. B	21. A
4. A	10. D	16. D	22. C
5. C	11. D	17. A	23. E
6. D	12. C	18. D	24. D

Section 3

1. **C**   3. **E**   5. **E**   7. **B**

2. **B**   4. **D**   6. **A**   8. **C**

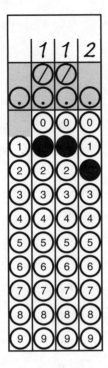

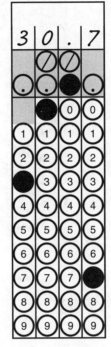

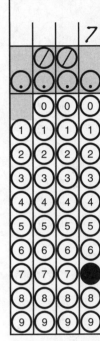

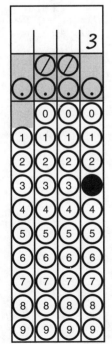

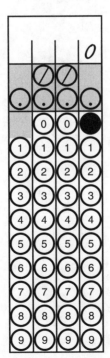

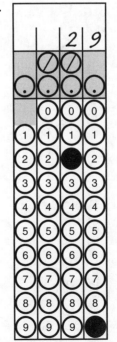

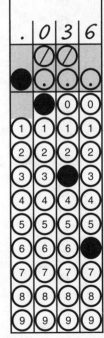

9. 5

10. 112

11. 30.7

12. 7

13. 3

14. 0

15. 29

16. .036

17.

18.

Section 4

1. D	10. B	19. A	28. E
2. B	11. B	20. A	29. D
3. C	12. D	21. C	30. B
4. D	13. C	22. A	31. E
5. B	14. B	23. C	32. D
6. E	15. C	24. D	33. E
7. B	16. E	25. C	34. A
8. E	17. D	26. B	35. D
9. C	18. C	27. B	

Section 5

1. B	7. B	13. D	19. A
2. A	8. C	14. C	20. D
3. C	9. E	15. C	21. E
4. A	10. A	16. B	22. D
5. E	11. C	17. B	23. A
6. D	12. D	18. D	24. C

Section 6

1. A	6. C	11. D	16. B
2. C	7. D	12. B	17. C
3. D	8. E	13. D	18. B
4. B	9. A	14. C	19. C
5. C	10. B	15. D	20. C

Section 7

1. B	6. E	11. A	16. A
2. A	7. E	12. E	17. C
3. E	8. D	13. B	18. C
4. B	9. B	14. C	19. B
5. D	10. E	15. D	

Section 8

1. D	5. D	9. E	13. E
2. B	6. B	10. D	14. C
3. C	7. D	11. B	15. B
4. D	8. C	12. B	16. A

Section 9

1. C	5. B	9. C	13. B
2. D	6. C	10. D	14. C
3. B	7. D	11. B	
4. E	8. B	12. C	

Detailed Answers

Section 2

Question 1: Answer **D** is correct.
Explanation: Knowing the definition of all five words certainly helps complete this sentence correctly. All five words could be used, logically, but only one best fulfills the logic of the sentence, and that's agrarian. An agrarian society is an agricultural society and therefore, would have little use for an engineer. The right answer is the best answer. At first glance, "barren" seems good; you might have trouble finding a job in a barren spot. However, "agrarian" contrasts more specifically with "engineer," so that word is better. Always search for the best response, not the first response that seems to work. Answers A, B, C, and E are all incorrect for the same reason—they offer nothing to help explain why an engineer would find it difficult to find employment.

Question 2: Answer **E** is correct.
Explanation: The word "despite" at the beginning of the sentence is your main clue. You know that despite their size, the girls are otherwise healthy. Answer A is incorrect because it's illogical—"petite" is an antonym for "enormous," not a synonym. In this case, the sentence requires a synonym or logical adjective. Answers B and D are incorrect. Although "petite" and "small" both work, neither "fragile" nor "frail" does. The second word must have a positive connotation to match healthy. Answer C is incorrect, although logically it might work. Remember, you want the best answer, not the first answer that might work. Answer D is incorrect for the same reason as B.

Question 3: Answer **B** is correct.
Explanation: The clues in this sentence aren't as obvious as the first two, but they're there, even though the two thoughts don't seem to be related. You should be able to glean the following: Alfred Nobel spoke and wrote many languages, and he wrote his own business letters. If you can ascertain that much of the sentence's purpose, answer B is easy to spot. If not, eliminating the other responses should help. Answer A is incorrect. Although "accomplished" might work logically, "speak" doesn't because the statement discusses letters, not public speaking. Admittedly, the word "speak" could fill in, but there's probably a better choice and you should keep looking. Answer C is incorrect. Both words could fit in a pinch, but neither really represents the thoughts. "Knowledgeable" is a bit contrived in this context, and "compose" suggests more original input than would be required for someone writing business letters for someone else. Answers D and E are incorrect because the sentence suggests that the first word is positive—"lacking" and "illiterate" are both illogical in this context.

Question 4: Answer **A** is correct.
Explanation: You know right from the start that the sentence is discussing more than one technology, so the word "combined" is the most logical choice for the first word, within the context of the entire sentence. In addition, the phrases "new crafts" and "the edge of space" are great clues, and "probe" completes that thought well. Answer B is

incorrect. There's no connection between abandoning the technologies and reaching new frontiers. Answer C is incorrect. Both words could be used, but the words in answer A create a stronger, more descriptive sentence. Answer C isn't the best response. Answer D is incorrect because "refurbished" is illogical in this context. You don't refurbish technology—you refurbish machinery. Answer E is incorrect. Like answer C, the words could fit, but within the context of the entire sentence, they're not the best response. Significantly, the word "pooled" means to gather, not necessarily to combine. In addition, you probably wouldn't use rocket and jet technologies to study outer space. You'd use those technologies to visit space, or at least try.

Question 5: Answer **C** is the correct answer.
Explanation: This sentence is a bit trickier than the others, but you must keep the context of the entire sentence in mind while reading. After reading the sentence, you should be able to ascertain that the first word refers to persons who did not actually attend a college. Answers A and B are incorrect because it's safe to assume that an educator would've completed college. Even the early colleges had standards that required a certain level of academic success for educators. Besides, the word "appreciated" within context is a bit illogical. Why would a person who didn't appreciate college become a professor? Answer D is incorrect—it's easy to determine that the first word probably refers to nonstudents. The words themselves almost fit logically, but even if you miss the nonstudent clue, this response simply isn't the best response. Answer E is incorrect because it's illogical. There's no way to support the idea that employees had faith in education as an ideal.

Question 6: Answer **D** is correct.
Explanation: Answer A is incorrect because the mention of history in the passages is only passing. Answer B is incorrect; the

passages assert that software is important, but they don't demonstrate this point. Answer C is incorrect because there is no material on actual computer programming in the passage. Answer E is incorrect because neither passage calls for any specific changes. Only answer D fits both passages.

Question 7: Answer **A** is correct.
Explanation: Recognizing that the two passages are directly opposed to one another lets you eliminate the relatively positive statements in answers C, D, and E. On the other hand, answer B is too negative; there's no evidence in the writing here that the author of passage 2 would want to convict the author of passage 1 of a crime. Answer A is a good way to state the disagreements between the two.

Question 8: Answer **C** is correct.
Explanation: Answer A is incorrect because the passage doesn't mention experience at all. Answer B is incorrect because the author of this passage opposed software patents rather than advocating them. Answer D is incorrect; there's no way to tell which software either passage is talking about specifically. Answer E may be tempting, but it's not justified by the actual content of the passages; be careful not to interject your own prejudices into the exam. Only answer C is taken from the passages themselves.

Question 9: Answer **E** is correct.
Explanation: The key to answering this one correctly is to sort out the question. The author of the second passage is in favor of patents and copyrights on software, and so would be unhappy if they were discontinued. This eliminates answers A and B, which are not states of unhappiness. The author could be confused or tired (answers C and D), but there's no reason to think so. Answer E fits: "Crestfallen" is a synonym for "dejected."

Question 10: Answer **D** is correct.
Explanation: Answer A is clearly untrue because the passage goes on to discuss the

remains of the civilization that have been found. Answers B and C are true statements, but they're not a good fit for the quoted phrase. Answer E is also supported by the passage, but is not a meaning for the quoted phrase. Only answer D explains what the author meant.

Question 11: Answer **D** is correct.
Explanation: The paragraph containing this sentence recites a number of facts intended to show how well organized the Indus River civilization was. Answers A and E may be true in the broader context of history, but cannot be inferred from this passage alone. Answer B is there to catch the unwary student who misreads the meaning of the word "uniform." Answer C is implied by the passage, but not the main point of the sentence.

Question 12: Answer **C** is correct.
Explanation: There is no evidence in the passage that the author is considering alternative explanations or not summarizing the latest research, which eliminates answers A and D. The tone of the passage indicates that it is meant to teach the reader, so answer B is not correct. Answer E could be correct, but it's too grandiose for what's presented in the passage. You don't know how the authors feel about archaeology as a whole, only how they interpret the evidence in this one particular case.

Question 13: Answer **C** is correct.
Explanation: Even if you didn't know before the exam that "polytheistic" means "worshipping many gods," you should be able to take a good guess at this one by recognizing that the root word "poly" means "many."

Question 14: Answer **B** is correct.
Explanation: One of the overarching themes of the passage is how little we actually know about this particular civilization. Answer A is incorrect because the civilization lasted for a thousand years. Answers C and D are not justified by the passage; it doesn't allow one

to draw any conclusions about modern civilization. Answer E is incorrect as well; although the group with horses defeated the group with writing, this does not imply that horses are more important than writing.

Question 15: Answer **B** is correct.
Explanation: In the context of the passage, the departing fishermen are commenting on the fact that the one man will be left at camp alone—that is, with only an imaginary companion. None of the other answers match this meaning.

Question 16: Answer **D** is correct because the phrase indicates figuratively that the man is scared. **Explanation:** Answer A is wrong because the shadows are not about to literally assault the man. Answer B is incorrect because there's nothing ironic about the phrase, and answer C is incorrect because this isn't an exaggeration; the shadows are not about to slightly assault him. Answer E doesn't fit the tone of the paragraph.

Question 17: Answer **A** is correct.
Explanation: By substituting the proposed answers in place of the word "magnified" in the sentence, you should be able to see that "emphasized" makes the most sense: The red of the fire made the red of the bear's mouth stand out. It did not literally make the mouth larger.

Question 18: Answer **D** is correct.
Explanation: In the context of the paragraph, it's clear that the boots of fear are meant to show the transition from standing still to "darting around the campfire." Answer A is incorrect because the man was not paralyzed. Answer B is incorrect because there's nothing in the paragraph speaking to lack of feeling. Answer C is incorrect because the man didn't conquer his fear. Answer E is incorrect because, although the story seems unlikely, it does not involve magical elements.

Question 19: Answer **E** is correct.
Explanation: Here again the easiest way to get the correct answer is to substitute the explanations for the original phrase. The man has been presented as the sympathetic figure and the bear as the villain throughout the piece, but the bear is gaining. Thus, the good guy is not winning.

Question 20: Answer **D** is correct.
Explanation: The bear is a formidable opponent. This one is a matter of the tone of the passage. The bear didn't do a bad job of snarling, which eliminates answers B and E. Answer A is not strong enough for the sense of a passage that also includes phrases such as "jowls dripping." Answer C is almost true, but the bear inspires fear rather than awe.

Question 21: Answer **A** is correct.
Explanation: The actions and thoughts portrayed for the little man all indicate that he thinks his life is in danger. Answer B is incorrect; although the bear does something playful in this paragraph, it is not the main point of the paragraph. Answer C is incorrect because we're not given any information to evaluate whether the dark is scarier than the daytime. Answer D is incorrect because the bear's actions don't arise from the party being split. Answer E might be a reasonable conclusion, but the lines indicated are more about the little man than about nature.

Question 22: Answer **C** is correct.
Explanation: The sentence containing this phrase is about the bear's roar, and it includes flowery language to tell you that the roar was very loud indeed. None of the other answers fits this sentence.

Question 23: Answer **E** is correct.
Explanation: Although Crane's language is characteristically overblown, the meaning should be clear. Just substitute simpler words for "overwhelmed" and "interrogations," and you'll get the right answer. The other choices are grammatically correct but change the meaning of the sentence if you insert them.

Question 24: Answer **D** is correct.
Explanation: This sort of question is best answered by outlining the passage as you go along so that you can pick out its main points. If asked to summarize the story, you might come up with something like "a man is left alone by his comrades to face a bear, but he survives and the joke is on them." This is close to "he who laughs last, laughs best," whereas the other choices don't fit the story.

Section 3

Question 1: Answer **C** is correct.
Explanation: Start by calculating the value of n. If 15% of n is 45, then $n = 45 \div .15 = 300$. Then you know that m is 250% of n, so $m = 2.5n = 750$. Finally, you can use this to calculate 12% of m: $.12m = .12(750) = 90$.

Question 2: Answer **B** is correct.
Explanation: If $\angle ACB = 60°$ and $\angle CBA = 90°$, then $\angle BAC = 30°$ (because you know that the sum of the angles in any triangle is 180°). Then $\angle CED$ must be 30° as well because the figure ACED is a parallelogram, and the opposite angles of a parallelogram are equal.

Question 3: Answer **E** is correct.
Explanation: If the black beans represent 75% of the total, the white beans are 25%, or $\frac{1}{4}$, of the total. Thus the total number of beans is $16 \times 4 = 64$.

Question 4: Answer **D** is correct.
Explanation: First consider the prime factors of 210. $210 = 2 \times 3 \times 5 \times 7$. The value of b must be some combination of these factors. But you know that a is $14 = 2 \times 7$ and the GCF of a and b is 7. This tells you that 7 must be one of the factors of b, whereas 2 cannot be a factor of b (otherwise the GCF of the two integers would be 14). What about the factors 3 and 5? These *must* be factors of b; otherwise, they would not appear in the factorization of the LCM. Thus the answer is $3 \times 5 \times 7 = 105$.

Question 5: Answer **E** is correct.
Explanation: To solve this, note that the four triangles make up a square (this must be the case because they are identical) and that each of these triangles is a 45°-45°-90° right triangle. Also note that the area of the shaded region is the area of the circle less the area of the square. Getting the area of the square is easy: If one side of the square (AB) is 2 units, the area of the square is $(2\sqrt{2})^2 = 8$ units. Now consider the circle. To get the area of the circle, you need to know its radius. If $AB = 2\sqrt{2}$, AO = 2 units—you can remember the relation for the special triangle or work this out via the Pythagorean Theorem by noting that AO and BO are the same length. So the area of the circle is $\pi 2^2 = 4\pi$, and the area of the shaded region is $4\pi - 8$.

Question 6: Answer **A** is correct.
Explanation: To answer this question, look at the difference between the stacks of cars for 1985 and 1987. There are three cars different, and the legend tells you that each car stands for 50,000 sales. So the total difference of 2 years is 150,000 sales, for an average of $150,000 \div 2 = 75,000$.

Question 7: Answer **B** is correct.
Explanation: Set B must contain all the elements from the intersection, so you know that it must at least contain the elements 7, 11, and 22. This eliminates answers C, D,

and E. You also know that every element in the union must come from either A or B or both. But set A does not contain 14 or 17, so these elements must be part of set B.

Question 8: Answer **C** is correct.
Explanation: By inspecting the equation of line ℓ, you know that its y-intercept is 4, so the y-intercept of line m must be either 2 or 6. If the two lines are parallel, they must have the same slope. Thus, the equation of m is either $y = 2x + 2$ or $y = 2x + 6$.

Question 9: Add the two equations to get a third equation, $2a^2 = 50$. Divide by two to get $a^2 = 25$. Thus, $a = \sqrt{25}$. Remember, there are two possible square roots of 25, but the grids do not allow you to enter negative numbers. So **grid 5** to receive credit.

Question 10: To answer this question, note that the angles along a line always add up to 180° and substitute the given value for angle y:

$$x + y + 2y + y = 180$$
$$x + 4y = 180$$
$$x + 4(17) = 180$$
$$x + 68 = 180$$
$$x = 112$$

Grid 112 to receive credit.

Question 11: Use the percent change formula to figure out the answer:

$$\text{Change} = \frac{(\text{final} - \text{starting})}{\text{starting}} \times 100\%$$

$$\text{Change} = \frac{(68 - 52)}{52} \times 100\%$$

$$\text{Change} = \frac{16}{52} \times 100\%$$

$$\text{Change} = 30.76\%$$

Remember, if there are more digits than will fit on the grid, you can either round or truncate the answer. So grid **30.7** or **30.8** to receive credit.

Question 12: The domain of a function is all points at which the function is defined. $f(x)$ is undefined when the denominator is zero, which happens at $x = 7$. **Grid 7** to receive credit.

Question 13: First consider the right triangle $\triangle ABF$. From the Pythagorean Theorem, $BF = \sqrt{(1 + 1)} = \sqrt{2}$. Now consider the right triangle $\triangle BCF$. Again, you can apply the Pythagorean Theorem:

CF is one side of the square, so the area of the square is $(\sqrt{3})^2 = 3$. **Grid 3** to receive credit.

Question 14: To calculate the median, add

$$CF = \sqrt{1^2 + \left(\sqrt{2}\right)^2}$$

$$CF = \sqrt{3}$$

the numbers and divide by their count: $(4 + 17 + 11 + 14 + 3 + 2 + 8 + 22 + 18) \div 9 = 11$. To calculate the mode, you must put the numbers in order—2, 3, 4, 8, 11, 14, 17, 18, 22—and then pick the number in the middle, which is 11. In this case, the median and the mode are the same, so the difference between the two is zero. **Grid 0** to receive credit.

Question 15: Start with the term inside the parentheses, and don't let the special symbols throw you. From the definition, $3><4 = 2 \times 3 + 2 \times 4 = 14$. Then $14><.5 = 2 \times 14 + 2 \times .5 = 29$. **Grid 29** to receive credit.

Explanation: Being a junior and having red hair are independent events, so you can just multiple the probabilities together: $.3 \times .12 = .036$. **Grid .036** to receive credit.

Question 17: The graph of $g(x + 3)$ is simply the graph of $g(x)$ shifted three units to the left. The graphs show the positive zeros of $g(x)$ as 2, 4, 6, and so on. If you subtract three from these, you get zeros of –1, 1, 3, and so on. The first positive number in this set is 1, so **grid 1** to receive credit.

Question 18: Each line from a point of the star through the center of the star is an axis of reflective symmetry because the figure won't change if it is reflected across that line. **Grid 5** to receive credit.

Section 4

Question 1: Answer **D** is correct.
Explanation: The phrase "in addition to" indicates a singular subject, so the verb must match the noun in number. Answer A is incorrect because the phrase isn't correct as is. Answer B is incorrect because it provides new words that offer nothing to the sentence, and doesn't use the appropriate verb. Answer C is incorrect because it uses the wrong verb and there's no reason to change "to" to "for." Answer E is incorrect because there's no reason to change "to" to "for."

Question 2: Answer **B** is correct.
Explanation: The verb tense isn't parallel between the two phrases. The first phrase implies something is going to happen, but then the action in the second phrase has already occurred. It doesn't matter which tense you change, but they must match. Answer A is incorrect because the phrase isn't correct as is. Answer C is incorrect because it still uses the wrong verb tense, and there's nothing wrong with the subject's number—it is irrelevant in this sentence. Answers D and E are incorrect. There's no reason to change the verb, just the verb's tense. In addition, there's no reason to change the subject's number.

Question 3: Answer **C** is correct.
Explanation: A definite noun and its antecedent must agree in number and kind. In this case, you're dealing with kind, a personal or impersonal entity. The pronoun "that" is referring to a definite noun, the

man. "That" is used with indefinite pronouns. The correct pronoun is "who." Answer A is incorrect because the phrase isn't correct as is. Answers B and D are incorrect because they repeat the same error as the original sentence. In addition, answer B changes the noun, which is unnecessary. Answer D changes "the" to "that," which is unnecessary. Answer E is incorrect even though it uses the right pronoun. There's no reason to change the noun. Remember, some of the responses may seem correct, but introduce new errors. In this case, both C and E are grammatically correct, but C is the most correct because there's no reason to change the noun as answer E does.

Question 4: Answer **D** is correct.

Explanation: Interrogative pronouns, such as "when," refer to a definite pronoun. As is, the sentence suggests that vaporization is a time, but it's a noun. The antecedent, vaporization, doesn't answer the question of time. By adding the verb "occurs," you correct the problem. Answer A is incorrect because the phrase isn't correct as is. Answers C and E are incorrect even though they might be considered grammatically correct. They are too wordy and awkward. Answer B is incorrect because the resulting sentence would be grammatically incorrect.

Question 5: Answer **B** is correct.

Explanation: The preposition "up" isn't necessary. Answer A is incorrect because the phrase isn't correct as is. Answer C is incorrect because it doesn't omit "up." Answers D and E are incorrect because there's no need to change the verb.

Question 6: Answer **E** is correct.

Explanation: The verb "concerned" requires the preposition "about," not "with." Answer A is incorrect because the phrase isn't correct as is. Answers B and D are incorrect because they don't use the correct preposition. Answer C is incorrect because it changes the sentence's meaning, even though it uses the correct preposition.

Question 7: Answer **B** is correct.

Explanation: The adverb "badly" modifies "feels," meaning she's not a good feeler. The adjective "bad" modifies the pronoun "she," and that is correct. Remember, as long as you use the word "feel" or "feels" as a linking verb, you can use "good," "well," and "bad" as an adjective. In Chapter 3, "The Critical Reading Section: Sentence Completions," we told you not to worry about the use of bad/badly and good/well because it won't show up on the exam. But, you should still know how to use them correctly. If you use them incorrectly on your essay, it could count against you. Answer A is incorrect because the phrase isn't correct as is. Answer C is incorrect because changing the verb's tense doesn't correct the problem. Answer D is incorrect because it adds more words without correcting the problem. Answer E is incorrect because it's wordy, albeit grammatically correct.

Question 8: Answer **E** is correct.

Explanation: When using the comparative form of an adjective, add "er." Answer A is incorrect because the phrase isn't correct as is. The sentence's intent is clear—the best response is to correct the comparative form, not remove it. Answers B and C are incorrect because they introduce other grammatical mistakes. Answer D is incorrect even though it's grammatically correct. Introducing the phrase "this morning" is unnecessary in order to correct the sentence.

Question 9: Answer **C** is correct.

Explanation: The subject of the opening modifying phrase should follow the phrase. Answer A is incorrect because the phrase isn't correct as is. Answers B and D are incorrect because there's no need to omit the phrase "in reality." In fact, doing so weakens the sentence. Answer E is incorrect because changing the preposition changes the sentence's meaning.

Question 10: Answer **B** is correct.
Explanation: The serial items aren't parallel. Answer A is incorrect because the phrase isn't correct as is. Answers C, D and E are incorrect. The phrase "little but" isn't the problem. In addition, D actually changes the sentence's meaning. Answer E is incorrect, changing "little" to "nothing" doesn't help the parallelism.

Question 11: Answer **B** is correct.
Explanation: The verb phrase "named Myra" is misplaced. As is, it seems to modify Virginia. Answer A is incorrect because the phrase isn't correct as is. Although acceptable grammatically, Virginia belongs with Myra, not the Mud River. The Mud River may flow through several states, not just Virginia. Answers C, D, and E are all incorrect because they omit important information.

Question 12: Answer **D** is correct.
Explanation: The pronoun "their" does not match the indefinite pronoun, "everyone," in number. "Everyone" is singular; "their" is plural.

> The park is usually more crowded and noisier on nice days when everyone shows up with <u>his or her</u> kids and dogs.

Question 13: Answer **C** is correct.
Explanation: You should avoid clichés. The phrase is also an idiom, but in either case, you could completely omit the phrase and not harm the integrity of the sentence.

> We thought the birds might reject this new seed, but none of the seed is left.

Question 14: Answer **B** is correct.
Explanation: The pronoun "he" isn't necessary. Of course, if you omit the pronoun, you must change the tense of the verb "wrote." Or, you could separate the two complete thoughts with a semicolon because in this case, the second thought develops the first.

> Lincoln Steffens was the pioneer investigative reporter, writing fearlessly on the abuses of government.

> Lincoln Steffens was the pioneer investigative reporter; he wrote fearlessly on the abuses of government.

Question 15: Answer **C** is correct.
Explanation: The verb tense in phase C is incorrect. The first verb phrase (B) is perfect present; the second (C) is progressive past. Verb tense must be parallel throughout the sentence. As a side note, if you were really using this sentence in an essay, you would want to define de facto.

> Until Woodrow Wilson was elected President, the United States had been in the habit of recognizing de facto governments.

Question 16: Answer **E** is correct.
Explanation: This sentence is a bit wordy, but there are no grammatical mistakes.

Question 17: Answer **D** is correct.
Explanation: The comparative phrase "than education" should follow its introductory phrase. You might be tempted to delete B, but there's nothing wrong with it. You should avoid repetition generally, but occasionally it works well to emphasize a point.

> Success in business, any business, no matter how small, played a more important role than education in the immigrant's daily life.

Question 18: Answer **C** is correct.
Explanation: Both of the ending preposi-tional phrases "of them" and "for herself" could be considered unnecessary. However, removing "for herself" changes the tone of the sentence a tad too much.

Gems are priceless in her culture, but she kept none for herself.

Question 19: Answer **A** is correct.
Explanation: The phrase "is to be" is passive. Use active voice. She isn't performing the action, which is the induction. In this case, the subject, whoever is doing the induction, is implied.

We will induct her as an initiate at noon on the first Sunday of March.

Question 20: Answer **A** is correct.
Explanation: Although it isn't grammatically incorrect, you should never use the phrase "in conclusion." Your reader knows you're done—if the reader doesn't know you're done, the rest of the essay needs a thorough edit.

Bertha von Suttner profoundly influenced Alfred Nobel, despite the fact that she married someone else.

Question 21: Answer **C** is correct.
Explanation: You should consider deleting this redundant phrase altogether. It is unnecessary and makes an already wordy sentence worse. This problem may not be readily apparent, but the process of elimina-tion might help. Because none of the other phrases appear to have any grammatical problems, omit each phrase from the sentence, one-by-one. The sentence is strong and stands fine without C.

In 1888, Massachusetts became the first state to use ballots that contained the names of all the candidates instead of using different colored ballots for each candidate.

Question 22: Answer **A** is correct.
Explanation: The first phrase is a misplaced participial phrase. This is easy to do when the subject is assumed, as it is in this subject. As is, the sentence literally means that the thunder and lightning were running madly through the forest.

She ran madly through the forest as the thunder shook the earth and the lightning pierced the night sky.

Question 23: Answer **C** is correct.
Explanation: A series of items should be parallel. None of the other verbs are modified by an adverb. To make the sentence parallel, omit "calmly."

Before you say something you'll regret, take a deep breathe, clear your mind, and count to 10.

Question 24: Answer **D** is correct.
Explanation: The pronoun "it" is too far from its antecedent "clock." Although you know perfectly well what "it" refers to, you should still replace the pronoun with a noun.

Cinderella looked at the clock but didn't realize it was midnight until she heard the clock chime.

Question 25: Answer **C** is correct.
Explanation: The pronoun "his" doesn't agree in number with "they." This is a tricky one because the phrase "to be the first" tends to make you think in singular terms.

Sam and Tom raced to the frozen Mississippi where they scrambled to be the first to don their skates and meet the ice.

Question 26: Answer **B** is correct.
Explanation: The verb phrase is passive. This one's a bit harder to find. The real subject of the sentence is "the fear," but the wording might make you think that "the excitement" is the subject.

> *The fear that the small and weak child might not survive the night challenged the excitement of the new baby's arrival.*

Question 27: Answer **B** is correct.
Explanation: This sentence would benefit from a transition, but "subsequently" is the wrong one. Transitions must match the tone of the sentence. "Subsequently" means in order of, not because of.

> *John had a talent for business and consequently met with great financial success, but he had little patience for family.*

Question 28: Answer **E** is correct because nothing is grammatically wrong with this sentence.

> *Samuel Clemens wrote under the pen name Mark Twain, which was a river-piloting term for deep, safe water.*

Question 29: Answer **D** is correct.
Explanation: The problem is the pronoun "they." First, it's unclear which antecedent "he" refers to, although you get the gist of the sentence. Second, "he" is singular. Is the word "any," which is used earlier in the sentence to modify the antecedent, singular or plural? Sometimes a word can be either singular or plural, and when that's the case, you must refer to the noun for more help. In this case, the noun is presidential nominations—plural. Besides, even in these days when political correctness is running amuck, it really is a bit insensitive to use the pronoun "he" in reference to the Supreme Court justices, even when it is grammatically correct. Although you won't run into this last problem on the exam, you might want to steer clear of it on the essay portion of your exam. Even though the readers are trained to look for specific keys, you never know when something that small might trigger a negative response.

> *The United States Constitution requires the Senate to confirm any presidential nominations to the Supreme Court before they can actually be sworn into office.*

Question 30: Answer **B** is correct.
Explanation: The two thoughts just don't mesh. It's okay to keep the sentence; it helps to develop the main thesis. However, the two phrases must be similar in subject and nature if you're going to use them in a comparative form. Answer A is incorrect; the sentence doesn't repeat the first; it helps develop the first. Answer C is incorrect; the sentence isn't too wordy. A long sentence is acceptable as long as all the words are truly needed. Answer D is incorrect. The mood needs to be set right at the beginning for this essay. Answer E is incorrect, although in the end, you might actually move this statement to the conclusion after you've decided whether you wanted to use "machinery" or "dance" as the subject.

Question 31: Answer **E** is correct.
Explanation: The passage needs to transition from the thesis—that life is a delicate balance—to the plight of the sea otters and what happened when the balance of their ecosystem was altered. Answer A is incorrect because the paragraph break, as is, is sound. Answer B is incorrect because it isn't true. Answers C and D are incorrect because neither sentence works as a transition. Sentence 7 has promise, but as is, won't do.

Question 32: Answer **D** is correct.
Explanation: A quick general statement is in order here to let the reader know that the explanation is coming. Answer A is incorrect; the sentence is important. Answer B is incorrect. You might replace the pronoun, but it won't improve the problem discussed in the question. Answer C is incorrect. The suggestion is a good one, but it doesn't resolve the problem in the question. Answer E is incorrect. The sentence is grammatically sound.

Question 33: Answer **E** is correct.
Explanation: Both would improve the sentence. Answer A is incorrect because it's incomplete. Remember, you're looking for the best answer, not the first one that works. Answer B is incorrect; you don't need two sentences when one will do. Answer C is incorrect; "feed" is vital to the whole discussion. Answer D is incorrect because it's incomplete.

Question 34: Answer **A** is correct.
Explanation: You need to make the point that they both share the same food source and that tipping the balance didn't favor one or the other, but actually devastated both populations. Answer B is incorrect. Combining the sentences would create a very long sentence, which is fine if it's clear and strong. However, sentence 9 already makes the point that the sea urchins eat kelp. Answer C is incorrect. Moving the sentence doesn't help the problem. Answer D is incorrect. Deleting the sentence won't resolve the problem of making the connection between the primary food source and the loss of balance.

Question 35: Answer **D** is correct.
Explanation: The passage still needs a lot of work—it needs a final paragraph to pull everything together. Answer A is incorrect because the passage isn't done. Answer B is incorrect. The fate might not be known. If it is, a sentence about it would be good, but it would not be the basis of the entire concluding paragraph. Answer C is incorrect because there's not a good transition into the concluding paragraph. Answer E is incorrect. Moving those sentences does set up a concluding paragraph, but you still need a final paragraph.

Section 5

Question 1: Answer **B** is correct.
Explanation: That sentence is the most logical. There's really no clue here—you either know the word or you don't. It would be difficult to guess. Process of elimination might help, but chances are, if you don't know the meaning of "exception," you won't know the other words. Answers A, C, D, and E are all incorrect because the thought would be illogical.

Question 2: Answer **A** is correct.
Explanation: The pair in answer A presents the most appropriate sentence. You must understand the nature of the word pledge and how you go about keeping a pledge—you honor a pledge. Answers B, C, and E are all incorrect because the words simply do not go together as well as A's. Answer D is incorrect because broken changes the meaning of the sentence.

Question 3: Answer **C** is correct.
Explanation: The pair in answer C presents the most logical sentence. If you're lucky enough to know Soviet history and politics, you could quickly eliminate answers A, B, D, and E because the equivalent office in the USSR is the General Secretary. If you don't know the Soviet political system, you can still use the process of elimination. Answer A is incorrect because it assumes that the assassin became the leader, and nothing in the sentence supports that. Although the sentence is logical enough, it isn't as strong as C. Answer B is incorrect because it's illogical.

If Gorbachev inaugurated Chernenko, the following phrase would be illogical. Answer D is incorrect because "preceded" is actually an antonym for "succeeded" in this context. Answer E is incorrect because it isn't as strong as the verb "succeeded."

Question 4: Answer **A** is correct.
Explanation: The second phrase lends a clue by referring to two time periods—year and decade. Thus, you should be able to deduce that the missing word has a connotation of measuring time, or at least time. Answers B, C, and D are incorrect. Even though they might all fit logically, none of them create the strongest sentence within the context of the second phrase. Answer E is incorrect because the sentence would be illogical.

Question 5: Answer **E** is correct.
Explanation: The two words in answer E work together to form the strongest possible sentence. The terms support one another. Answers A and B are incorrect. Their logic is sound enough, but the end result isn't as strong as E. Answer C is incorrect; "pondered" doesn't fit the tone of the sentence. Answer D is incorrect because "hullabaloo" has a connotation of chaos.

Question 6: Answer **D** is correct.
Explanation: Answer D most appropriately expresses the political structure. Answers A and B are incorrect. They are synonyms, but "dominion" is stronger. Answers C and E are incorrect because they change the meaning of the sentence.

Question 7: Answer **B** is correct.
Explanation: The terms in answer B support one another within the context of the sentence, using the most appropriate terms for the subject. Answers A, C, and D are incorrect. The paired words might create a logical sentence, but the words aren't as appropriate to the discussion as B. Answer E is incorrect because it uses the term "circumnavigate" incorrectly.

Question 8: Answer **C** is correct.
Explanation: It creates the most logical sentence. The second phrase, "safeguarding the rights of all citizens," is your best clue because "safeguarding" is a synonym for "bulwark." Answers A, B, and D are all incorrect. They might create a logical sentence, but the result is not as strong as C, given the context of the second phrase. Answer E is incorrect because it's illogical.

Question 9: Answer **E** is correct.
Explanation: These two areas encompass the two western frontiers in 1960. Answer A is incorrect because neither were considered frontiers in 1960. Answers B and C are incorrect because they are both incomplete. Answer D is incorrect because these areas were not considered a frontier.

Question 10: Answer **A** is correct.
Explanation: The crux of the entire paragraph is the emptiness of the area between the two existing frontiers. Answer B is incorrect because it isn't as specific as A. Answers C and D are incorrect—the discussion is of the land, not the people settling it. Answer E is incorrect. The paragraph isn't about discovering; it's a comparison of existing settlements and the empty land in between.

Question 11: Answer **C** is the most correct interpretation of the term "sexual license" within the context of the passage.
Explanation: Answer A is incorrect. The sexual revolution saw an increase in promiscuity, but it wasn't the essence of the philosophy. Answer B is incorrect because no one can escape the consequences. Answer D is incorrect because some of the behavior was very irresponsible, even by today's standards. Answer E is incorrect because prostitution plays no part in the philosophy.

Question 12: Answer **D** is the most correct answer. **Explanation:** There was no cure for AIDS. The only way to slow the spread was to educate the next generation. Answer A is incorrect because it's incomplete. Answers B and C are incorrect because they're not supported by the passage. Answer E is incomplete because it's vague.

Question 13: Answer Ⓓ is correct.
Explanation: The author states that Washington became convinced of the colonists' position but that he still hoped that the British would realize they were making a "mistake" and that war only arrived "at length." Answer A is incorrect because that contradicts the assertion that Washington was not a sudden clamorer for independence. Answer B is incorrect because the information in the passage is that Washington was asked to command the army, not that he lobbied for the post. Answer C is incorrect because the author made it clear that his devotion to independence was a gradual process. Answer E is incorrect because the mistake mentioned in the passage is that of the British, not of the colonists.

Question 14: Answer Ⓒ is correct.
Explanation: The best way to get this one right is to substitute the given answers back into the original sentence and to see which of them does not change the meaning of the paragraph. The word "scrupulous" is also a clue that the correct answer involves making a principled choice, which only fits answer C.

Question 15: Answer Ⓒ is correct.
Explanation: To get this one right, follow the author's argument: Washington insisted on respect and dignity for the office. His enemies sneered at this. Things might have been different were Jefferson the first president. This makes it clear that the reason for mentioning Jefferson is to note that different men would have left a different stamp on the presidency—and rules out answer E, which directly contradicts that assertion. Answers A, B, and D are potentially true, but they are not directly supported by the passage.

Question 16: Answer Ⓑ is correct.
Explanation: The three monarchs that the author lists are respectively, vicious, crazy, and insane. The author is writing in glowing terms about Washington, so it is unlikely that he would say anything positive about such a collection of monarchs. Answer B is the only answer that casts these monarchs in a negative light.

Question 17: Answer Ⓑ is correct.
Explanation: The phrase referring to a deficiency follows directly after a sentence stating that Washington had a lack of imagination. The other answers are incorrect; they all contain words from the paragraph, but none that are referred to from that phrase.

Question 18: Answer Ⓓ is correct.
Explanation: The author of the passage states that well-intentioned people argued that Washington never swore in order to portray him as a faultless being, and then goes on to give evidence that Washington swore. The logical conclusion from this set of statements is that Washington was not a faultless being. Answer A is incorrect because of the evidence presented that Washington swore. Answers B and E are incorrect because those are statements about the well-intentioned people, not about Washington. Answer C is incorrect because the portion of the sentence about attracting attention refers to arguments, not to Washington.

Question 19: Answer Ⓐ is correct.
Explanation: A knowledge of the word "propriety" (which means "the quality of being proper") will help you focus in on the right answer immediately; only answers A and D concern what is right. From the construction of the sentence, A is a better choice because the sentence is not solely about the speaker.

Question 20: Answer **D** is correct.
Explanation: The author of the passage argues that Washington maintained an unruffled spirit despite his love for life because of his faith in an afterlife. The key word "but" tips you off that he feels this faith is necessary for the unruffled spirit. Answer A is contradicted because the passage says Washington enjoyed life even though he regarded death with calmness. Answer B is incorrect because no connection is stated between the love for life and the courage. Answer C is incorrect because the courage referred to in the passage is not tied to the judgment of posterity. Answer E is incorrect because the passage's author doesn't tell readers what they should believe; it only states what Washington did believe.

Question 21: Answer **E** is correct.
Explanation: The author of passage 2 goes to some effort to portray Washington as a human being with human failings, even though he also mentions superior qualities that Washington had. By contrast, the final paragraph of passage 1 paints Washington as an almost superhuman figure. Thus the author of passage 2 would probably think the author of passage 1 was overstating the case. Answer A is incorrect because the paragraph is a matter of opinion, not fact. Answer B is incorrect because it's exactly the reverse of the truth. Answer C is incorrect because no humor is implied. Answer D is incorrect because "prescient" means "having knowledge of the future," which is inappropriate here.

Question 22: Answer **D** is correct.
Explanation: Passage 1 speaks of Washington's silence in the first paragraph (where the author calls him taciturn), and passage 2 mentions Washington's silence at the start of its second paragraph. Answers B and E are true of the first passage, but Washington's courage and dignity in office are not mentioned in the second passage. Answers A and C are true of the second passage, but Washington's temper and faith are not mentioned by the first author.

Question 23: Answer **A** is correct.
Explanation: The author of the first passage is mainly concerned with identifying Washington's place in the broad sweep of history, whereas the second passage provides a more personal evaluation of Washington as a man. Answer B is incorrect because neither passage gives preference to acts over words. Answer C is incorrect because both authors credit Washington as being a victorious military leader. Answers D and E are incorrect because passage 1, not passage 2, concentrates more heavily on those areas.

Question 24: Answer **C** is correct.
Explanation: The first passage takes a very positive view of Washington and cites his neighbors and acquaintances to support this view. There's no hint of scandal in anything the first author says, nor any indication that he views Washington as imperfect. Answers A, D, and E are incorrect because they assume the truth of the scandals. Answer B is incorrect because there's no indication that the author of the passage would like to hide evidence.

Section 6

Question 1: Answer **A** is correct.
Explanation: To solve, multiply the second equation by –2 and add it to the first equation. This cancels out the x term, and the remaining equation is 3y = 9. Divide by 3 to confirm y = 3.

Question 2: Answer **C** is correct.
Explanation: The acute angles of an isosceles right triangle are each 45°. (If you don't remember this, you can determine it by knowing the total angles in the triangle add up to 180°—the right angle itself is 90°, and the other two angles are equal.) Because ∠x and ∠ACB are alternating interior angles of a line through B and C cutting across parallel lines, they must be equal. So x is also 45°.

Question 3: Answer **D** is correct.
Explanation: Remember, to raise a power to another power, you multiply the exponents together, so answer D is equivalent to 3^9. This is clearly much larger than any of the other choices, though you can confirm that with your calculator if you're unsure of the result (which is 19,683).

Question 4: Answer **B** is correct.
Explanation: You should be able to answer this one as fast as you can read the question; don't get tricked into performing any calculations or drawing anything. Two points in the plane always define precisely one line.

Question 5: Answer **C** is correct.
Explanation: You don't actually need the graph to answer this question. Start from what you know and reason to what you need: If there are 20 mammals and 4 times as many birds as mammals, there are 80 birds. If there are $\frac{3}{4}$ as many reptiles as mammals, there are 60 reptiles. If there are the same number of reptiles and fish, there are 60 fish.

Question 6: Answer **C** is correct.
Explanation: The easiest way to solve this one is probably to just write down a list of prime numbers and inspect to see which set of four sums to about 72. The first few primes are 2, 3, 5, 7, 11, 13, 17, 19, 23, 29, and 31. A little work with your calculator will show that 13 + 17 + 19 + 23 = 72. Then take a look at the question—it asks for the smallest of the four, so the answer is 13.

Question 7: Answer **D** is correct.
Explanation: By the Pythagorean Theorem, AC is $\sqrt{(3^2 + 4^2)}$ = 5. (You may also just recognize the 3-4-5 triangle.) If the center of the circle lies on this line, AC is a diameter of the circle, and the circumference is π times the diameter of the circle.

Question 8: Answer **E** is correct.
Explanation: If the mean of all 10 numbers is 18, the sum of all 10 numbers is 180 (because the mean is the sum divided by the count). Similarly, the sum of the remaining 7 numbers is 7 × 22 = 154. The three removed numbers must account for the difference between 180 and 154, which is 26.

Question 9: Answer **A** is correct.
Explanation: If the answer isn't immediately evident, you can substitute x and y into the function definition for each answer to simplify. Answer A evaluates to 18, B to 0, C to 9, D to 0, and E to 0. Thus A is largest.

Question 10: Answer **B** is correct.
Explanation: Because the triangles are similar, their sides have a constant ratio. From the information given, BC = 2. Because BD = 1, this means that the large triangle is twice as large as the small triangle. Thus DE = .5(AC) = .5(1.5) = .75. The area of CDEF is then .75 × 1 = .75.

Question 11: Answer **D** is correct.
Explanation: You can use the information about the intersections to determine two points on the line by finding the corresponding points on the curve. For x = –1, x² = 1, and for x = 3, x² = 9. So (–1, 1) and (3, 9) are two points on the curve. Now recognize from the equation that the desired quantity, *a*, is the slope of the line. You can figure the slope from the expression "rise over run" as follows:

$$a = \frac{(9-1)}{(3--1)}$$

$$a = \frac{(9-1)}{(3+1)}$$

$$a = \frac{8}{4}$$

$$a = 2$$

Question 12: Answer **B** is correct.
Explanation: Start by considering *z*. 3 🍎 z = 5 means |3–z| = 5. From that, 3–z = 5 or 3–z = –5, giving two possible values for *z* (–2 and 8). Now take each of these two possible *z* values and repeat the process for *w*. This leads to four possible equations for *w*:

- –2 – w = 2
- –2 – w = –2
- 8 – w = 2
- 8 – w = –2

The four possible values of *w* are then –4, 0, 6, and 10. Only one of these appears in the answer set, so B is the correct answer.

Question 13: Answer **D** is correct.
Explanation: Knowing the zeroes of the polynomial lets you immediately determine that its factors are x + 4 and x + 2. This means that the actual polynomial f(x) = (x + 4)(x + 2) = x² + 6x + 8. So f(9) = 9² + 6(9) + 8 = 143.

Question 14: Answer **C** is correct.
Explanation: When tossing a coin eight times, there are eight different ways in

which you can get a single head: The first toss may come up heads, or the second, and so on. The eight tosses are independent events each with two possible states, so the total number of different possible results is 2⁸ = 256. The probability of a single head is then

$$\frac{8}{256} = \frac{1}{32}$$

Question 15: Answer **D** is correct.
Explanation: The volume of a right circular cylinder is πr²h. (This is one of the formulas that the SAT gives you at the start of each math section.) The cylinder in the question has a diameter of 2 units, so its radius is 1 unit. With a height of 2, that means its volume is 2π. For a cube to have the same volume, its side must be the cube root of this quantity, which is answer D.

Question 16: Answer **B** is correct.
Explanation: The two white faces are opposite one another on the cube. This means that they cannot be adjacent to one another when the cube is flattened out to the plane, no matter how the flattening is done.

Question 17: Answer **C** is correct.
Explanation: If *m* and *n* are even integers, their sum and difference must also be even integers. But (m + n)/2 can be odd—for example, substitute m = 4 and n = 2 to get 3, which is an odd number.

Question 18: Answer **B** is correct.
Explanation: Start by calculating the area of the entire circle. From the formula A = πr², this area is 25π. The sector is thus $\frac{1}{5}$ of the circle, and its arc must be $\frac{1}{5}$ of the total circumference. Calculate the circumference from the formula c = πd = 2πr. The circumference is thus 10π, so the length of the arc must be 2π.

Question 19: Answer **C** is correct.
Explanation: There are $30 \times 29 \times 28 =$ 24,360 ways to select three books from the shelf. But in composing sets, the order of books doesn't matter. For each set of three books, there are six different ways to get the set; if you call the books A, B, and C, they are

- A B C
- A C B
- B A C
- B C A
- C A B
- C B A

So the final answer is $24,360 \div 6 = 4,060$.

Question 20: Answer **C** is correct.
Explanation: If the diameter of the circle is an integer, its radius is an exact multiple of .5. Given the formula for the area of a circle, $A = \pi r^2$, you know that $r = \sqrt{(A/\pi)}$. For A = 10, this means r = 1.79 is the largest radius that would work. So the possible radii that will work here are 1.5, 1.0, and .5.

Section 7

Question 1: Answer **B** is the most correct answer. **Explanation:** Corrosive chemicals have the potential to be dangerous if they touch your skin or get in your eyes. Answers A, C, and D are all incorrect because they create illogical statements. Answer E is incorrect because "acrid" doesn't fulfill the sentence's purpose. Chemicals may stink, but smell alone won't hurt you.

Question 2: Answer **A** is the most appropriate response. **Explanation:** You might expect the public to be mistrustful and cautious about any politician's promises, not just those involved in scandal. Answers B, C, and E are

incorrect because they aren't believable within the context of the sentence. Answer D is incorrect because it's illogical—being silent is probably the last thing the public would be.

Question 3: Answer **E** is correct.
Explanation: It creates the strongest most logical sentence of all the sets. Answer A is incorrect because the clerk complained about the work—surely the clerk wouldn't find the work relaxing. Answer B is incorrect because it's a tad illogical. Reading illegible symbols doesn't sound like dangerous work unless you're in the middle of a science fiction melt-down. Sometimes you just have to apply a little common sense. Answer C is incorrect because "impenetrable" is an inappropriate adjective for the noun "symbol." Answer D is incorrect for the same reason as A. It's not likely the clerk would complain about interesting work.

Question 4: Answer **B** is correct.
Explanation: The sentence suggests a woman of many talents, and that would be "eclectic." Answer A is incorrect. If you were tempted to choose A, read the sentence again and then review the definitions of both "eccentric" and "eclectic." Although the same person might be both, the sentence isn't a good definition of an eccentric person. Answers C, D, and E are incorrect because the sentence would be illogical.

Question 5: Answer **D** is correct.
Explanation: The sentence is looking for a pair of antonyms, and this pair is the only pair of true antonyms. Answers A and C are incorrect. You can easily eliminate them because they're not good antonym pairs. Answer B is incorrect because "aloof" and "reticent" are synonyms. Answer E is incorrect because neither word fits, nor are they antonyms.

Question 6: Answer **E** is correct.
Explanation: Although "dogmatic" is not necessarily a bad thing to be, the context of the sentence tells you that in this case, it is. Answer A is incorrect because "notorious" is illogically used in this context. Answer B is incorrect because the two words clash instead of support one another. Answers C and D are incorrect because at least one of the words has a positive connotation.

Question 7: Answer **E** is correct.
Explanation: The question asks specifically about the first paragraph, so it needs to be answered based only on information in that paragraph. Answer A is incorrect because, although the paragraph mentions that some people do not wish him well, it's not possible to conclude that there are many of those people. Answer B is incorrect because the information on his loving leisure and women is later in the passage. Answer C is incorrect because the envy mentioned is that of other people, not of Harrison Blair. Answer D is incorrect because the information that he wrote a book with an unusual treatment of its subject implies that he is not lacking in imagination. That leaves answer E, which is a reasonable conclusion from the paragraph.

Question 8: Answer **D** is correct.
Explanation: The passage makes it clear that the book was successful because Blair is talented and that its success was deserved. Thus you need to pick a positive synonym from the list. Only "unexpected" fits. Answers A, B, C, and E are incorrect because they all imply that the book's success was undeserved.

Question 9: Answer **B** is correct.
Explanation: If you take some notes as you read the passage, you'll discover that Blair was a rich young man who was expected to just coast through college, and he was a "jock" to boot. But his undergraduate work

in English was good enough that those who knew about it were not surprised by the success of his book. Thus his teachers were impressed despite themselves. The other answers require you to guess at facts that are not present in the passage or not supported by what is present.

Question 10: Answer **E** is correct.
Explanation: You can get this one right if you know the meaning of either "vouchsafed" or "remonstrated" (or both, of course). Even if you don't, you should be able to eliminate a couple of the choices to increase your chance of guessing properly. The statement isn't a promise, so answer A is unlikely to be correct even if you know nothing about the words. Similarly, there's no hint of an offer, which eliminates answer C.

Question 11: Answer **A** is correct.
Explanation: Answer B is incorrect because there's no evidence in the passage of Blair spending excessively. Answer C is incorrect because the passage does not speak of any delaying behavior. Answer D is incorrect because the evidence in the passage is that Blair is not spoiled; rather, he is making his way through the world on his own. Answer E is incorrect because the author paints Blair in a positive light.

Question 12: Answer **E** is correct.
Explanation: "Sympathy" refers to sharing the feelings of another, and by calling it a technical sympathy, the author implies that it was developed as part of his being a writer. (This is further confirmed by the use of the word "vocation.") Answer A is incorrect based on a poor reading of the word "technical." Answers B and C are based on other possible meanings of "sympathy" that do not fit the passage. Answer D is incorrect; although possibly true, this explanation does not fit the words in question.

Question 13: Answer **B** is correct.
Explanation: Though any of the answers given might be a plausible explanation for wanting a smaller room, the clerk explains late in the passage that the expense of staying prevents her from finishing her work. The mentions of her shabby hat and bag serve to emphasize her poverty. This implies that a smaller room, being less expensive, is preferable to her.

Question 14: Answer **C** is correct.
Explanation: In the context of the passage, Blair is annoyed because the clerk has presumed to ask him an insulting question ("familiarity" here means "impropriety"). Answers A, D, and E are incorrect because the passage does not show the clerk with these qualities. Answer B is incorrect; although the clerk is said to be amused, it doesn't mean that he is attempting to be funny.

Question 15: Answer **D** is correct.
Explanation: The reasonable conclusion from the start of the passage is that Blair has come to the island to pursue his own work on Indians; he was thus interested to find out that someone else was there on a similar pursuit. The other answers are not supported by the text, though you might find any of them reasonable conclusions on their own.

Question 16: Answer **A** is correct.
Explanation: The author spends much of the passage establishing that Blair is an unusually good author and that he makes writing his vocation. Answers B and C are incorrect; though his looks and money are mentioned in passing, they are not portrayed as his essential qualities. The same applies to his sporting ability (answer E).

Answer D is incorrect because there is not enough information in the passage to draw a conclusion about his attention to detail.

Question 17: Answer **C** is correct.
Explanation: Answers A, D, and E are incorrect because the author does not give much, if any, detail of the setting of the story in this passage. Answer B is incorrect because Blair's motivations are not established in the passage beyond a cryptic reference to a letter from the Atlantic. Answer C fits because most of the passage is concerned with introducing and describing characters in the story.

Question 18: Answer **C** is correct.
Explanation: Answers A, D, and E are all statements that are supported by the passage—which means that the author is not concerned with counteracting them. There's no evidence one way or the other as to the author's view of vacation spots, which eliminates answer B. The passage directly contradicts answer C by showing how Blair works hard despite inherited wealth, so the author is evidently concerned with counteracting this idea.

Question 19: Answer **B** is correct.
Explanation: By writing about Blair's father, the author is able to discuss the type of man Blair is and to give Blair's reason for working a menial job. Answer A is incorrect because the father and son are portrayed as distinctly different. Answer C is incorrect because there is no indication of this fact in the passage. Answer D is incorrect because the father, though wealthy, is not described in terms that would brand him a miser. Answer E is incorrect because you can't know from the passage whether family plays a role in the remaining story or not.

Section 8

Question 1: Answer **D** is correct.
Explanation: The main thing to watch for in this sort of problem is not to go too fast and answer the wrong question. In this case, you know that $.4x = 10$, so $x = 10 \div .4 = 25$. Then $3x + 7 = 3 \times 25 + 7 = 82$.

Question 2: Answer **B** is correct.
Explanation: Because the angles of a triangle add up to $180°$, you know that $\angle ACB = 60°$. $\angle DEC$ is then also $60°$ because it is a vertical angle to $\angle ACB$. Then $3x = 60°$, so $x = 20°$.

Question 3: Answer **C** is correct.
Explanation: No matter how you attempt to draw an axis for reflective symmetry, there is no way to divide the figure into two mirror images. But a rotation of $180°$ leaves the figure unchanged, so it has rotational symmetry.

Question 4: Answer **D** is correct.
Explanation: Solve the inequality for x:

$-4x + 12 < 16$

$-4x < 4$

$x > -1$

Remember, when you multiply or divide an inequality by a negative number, you must change the direction of the inequality.

Question 5: Answer **D** is correct.
Explanation: After three quizzes, the total points earned by the student are $88 \times 3 = 264$. For an average of 90, with the exam counting for two quizzes, she must have a total of $90 \times 5 = 450$ points. This means that 186 points must come from the final exam. Divide that by 2 to get the final exam score of 93.

Question 6: Answer **B** is correct.
Explanation: Increasing the price by 10% sets the new price to $90 + (.1 \times 90) = 99$. But then decreasing by 10% does not return to the original price because the 10% is based on the new price. So the final price is $99 - (.1 \times 99) = 89.1$.

Question 7: Answer **D** is correct.
Explanation: You don't actually need to do any calculations to solve this one. Remember, the area of a triangle is $\frac{1}{2}$ bh and the area of a parallelogram is bh. The triangle and the parallelogram share the same base and the same height, so the area of the parallelogram is simply twice the area of the triangle.

Question 8: Answer **C** is correct.
Explanation: The percent increase is measured by the amount of change compared to the base year. Although it's impossible to calculate this precisely for each pair of years on the graph, it's obvious that the 1988 to 1989 change is the largest proportion of its base year.

Question 9: Answer **E** is correct.
Explanation: Each of the blocks has a volume of $1 \times 1 \times .5 = .5$. The box itself has a volume of $12 \times 12 \times 12 = 1,728$. Thus, you will need $1,728 \div .5 = 3,456$ blocks to fill the box.

Question 10: Answer **D** is correct.
Explanation: To see this, express each of the integers in terms of a. They then become

- a
- $a + 1$
- $a + 2$
- $a + 3$
- $a + 4$

The sum of these integers is then $5a + 10$, or $5(a + 2)$. With a suitable choice of a, that can be made to equal any value that is a multiple of 5. The answer is the one choice in the list that is not a multiple of 5.

Question 11: Answer **B** is correct.
Explanation: Ignore the circle and just concentrate on the two squares. The outer square has an area of 4, so its side is equal to 2, as is its height. This is also the diagonal of the inner square. From the Pythagorean Theorem, you know that the diagonal of a square is $\sqrt{2}$ times the side, so the sides of the small square are $2/\sqrt{2} = \sqrt{2}$. Then the area of the inner square is $\sqrt{2} \times \sqrt{2} = 2$. You can also see this by geometric reasoning: The four triangles surrounding the inner square have a total area exactly equal to that of the inner square, so each of them accounts for half of the total area of the outer square.

Question 12: Answer **B** is correct.
Explanation: Remember, the formula for the nth term of an arithmetical sequence is a + (n – 1) × b. In this case, the first term is 2, which gives 2 for a. Plugging in 6 for the second term then gives

$$6 = 2 + (2 - 1) \times b$$

$$4 = b$$

Now, knowing a and b, you can calculate the 49th and 50th terms of the series:

$$2 + (49 - 1) \times 4 = 194$$

$$2 + (50 - 1) \times 4 = 198$$

The sum of these two numbers, 392, is the desired answer.

Question 13: Answer **E** is correct.
Explanation: Start by calculating the side of each square by taking the square root of the area. The smaller square then has a side of 2, and the larger square has a side of 4. The perimeters are four times the side, 8 and 16, respectively. Then the ratio of the perimeters is 8:16, which reduces to 1:2.

Question 14: Answer **C** is correct.
Explanation: Suppose that the roll of film were sufficient to take only a single picture; the cost per picture would then be simply f. If it could take two pictures, each picture would cost half as much, or $\frac{f}{2}$. Similarly, if the roll could take three pictures, they would each take $\frac{1}{3}$ as much, or $\frac{f}{3}$. Note the progression here; the number of pictures is the denominator. So the answer is $\frac{f}{p}$.

Question 15: Answer **B** is correct.
Explanation: You need to treat this as a weighted average problem rather than simply taking the mean of the two speeds, because the time spent en route is different on the two legs of the trip. On the way out, the plane flies 2,000 miles at 400 miles per hour, which takes 5 hours. On the way back, the plane flies 2,000 miles at 500 miles per hour, which takes 4 hours. The total flight is thus 4000 miles in 9 hours, for an average of $444\frac{4}{9}$ miles per hour.

Question 16: Answer **A** is correct.
Explanation: Each triangle must be an equilateral triangle because it is composed of three identical sides. Because of the symmetry of the figure, the line segment AB will go through the center of two sides of the square and will include the height of each triangle. Consider the right triangle made up by one side of the equilateral triangle, half of the side of the square, and the height of the triangle. You can now calculate the height using the Pythagorean Theorem:

$$1^2 = h^2 + \left(\frac{1}{2}\right)^2$$

$$h^2 = 1 - \frac{1}{4}$$

$$h = \sqrt{\frac{3}{4}} = \frac{\sqrt{3}}{2}$$

The desired distance is then 2h + 1, or $1 + \sqrt{3}$.

Section 9

Question 1: Answer **C** is correct.
Explanation: Although the sentence doesn't break any concrete grammar rules as is, the phrase "that which you" is terribly wordy. Answer A is incorrect because the phrase is incorrect as is. Answer B is incorrect because it omits the pronoun "you." Answer D is incorrect because the use of "is" instead of "you" makes the sentence awkward. Answer E is incorrect because it's just horrible. If you selected E, go directly to jail and do not pass Go.

Question 2: Answer **D** is correct.
Explanation: Repeating the noun is redundant (although not actually breaking any rules). Answer A incorrect because the phrase could be better. Answers B, C, and E are all incorrect, although they would all work grammatically. Remember, you're not looking for just any right answer. You're look for the best response.

Question 3: Answer **B** is correct.
Explanation: The pronoun "their" doesn't match the noun, "band," in number. In this case, "band" is singular, although it's composed of many individuals. Answer A is incorrect because the phrase isn't correct as is. When using the phrase "in addition to," the verb and pronouns must match the first noun in tense and number. "Band" is singular; "are" is plural. Answers C, D, and E are all incorrect because they change the nature of the sentence.

Question 4: Answer **E** is correct.
Explanation: Although the sentence isn't grammatically incorrect, the use of the possessive pronoun "their" makes the sentence stronger. Answer A is incorrect, because the original phrase isn't as strong as E. Answer B is incorrect, replacing "so" with "and" actually changes the tone of the sentence, although it isn't incorrect. Answer C is incorrect because it doesn't correct the problem. Answer D is incorrect because there's nothing in the sentence to indicate the teacher's sex.

Question 5: Answer **B** is correct.
Explanation: "Neither of the girls" in itself is an incorrect usage, although it seems perfectly fine. "Neither" is singular; "of the girls" implies plural. Answer A is incorrect because the phrase isn't correct as is. Answer C and D are incorrect because "none" is plural and the verb "is" is singular. You have to correct the underlined portion, so you have to work with the rest of the sentence as is. Answer E is incorrect even though it's grammatically correct. The girls aren't mentioned by name; you can't make stuff up.

Question 6: Answer **C** is correct.
Explanation: When combining a plural and a singular subject with neither and nor, the verb must match the second subject. In this case, the verb is singular, so transposing "cows" and "dog" does the trick. Answer A is incorrect because the phrase isn't correct as is. Answer B is incorrect because it changes the nature of the sentence. We don't know about the rest of the animals. We only have information about the cows and the dog. Answer D is incorrect as using either/or in this context is wrong. Answer E is incorrect because you can't take liberties with the subject. The sentence says that there's more than one cow—you have to work with that.

Question 7: Answer **D** is correct.
Explanation: The preposition "up" isn't necessary. Answer A is incorrect because the phrase isn't correct as is. Answers B and E are incorrect because there's no need to change the wording. Answer C is incorrect because it's illogical. Something doesn't "take sprout"—it takes root.

Question 8: Answer **B** is correct.
Explanation: There are two things going on with this answer. First, the serial items should be parallel. Second, repeating the word "different" with each item is acceptable, but redundant given the prior use of the word "diverse." Answer A is incorrect

because the phrase isn't correct as is. Answers C and D are incorrect because they're not parallel. If you are going to use the adjective "different," you'll need to repeat it with each item. Answer E is incorrect because there's no need to include the word "and" before each subsequent item.

Question 9: Answer **C** is correct.
Explanation: Depending on the context, some verbs are timeless. When this is the case, you should always use present tense. God is timeless. The transcendentalists may no longer be a powerful movement in modern times, but their God is just as timeless as any modern rendition. This is a hard one—don't feel bad if you missed it. Answer A is incorrect because it isn't correct as is. Answer B is incorrect because changing the verb "believe" to present tense isn't necessary. Answer D is incorrect because it changes the meaning of the sentence. Answer E is incorrect as the word "that" is inconsequential in the sentence—its use is preferential, not incorrect.

Question 10: Answer **D** is correct.
Explanation: This one's a bit tricky. As is, the sentence doesn't really sound wrong. However, the phrase "By 1929" implies an ongoing state. The date clues us in that the ongoing state is in the past. We know the event occurred in the past, but the phrase "by 1929" is inconclusive. It is difficult to discern from the one sentence if the phrase indicates an end or just a stage of this spending phase. The most appropriate tense should be progressive past—which indicates an ongoing state in the past. The verb phrase "had been spending" is perfect past—indicating an event that began and ended in the past. Even if you decide that the proper verb phrase is present past, keep in mind that this tense is rarely necessary and can usually be rewritten in a clearer form without changing the timing. That's what D does. Even if you decide that the verb tense,

as is, is acceptable, D is better. Answer A is incorrect because the phrase isn't correct as is. Answer B is incorrect because it's perfect present, indicating that it began in the past but extends to the present. We don't know that to be true. Answers C and E are incorrect because they're grammatically incorrect. Neither represents a valid verb tense within the context of this sentence.

Question 11: Answer **B** is correct.
Explanation: The first phrase is a participial phrase, and the rule is: When using a participial phrase to begin a sentence, you must follow the phrase with a comma and then the noun it modifies. As is, the subject is unclear. Who is returning to America: we or he? The clue is in the first phrase. A singular subject is returning to America; therefore, he must be the subject. We did take a bit of license with this one, and you probably won't run into a question quite so ambiguous as this one on the real exam. We're just trying to emphasize the grammatical rule. Answer A is incorrect because the phrase isn't correct as is. We wanted to trick you a bit with answer C, which is incorrect. Remember, the exam will *not* use a preposition at the end of a sentence as an error. Answer D is incorrect because it changes the meaning of the sentence, and the subjects don't match in number. Answer E is incorrect, but you might have been tempted by this one. It is grammatically correct, but it does change the meaning of the sentence more than A.

Question 12: Answer **C** is correct.
Explanation: The preposition "up" is unnecessary. Answer A is incorrect because the phrase isn't correct as is. Answer B is incorrect because it doesn't omit the unnecessary preposition. Answers D and E are incorrect, even though they are grammatically sound, because it is unnecessary to change so much.

Question 13: Answer **B** is correct.
Explanation: The prepositional phrase "of post-war Europe" is used as an adjective to further define the subject, which is "The sagging economies." When this is the case, the prepositional phrase can almost always be omitted. Answer A is incorrect because the phrase isn't correct as is. Answer C is incorrect because post-war should describe Europe, not their economies. Answers D and E are incorrect because the noun "economies" isn't the problem.

Question 14: Answer **C** is correct.
Explanation: When using an adjective in comparative form, precede the adjective with more or most; don't add "er" to the adjective. Answer A is incorrect because the phrase isn't correct as is. Answers B and E are incorrect because the verb "was" and the subject "immigrants" don't match in number. Answer D is incorrect because "most" is not comparative; it is absolute.